"The *Travelers' Tales* series is quite remarkable."
— Jan Morris, author of *Journeys*, *Locations*, and *Hong Kong*

"For the thoughtful traveler, these books are an invaluable resource. There's nothing like them on the market."
— Pico Iyer, author of *Video Night in Kathmandu*

"This is the stuff memories can be duplicated from."
— Karen Krebsbach, *Foreign Service Journal*

"I can't think of a better way to get comfortable with a destination than by delving into *Travelers' Tales*...before reading a guidebook, before seeing a travel agent. The series helps visitors refine their interests and readies them to communicate with the peoples they come in contact with...."
— Paul Glassman, Society of American Travel Writers

"...*Travelers' Tales* is a valuable addition to any pre-departure reading list."
— Tony Wheeler, publisher, Lonely Planet Publications

"*Travelers' Tales* delivers something most guidebooks only promise: a real sense of what a country is all about...."
— Steve Silk, *Hartford Courant*

"These anthologies seem destined to be a success... *Travelers' Tales* promises to be a useful and enlightening addition to the travel book-shelves. By collecting and organizing such a wide range of literature, O'Reilly and Habegger are providing a real service for those who enjoy reading first-person accounts of a destination before seeing it for themselves."
— Bill Newlin, publisher, Moon Publications

"The *Travelers' Tales* series should become required reading for anyone visiting a foreign country who wants to truly step off the tourist track and experience another culture, another place, first hand."
— Nancy Paradis, *St. Petersburg Times*

"Like having been there, done it, seen it. If there's one thing traditional guidebooks lack, it's the really juicy travel information, the personal stories about back alleys and brief encounters. The *Travelers' Tales* series fills this gap with an approach that's all anecdotes, no directions."

—Jim Gullo, *Diversion*

LOVE &
ROMANCE

TRUE STORIES OF PASSION ON THE ROAD

TRAVELERS' TALES

LOVE &
ROMANCE

TRUE STORIES OF PASSION ON THE ROAD

Collected and Edited by

JUDITH BABCOCK WYLIE

Series Editors

JAMES O'REILLY AND LARRY HABEGGER

TRAVELERS' TALES, INC.
SAN FRANCISCO, CALIFORNIA

Distributed by
O'REILLY AND ASSOCIATES, INC.
101 MORRIS STREET
SEBASTOPOL, CALIFORNIA 95472

*Underlying every conflict is an avoidance of
commitment and a simultaneous yearning for it.
Love is more than finding a mate and settling
down in paradise. Love is embracing life, jumping
into the adventure of it, tasting the great banquet,
opening your senses to nuances, pain, pleasure,
wonder—it's the commitment to living fully,
and doing something with experience.*

Rebecca Bruns (1951–1994),
The Sensuous Traveler

*Dedicated to the loving
memory of my mother,
Louise Boynton
(1914–1997)*

Table of Contents

Part Four
IN THE SHADOWS

Part Five
THE LAST WORD

Introduction

For those of us who love to travel every trip is a small romance. It begins with the seduction of seeing ourselves in a new way in a foreign place. We know in our bones that when we stand hidden by sago palms near a glistening bank of the Amazon, crocodiles lurking below with golden eyes, we will be slimmer, stronger, surer, and more captivating than when we stand at the water cooler brushing aside plastic ivy from a cubicle divider.

We believe that we can be somehow truer to ourselves when we are not in our true environment. We may be terrified to ask for intimacy as we sit in our own living rooms, but are convinced that the simple act of boarding a flight of over a thousand miles will loosen our tongues and make us suddenly able to see deeply into the soul of another and discover them looking back at us with fascination and surprise. And in some ways, we're right. The proof is in these true stories.

As we pack our travel wardrobe, we pack a new attitude, one more open, more vulnerable, more willing to be touched by who and what we see.

When happily-married Beth Clark finds herself inexplicably drawn to a deeply tanned Tahitian guide with palm frond ankle bracelets and a tattoo on his backside peeking above his low-slung sarong, it creates a crisis of conscience. Whose life is this anyway? What will it mean if she gives in to her first impulse? Will she be the same person? And does she want to be? In a carefully constructed life can you make detours and still find your way to your final destination?

Other stories tell of not just flirting with the exotic but embracing it. Joana McIntyre Varawa has always been drawn to dark skin, and had the courage to make a remarkable journey to love and then marry a tribesman in Fiji.

For most of us, loosened from the strictures of home rules and away from the eyes of those who know us as we've always been, taking small chances is the essence of the romantic travel experience. When Robert Strauss and his bride miss getting back to their intended hotel in Tokyo one dark night, they stumble instead into a bizarre lodging with peculiar objects on the room service menu and a mysterious clock on the wall that ominously ticks backwards. We learn with them what this hotel is and why Japan has so many of them. In the process, we also learn to laugh.

A yearning for romance lies in all of us as we travel, even if we do not seek a relationship. Romance can be touched off by a gentle gesture, the sudden blush on a cheek, making the emotional gears turn, but often external cues are enough. The Moroccan city of Fez comes to mind. Even if you travel there alone, the city swirls in exotic splendor around you. A look, a pair of lowered eyes, the rustle of a *djelaba,* a taste of sweet tea, the scent of musk all create a small romantic drama. Romance is a word that originally meant a story, a tale. We want our travels to have a plot, to mean something when we come home. We want travel to make a heroine or hero of us, to change us, and the best travel does.

But change does not come easily, especially when you are learning life lessons in a foreign language. When Glenn Leichman discovers his hiking companion and lover is pregnant as they are trekking in Nepal, he doesn't want to believe it. He doesn't understand why she won't leap up and follow him up the trail once again. Slowly he realizes she is growing up and that this time it is she who will lead them out—on the treacherous route to adulthood.

Readers will learn a lot in these pages about risk, vulnerability, and the fierce delight of finding that passion has chosen you. But meanwhile, you will also discover how it feels to sink into a bubbling hot spring in the Himalayas after a cold trek, the magic sight of Hong Kong at night from a *sampan* in Aberdeen Harbor, the draw of hearing an old love story while snow beats softly against the window in a pine lodge in the Cook Forest of Pennsylvania.

One of the great pleasures of reading more than 700 possible stories for this book was to find that men are just as romantic as women. When Travelers' Tales Guides and United Airlines held a contest on the most romantic travel experience people had encountered, our winning entry came from a man—Frank X. Case is a former NFL football player who describes an epiphany in his marriage when he and his wife traveled to Cozumel over New Year's, learning a small but important lesson from the Mayan culture that changed their relationship.

What makes this possible? Chemistry. When two people fall in love, phenylalanine floods the brain in response to fear and excitement, the main fear being rejection. But when the initial danger passes, and a couple settles down, this chemical marvel subsides. The way to rev up a long-term relationship, biochemists tell us, is to put ourselves in a challenging situation together, and discover the chemical boost that once marked love in the making.

Nothing is more challenging than travel. There are odd verb forms to learn, lumpy new beds to sleep in, sea urchin dishes to try together, and cliffside roads with hairpin curves to survive. A couple returning from safari know they are different. They are now the kind of people who have heard the electrifying breath of a lion on the other side of a thin tent wall.

As you read these stories you will learn the alarming, funny, tender and frightening forms that love can take when you're traveling. "Be careful what you wish for, you might get it!" is never more true than when traveling. As Mary Ellen Schultz strikes up an innocent conversation in a Spanish train station, she has no idea that the red tablecloth next to the handsome young man she meets is his bull-fighting cape, and she is soon swept into the stands of a bull ring and an unusual dilemma. What exactly do you do with a freshly presented bull's ear?

In researching sidebar material on romance for this book, I discovered not much has changed in the romance advice area for thousands of years. Ovid, who wrote *Ars Amatoria,* a book of love advice in the year 1 B.C., sounds suspiciously like the authors of the recent bestseller, *The Rules.* Men, take courage, woman, step back.

You will find few women in this book who took that advice. The story that begins the book, "Leaving Los Pájaros," by Iris Litt, shows us the power of romance over practical thinking as the writer chooses to act on the dictates of her heart.

And the book ends with Jo Beth McDaniels' touching story of how shared travel memories defined a couple's life-long love, forever connecting them with a bond strong enough to win over the body's frailties.

Whether to seek another, seek a new understanding with a partner, or to seek ourselves, travel itself can be the ultimate romance.

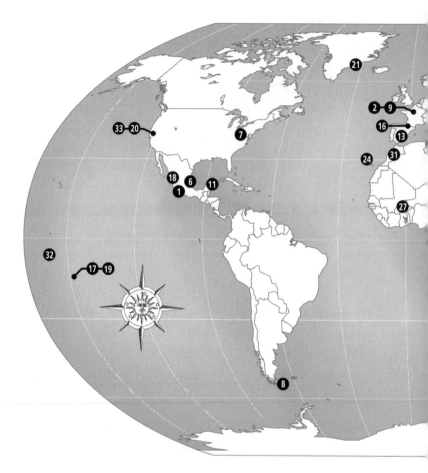

PART ONE

ESSENCE

IRIS LITT

* * *

Leaving Los Pájaros

The rhythm of Mexico can make
the future tentative.

IT WAS ONE OF THOSE MORNINGS WHEN I WOKE UP FAR TOO early, four-thirty to be exact. I decided to get up and go to the john and then try to sleep some more. When I hit the light switch and the bare overhead bulb went on, a startled lizard streaked across the wall. I opened the wood shutter and peered out to see if there was any early light, even though I knew there wouldn't be.

With the consolation of an empty bladder and the luxury of silence outside, I got back into bed and put on my eyeshade and earplugs, preparing for a Mexican dawn. Soon the roosters' crowing would wake the dogs whose barking would wake the babies whose crying would wake the adults who would shout to each other and turn on their radios and move furniture around on the bare tiles and sing.

I lay there and thought, I could leave today. I could pack up now. I could take the long bus ride to Puerto Vallarta. I could have my *siesta* on the bus. I could check into the Rio or Roger's, and tomorrow I could be on the 1:45 plane for New York, which is usually late getting in, but at least by 3 a.m. or so on Monday night, which by that time will have become Tuesday morning, I could be home.

Home. The cold air would sting my cheeks. There would be a toaster oven and a computer. And an endless supply of books and magazines containing conceptual material. *Agua caliente* twenty-four hours a day. Telephone, TV, poetry readings, lectures, museums, real movies—not just *Desperados*. And the poems and stories I'd been mailing home to myself, in case my baggage got lost or stolen, would be there in the shopping bag Edmund piled them into when he came over to check on my apartment.

Yes, I could do it. I could go home. There was nothing, really, to stop me. Alfonso would put on his mortally-wounded face when I told him. Suddenly his Mexican-male insistence on his right to have other women would become my advantage instead of the constant threat it had been. It meant I didn't have to feel quite as guilty when I told him. I would keep reminding myself of it to help me handle the pain, his and mine.

I rehearsed it in Spanish:

Pero es que tu insistes en estar con las otras mujeres: But you insist on having other women.

He would say: It doesn't matter.

I: Maybe next winter I'll come back.

Maybe, or its approximations, appears in many forms in Mexican. *Puede ser. Más o menos. Quién sabe?* I called it a whole different part of speech: Future Tentative.

When he realized I meant it, he'd offer to give the others up.

But all this very *norteamericano* reasoning was silly anyway. I didn't need a reason. I had just decided I wanted to go home. I was filled with a wild happiness. I took off the eyeshade and earplugs. I got out of bed faster than I had in three months and put on my white sandals, the northern, cushioned kind you can walk in on city sidewalks. I took my big leather handbag from the back of the closet. It was for traveling, too good to ruin in dirty *cantinas* or scratch up on jungle paths.

By now it was almost six, and I opened the front shutter. The light glittered on the Pacific. The surf was loud today, frighteningly so, bringing to mind the time it had jumped the beach, spewed through the stucco basketweave of the wall and flooded the scruffy yard right to the edge of my tile veranda. Next time it might not stop there, which was another reason I should flee immediately to the relative safety of New York City.

I slipped into my shift of embroidered *manta.* I set a pot of water to boil, wiped the iguana droppings off the sink, measured out a heaping teaspoon of Nescafé, sliced a *bollillo,* speared it with a fork and toasted it over the other burner. I smeared the *bollillo* with strawberry marmalade. I mixed the powdered milk for the coffee.

Then I turned out the light and opened all the shutters. It was safe, now that there was no light indoors to attract mosquitoes, to open the door and step out.

This was the rare moment of each day in Los Pájaros, like writing a near-perfect poem or falling in love, the rediscovering each morning of the world as the proverbial garden with its crawling walking flying chirping squawking crowing creatures living harmoniously, I liked to think, even though I knew they were all eating each other. The sun brightened the sky like a camera flash, brilliantly backlighting the green of the palm fronds and the cerise, coral, and yellow of the flowers, changing the sea from blue-grey to green-blue. The brilliantly-colored birds from which the town took its name whooshed among the tree branches. Seagulls glided, pairs of iguanas sat on rocks looking out to sea, roosters strutted, each living body propelled by the one miracle not completely explained by science: energy, life, eagerness.

I brought my coffee and *bollillo* outside and sat in the unraveling wicker chair. In New York, there would be that other energy; in New York, there was purpose, as though life had one. That's what I was going back to—today, yes, today!—that energy, and the stuff I wrote that seemed part of that energy, and a guy named Edmund (if he'd been able to wait for me this time as he had the times before), whose mind was a constant surprise and delight.

It was almost seven-thirty and the full yellow and blue and green day had arrived in Los Pájaros. Soon I would put on my straw hat and go to the post office. I'd check my mailbox, and I'd mail to my address in New York the pieces I'd written last week. I'd stop at the market for my daily bottle of drinking water, at the fruit store for the Mexico City newspaper. Maybe I'd lie in the *hammaca* on the beach and read or write. I'd have lunch at La Palapa on the beach, fresh-caught fish and a Sidral, with Serena and Lupe or any of the fifty or so other *gringos* and Mexicans who might be there. Then I'd come back, close the shutters and sleep the extraordinarily sound sleep of *siesta*. Maybe Alfonso would join me. When I opened the shutters, the light would be softer, the sea gentler. Early fishing boats would be coming in. On the horizon, the big shrimp boat would be raising its derricks. Unlike the brilliant light of morning, a rose tint would paint the same scene, like the progressive versions of a monotype. Maybe I'd sit in the wicker chair and write some more. If it was driving me, I'd write all evening. If not, I'd put on my blue and white gauze skirt, my slinky white rayon halter top and walk, feeling as though I were floating, to Jim and Pam's café, Mi Casa, where the crowd would be gathering, maybe some new *gringo* faces with stories of adventure and misadventure, and the familiar ones with their newest stories of local happiness found and wrecked. Later, we'd all pile into Bob's pickup truck and go to the fiesta in El Rio, or if the *mariachis* showed up at Mi Casa, we'd stay there and drink and dance and laugh. Around 10:30, I'd walk through the streets with my flashlight picking out the thin tired dogs huddled in the potholes, stepping over the mule and horse manure, hearing soft guitar music from the houses that weren't yet shuttered, through the garden and into a sound sleep. I would do all this today, not much in the way of accomplishment by New York standards. But it felt like a lot.

Yes, I'd do all this today. If I stayed, that is. Was I wavering again? Could I endure another day here? I reached again for the taste of New York. For Edmund, the arms that held me warm, the strong, confident voice, the sense that he delighted in my quick mind, nutty imagination and, in his words of course, superb body.

If I didn't get ready immediately, it would simply be too late to leave today. I laid out my traveling clothes on the extra bed. I heard the stirring of palm fronds, footsteps on the path. Alfonso stood there, large and sturdy, with a smile as warm as all Mexico. His muscular brown shoulders and thighs gleamed after his morning swim. He scooped me up and carried me to the bed. He took off my shift. Then he closed the shutters, put the padlock on the inside of the door because he knew that I, *la gringa,* liked it safe and private that way, and came to me. Far off, somewhere beyond the whir of the ceiling fan, I heard the soft rhythms of Latin music above the surf and birdsongs. Another day had begun in Los Pájaros.

Iris Litt is the author of a book of poems, Word Love, *and has had poems and short stories appear in numerous magazines. She lives—and teaches poetry workshops—in both New York City and Woodstock, New York.*

✳

A Latin Lover will fill your life with passion, every day. He will make you feel sensuous and erotic whether you are young, old, wrinkled, smooth, fat or thin. A Latin Lover will make you feel beautiful. He will make you feel glorious even when you're not.

If you are overweight, a Latin Lover will tell you that you are succulent. If you are wrinkled, he will tell you that you are ripe. If you are old, he will tell you that you are wise. If you have cellulite, he will tell you that your skin is like a beautiful fruit. A Latin Lover will bring you coffee and a sesame cake and a flower in bed.

A Latin Lover will always take time to stop and watch the sunset. He will buy you a paper cup of fresh strawberry juice to sip while you stroll through the market. A Latin Lover will build a love on moments...on tastes and touches and smells and sunsets. A Latin Lover will stroke your body with a peacock feather one long, rainy afternoon.

—Paula McDonald, "Why Every Woman Should Have a Latin Lover"

JUDY WADE

* * *

The Working Class

*Some of the best surprises of Paris
are just outside your window.*

PARISIANS HAVE A UNIQUE SENSE OF THE APPROPRIATE. FROM THE fellow in green coveralls giving the cobbled streets an early-morning wash to the nattily dressed chap popping into the Hotel de Ville, the city's town hall, they seem to possess a feeling for what's fitting. I learned the extent of their sensibilities on a recent visit.

The tiny Hotel Saint-Louis on the fabled Ile St-Louis occupies one of the island's former 17th-century townhouses. It nestles agreeably between other such structures, giving no hint that the island was once a bucolic pasture where devout King Louis IX, the island's namesake, strolled as he read his breviary.

I hauled my duffel up three flights to a little room that faced the island's single narrow main street. The Ile itself is just six blocks long and two wide, making it more of an isolated village than a part of bustling Paris. I pulled back the lacy white curtains and opened the wood shutters. In this centuries-old setting, the buildings across the street seemed almost within touching distance.

On the street below I watched a woman in a green sweater walking her sleek brown dachshund. In a city where there are more dogs than people the little creature's "calling card" would not be remarked on. At eye level, I could see into a series of rooms across the street that obviously were being remodeled. The sounds of hammering and of a radio playing American rock drifted across the way. A young workman appeared at the window and surveyed the scene below as he lit a cigarette. He looked over at me, grinned, and saluted me with a cheery *bonjour*. I smiled, waved a reciprocal greeting, and turned to unpacking.

Late that afternoon after a trip to the Musée d'Orsay, I could see my workman friend, along with three others all in white overalls, lounging in a series of three windows. They obviously were enjoying a rest at the end of their day. I placed two of them in their twenties, one was plump and middle-aged, and a grandfatherish fourth wore a navy blue beret over a grizzle of gray hair.

My appearance at the window was a cause for calls and gestures inviting me to share a glass of wine at the little corner bistro. Between my fledgling French and their sketchy English I managed a gentle refusal, blaming jet lag and fatigue. When I started out the next morning around eight, the shutters across the street were closed.

That evening the four workmen were once again eagerly at the window. This time I explained as best I could that there were four of them and just one of me, which really didn't equate for a comfortable cocktail date. They nodded contemplatively. I got the distinct impression they were thinking it over.

Although it wasn't a weekend, my new acquaintances didn't appear for the next two days. I thought perhaps they'd finished the job, which my hotel concierge/owner had explained was the renovation of an apartment for a businessman and his wife.

As I returned to the hotel the next evening and passed through the small lobby-cum-breakfast room, Madame the proprietress called my name. She handed me a tissue-wrapped package of four dewy long-stemmed roses...one red, one white, one yellow, one pink. "*Les ouvriers*," she explained and pointed across the street. The workmen.

I carried the roses up to my room and threw open the shutters. In the window were my overalled friends. The two younger ones each held a pink and a red rose, the middle-aged fellow waved a yellow one, and the grandfather had a white one tucked behind his ear.

"*Choisis! Choisis!*" they chorused.

Choose? Ahhh. I looked down at the four roses in my arms and back at the workmen. Their smiles were sunshine. Without hesitating I extracted the white rose from the bunch and placed it behind my ear.

Over the glass of wine I later shared with Philippe, for that was his name, I learned that he was indeed a grandfather, and a craftsman in renovation. He asked about my travels and my job as a journalist. Later, when he walked me to my hotel, he folded my hand in both of his and kissed it gently. My last glimpse of him was as he rounded the corner, the white rose still balanced beneath his beret.

Judy Wade is a freelance travel writer who prefers to write about outdoor activities, including "mellow strolls through interesting countryside." She is a contributing editor of Travel 50 & Beyond, *a contributing writer for* Physicians Travel & Meeting Guide, *and a columnist for* Travel America. *She's the author of three books and lives in Phoenix.*

★

It must be genetic with French men. No matter what their station in life, they all seem to be capable of the grand romantic gesture. One afternoon I stood on the deck of a large cruise ship docked in Marseilles, as passengers toting parcels streamed back aboard, chatting about their day in port. Two aproned French women, one bent with age, sold fresh iris and lilies from large buckets next to the gangway. Children deftly steered bicycles among cargo stacked on the quay that was waiting to be hooked by a large crane and swung into an open hold.

As I leaned against the ship's rail, mildly engrossed in the busy scene, I watched the dark-eyed operator in his little enclosed cubicle atop the crane. Skillfully he handled the levers that caused it to swing into position. After a moment his glance took me in. On the next pass, the glance was accompanied by a smile. I smiled back. Between maneuvers he managed to doff his beret. I waved. He blew a kiss. I caught it to my heart.

As he worked, I watched, smiles and mouthed kisses flying back and forth in a flirtatious game. By the time he deposited the remaining bulky bale into the hold, our eyes were inseparable. And then the sharp blast of the ship's whistle said it was time to go. The last passengers straggled aboard and the gangway was removed. I felt a little stab of sadness as he turned the crane away with never a backward look.

Then suddenly he swung the giant hook down to the quay one last time, near to the old flower women. As they looked up, he called out and waved a fistful of francs. Quickly the pair put the remaining flowers in a single bucket and looped its handle over the crane's hook. As the ship began to inch away from the quay he swung the bucket of flowers to the liner's rail and presented them to me.

Thrilled, I cradled the blue bundle against my yellow summer dress as a tear slid into my smile. He grinned and waved as our ship slipped into the twilight.

—J. L. Wittmayer, "A Gallic Goodbye"

FRANK HAHN

✦ ✦ ✦

The Bridge at Mostar

Life and hope are renewed
in a special place.

DRIVEN BY THE STRESS OF LOS ANGELES LIFE AND PERHAPS BY AN unconscious attempt to save our marriage, we left home, jobs, and friends to travel. I had applied for and been granted a fellowship and a stipend to attend the Doxiodos Institute in Athens, Greece. At the age of thirty-six, after twelve years of marriage and a two-year-old daughter, the sixty-hour work weeks and constant commuting had gnawed at our relationship. Infidelity was an escape but not a cure. My wife Betty felt my distance and turned to work. Daughter Trina was badly affected by the L.A. smog. Our marriage was threatened.

Ignoring the advice of friends, the house was rented, belongings stored, and career abandoned. We departed for Europe, seafreighting clothes, a radio, transformers, and other essentials to Athens in two fifty-gallon drums. We left the life we knew in the hope of finding what we knew not.

A cheap flight took us to Frankfurt where we bought a well-used VW beetle. Purchasing sleeping bags and a small stove at a German store, we headed south to Greece. Betty and I slept outside and Trina slept on the rear seat. The VW broke down and its repair used up much of our spare cash. So camping was necessary and stays in *pensions* were rare. The campgrounds were full, the ground hard and the circumstances not conducive to love or romance. Two-year-old Trina needed constant attention and one of us would stay with her while the other shopped. The opportunities for intimacy were nil.

Driving down through Germany and Austria into what was then Yugoslavia, we stopped at Hadrian's Roman palace at Split and then went on to Dubrovnik. There we were told about a new road to Bulgaria which would make our journey over the mountains easier. Following directions and smoke-spewing buses we left town on a well-paved road. As the miles went by, the traffic and the road diminished, first to a one-lane road then to a dirt path, then to a track. Finally we found ourselves following bulldozer tracks and road construction vehicles. The road was not yet linked to the Bulgarian side and we were deep in the mountains.

Backtracking, we wove our way on back country paths north and east in the hope of finding a main artery. Then we crested a rise and as if we had come across a middle eastern Brigadoon, saw a town of mosques, minarets, bell towers, and church spires. The town was Mostar, not then known to many tourists or known to the world as it would become during the Balkan war. The four hundred plus-year-old Turkish bridge arched high over the river gorge looking

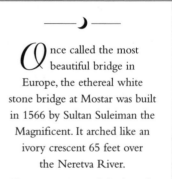

*O*nce called the most beautiful bridge in Europe, the ethereal white stone bridge at Mostar was built in 1566 by Sultan Suleiman the Magnificent. It arched like an ivory crescent 65 feet over the Neretva River.

This steep stone arch built without cement or concrete became a symbol for bridging the town's many cultures, as citizens of Mostar lived for centuries in unusual harmony.

The graceful bridge was destroyed by tank fire from Croat forces in November, 1993. It took two days to bring it down.

♦

—JBW

like a golden brown rainbow. The town was an exotic mix of diverse backgrounds. The food, architecture, customs, and dress of the people reflected their Moslem and Christian upbringing. The call to prayer sounded five times a day, sometimes punctuated by the ringing of church bells. Vendors carried sesame bread rings or baklava on their heads while others grilled meats over sidewalk barbecues. There were no signs of hate or animosity. The bridge linked the peoples and bonded the town.

That night we decided to get a room rather than camp. The campgrounds were far from town and the opportunity to explore the town too inviting. The place we found had been a grist mill. The old wooden water wheel still clunked and rumbled, pushed by the water. Various grain storage huts had been converted to sleeping areas simply by adding windows and beds. We rented one. After wandering around the town and eating kebabs and rice we went back to the mill and put Trina to bed. But the night held too much magic for us to sleep, so we took our sleeping bags and went outside. There the thunking beat of the wooden gears, the splashing of the wheel, the chorus of the frogs, and the river's whisper created a symphony as we snuggled down. The mountain sky was heavy with stars and the brisk night was clear. With a bottle of wine and our bodies for warmth we were truly together for the first time on the trip.

We made love that night on a hill not far from the lighted towers of that town. It was as if the god of each of the two religions had conspired to put us on an impassable road to get us here. It was a tender night just for ourselves, our bodies longing for the familiar touches, our minds remembering what we once had. A slower, more familiar yet exciting anticipatory love. Love like we had made before the daily pressures began to squeeze our feelings away. Love that renewed our bond and bridged the differences that had deepened the gorge between us. Perhaps aided by the acceptance between us and the magic of the moment, the mystery of conception took place. We know this because even though our love was renewed, the events and pace of the remaining trip kept us apart until we got to Athens.

Our second daughter Stephanie was conceived that night near the Mostar bridge. Some say souls waiting to be born choose their parents and the time of conception. If so, she picked a time of our need in a place that may never be the same again. When she was old enough to understand we told her of Mostar and for the rest of our married life she remained the reminder of that place.

Now Betty is gone, dead of cancer at a young age. The bridge at Mostar is gone, blown up by hate for all the world to witness on TV. The town we knew is gone. Its buildings shell-pocked, its towers destroyed, it harbors hate, not love. Yet I have living proof of that time and have only to reach out to revive my memories of Mostar and recall what love is.

An international energy consultant, Frank Hahn has lived and worked in Africa, the Middle East, and Eastern Europe. Extensive personal travels have taken him and his family camping around the world. His hobbies are whitewater rafting, hiking, and history. He has two daughters and lives in Northern California.

✳

To me there are three kinds of marriage: first, worldly ambition; that is, marriage for fortune, title, estates, society; secondly, love; that is the usual pig and cottage; thirdly, which is my ideal of being a companion and wife, a life of travel, adventure, and danger, seeing and learning, with love to glorify it; that is what I seek, *L'amour n'y manquerait pas!*

—Isabel Burton, *The Romance of Isabel Lady Burton:
The Story of Her Life* by W. H. Wilkins (1897)

_✳

Sachiko-san

In Japan, even a love affair must
bow to the right rituals.

MAKING PLANS WITH SACHIKO-SAN WAS ALWAYS, I HAD FOUND, AN uncertain business, not least because whenever she called me, both of us would engage in a polite, but ruthless, tug-of-war as to which should be the medium of confusion. Both of us were determined to speak the language we didn't know (she to practice her English and I to try out my Japanese), and so, very often, we ended up communicating in a kind of jangled bilingual hybrid in which nothing was lost except meaning.

Whenever we tried to fix meetings, therefore—she confusing "Tuesday" and "Thursday," I mixing up *ka-yobi* (Tuesday) with *kinyo-bi* (Friday), she routinely transposing "yesterday" and "tomorrow"—the result was madness. "Where would you like to meet?" I would ask her, in Japanese, and she would reply, in English, "You want to come here my house?" in a tone that suggested more apprehension than delight. She would say she was free at two, and I would arrive, for a brief encounter, only to learn that she was free for two hours. I would say that I was leaving for three days, and she would assume I was leaving on the third. That first day, when she had casually invited me to drop in on her daughter's birthday party at around two and I had casually dropped in at two forty-five, only to find that there was no party at all and I was forty-five minutes late, increasingly seemed an augury of all that was to come.

Once we met, of course, the craziness would only accelerate. For one thing, Sachiko-san was as unabashed and unruly in her embrace of English as most of her compatriots were reticent and shy. Where they would typically refuse to utter a single sentence unless they could deliver it perfectly, she was happy to plunge ahead without a second thought for grammar, scattering meanings and ambiguities as she went. Plurals were made singular, articles were dropped, verbs were rarely inflected, and word order was exploded—often, in fact, she seemed effectively to be making Japanese sentences with a few English words thrown in. Often, moreover, to vex the misunderstandings further, she spoke both languages at once, as if reading simultaneously from both columns of a phrasebook: "*Demo* but where are you *ima* now?" she sometimes asked, hardly stopping to bother about the fact that *demo* means "but" and *ima*, "now." Other times, she suddenly came up with an affirmative "*Sí!*" suggesting that somehow or other she had got hold of a French or Spanish phrasebook instead of an English one. Often, too, I could see in her sentences the scorch marks of an all-too-hasty trip through the dictionary: "Is America very high?" she asked me (since *takai* in Japanese means both "expensive" and "high"), or, to more alarming effect, "The bullet train is always very early" (since *hayai* in Japanese means "early" as well as "fast"). Sometimes, when she said something like "I have this happy feeling touch," I could tell that she had whizzed through a list of synonyms fatally unseparated (in her mind at least) by a comma.

I, of course, was hardly better, turning Japanese nouns into adjectives, using feminine forms for myself, and sometimes just deploying English words, with random vowels hopefully stuck in at the end, foolishly confident in the belief that Japan had incorporated an enormous number of English terms (*Hamu to tosto, kudasai!*). Having picked up most of my Japanese from a businessmen's handbook and bilingual editions of poetry—a fitting combination,

I had thought at the time—I was able to deliver nothing but sentences like "Please give your secretary the autumn moon."

To complicate matters even further, Sachiko-san, in the classic Japanese manner, contrived to make everything as ambiguous, as circumspect, as consensual as possible—even in English. If ever she wanted to use the English word for *itsumo*, which I had been taught meant "always," she always said, "usually," so as to soften the assertion and allow for the exception that might one day prove the rule (leading to such statements as "Usually, the first day of the year is January one"). And where we would say yes, she always said *tabun*, or "maybe." When once she told me that Yuki was sick, I replied, with empty assurance, "I'm sure she'll be better soon." "*Tabun*," she replied. "Maybe." "No, really," I insisted, "I'm sure there's no problem." "Maybe," she replied, all caution. The effect was one of instant melancholy, though really she must have been as sure as I that all would be okay. And of course, every adjective that was less than entirely positive—and much else besides—was qualified with a *chotto*, meaning "little," so that Frankenstein became "a little strange," and traveling to the moon "a little difficult."

Much of this, clearly, was as much an act of courtesy as of caution, and not so different, really, from the reflexive softenings in which I too had once been trained in England. Always prefer a rhetorical question to a bald assertion ("Might it not be easier perhaps to try this road?"). Never disagree outright ("I'm not absolutely sure that's true"), and sometimes soften the dissent further, with—what else?—a rhetorical question (It's so hard to know for certain, don't you find?"). If absolutely forced to say no, say anything other than "no," diluting every term in the sentence ("I'm very sorry, but I'm afraid it might be just a little difficult"). None of these were lies, as such, only stratagems for easing the social machinery.

Thus the intricacies of Japanese protocol were compounded by those of my own English training, and both were made nonsensical by the relentless exchange of gibberish. Whenever I said anything that made her happy, she assumed I was being polite, and whenever she replied, I assumed this was mere Japanese indirectness. So I would say, "Do you want to have some coffee?" and she would answer, "Okay. Do you want some coffee?" and I would have to say, *Iie, kekko desu* ("No, thank you, I'm fine as I am"), and both of us would end up exactly where we had started.

"Should we meet on Tuesday?" I asked her. Sachiko-san gave me a smile. "No problem! Yesterday, Thursday, okay!"

A few days later, as the month drew to its end, I awoke at dawn to find my window all fogged over: the first hard frost of winter. Longing to share the moment with someone—I had not experienced winter for three years now—I hurried out into the mild invigoration of the morning to visit [my friend] Mark. It was a joy undiminished to awaken

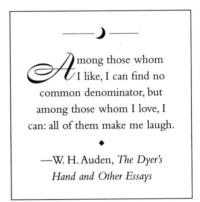

*A*mong those whom I like, I can find no common denominator, but among those whom I love, I can: all of them make me laugh.

♦

—W. H. Auden, *The Dyer's Hand and Other Essays*

in the cloudless blue and see the mountains sharp in the distance, to feel the briskness of a winter morning in the sun. The whole world felt uplifted and refreshed: the narrow lanes alive with oranges, old women chattering away below the muted sun, and everywhere a sense of purpose.

My only disappointment, I told Mark as I came into his house, was that I would not be able to see the *hatsu-yuki*, or first snowfall of the year. I would be leaving Kyoto the following day, not to return for a month, and I knew that I would miss the winter's first moment of silent transformation.

The next day, my last day in Kyoto, Sachiko came to my room again, bringing with her a book by A. A. Milne and a textbook for an English lesson. I led her up to my tiny space, and there, in the winter dark, I tried to teach her again the words that she might need. We sat on cushions on the *tatami*, the dark room lit by the glowing orange bar of my single-element heater. Often, in explaining the terms of my own language to her, I felt as if I were explaining them to myself. As I began, slowly, to speak English as a second language, my own tongue came to seem as new to me, and mysterious, as Japanese.

Patiently, sometimes frowning over the words and muttering, "*Muzukashii!*" sometimes giggling away the difficulty, she stumbled through a text about fishermen in Holland. When we were through, she looked at me, there was a long silence, and I stood up in the darkening room to make some tea.

As she wandered round the tiny space, inspecting the *gaijin* in his native habitat, I tried to divert her with some questions. I held up a Christmas card. "Ah, Monet!" she cried. Then a postcard I had bought in a museum. "Rodin!" Then a paperback I had found downtown, in Sony Plaza. "Paddington Bear!"

After the kettle had boiled, I put down two mugs on the table and knelt down on the *tatami* to show her some earrings I had bought for my mother. She leaned forward till her hair was tickling my face. In the winter darkness of the tiny room, the fire glowing, I brushed back her hair, felt her lips touch mine, her body shaking as if electrified.

Later, we walked along the river in the dusk. Turning, we saw the eastern hills, thick with orange trees, glowing in the dying light. Then, sitting down beside the red-lit river, she sang me a melody from *The Sound of Music*—"Something Good"—about Maria's escape from her abbey, in a quavering, high, but steady voice. "When I little children size," she said, "this song my favorite. But I never think I find this feeling. I think I cannot. I always 'lost lady.' Now I feel this song more. Thank you very much."

There was a long, charged silence on the riverbank. "Autumn now ending," she said, as we watched the last light leave the hills. And that night, it snowed.

Sachiko's goodbye, when it came, was as perfectly planned, as exquisitely decorated, as everything else in this land of ceremonies.

One day, towards the end of spring, she invited me and Matthew to join her and Hideko at a tea ceremony. She appeared in the hotel lobby in a radiant blue kimono, hair done up the style of a Meiji maiden, her steps in pure-white socks and formal sandals slow and reticent. We watched a woman in a white peacock kimono glide along against the paper screens, flooded now with early-morning sun, and we entered our names with thick brushes in a visitors' book. Then, with a bow, we were ushered into a room full of bowing matrons, all beady-eyed and kimonoed, as used to this as we might be to church. Seated cross-legged, we sipped at our tea, dutifully inspecting the lacquer tea box, inscribed with a scarcely visible tracery of cherry blossoms. "Night cherry," Sachiko whispered under her breath, and the matrons leaned a little closer. "Little *monoganashii* feeling." We inspected a scroll that told of a flower and a butterfly, and, eyes bright, she looked over at me meaningfully as the springtime message was translated.

Matthew, meanwhile, was his usual engaging self, and as the matrons looked at us in wonder, he started pulling at the legs crossed under him, forming a hideous frown and delivering, in loud stage whispers, a moving account of his torments. "Can't understand it. Terribly simple, actually. Legs quite dead. Can't move. Don't know if I'll ever recover!"

"Are you okay?" Sachiko asked anxiously, leaning over me towards him, to extend a hand.

"Oh, yes," he said, smiling tightly. "Fine, fine. Just a little stiff. Can't move, you see. Awfully painful, actually. Quite extraordinary."

The pantomime continued, I as ill at ease as Matthew, and the matrons staring over at us with quickened excitement, exchanging happy glances and then looking back at us, in awe; for them, I imagined, hardened veterans of these rites, the presence of two galumphing foreign males, banging against walls, attacking their tea with chopsticks, and pulling at their limbs like pretzels, was doubtless a welcome gust of comic relief in what was otherwise dull routine. "Terribly sorry, awfully embarrassing," Matthew apologized, smiling unhappily back at them. "Not sure, actually, whether I can move!"

"This was something Merchant Taylors' never prepared you for," I whispered back.

"No, quite," he answered, tight-lipped, then erupted into schoolboy chortles.

The tea bowl went round and round for our admiration, we munched at our sweets, scattering crumbs, which we proceeded to fold ineptly in the napkins Sachiko gave us. Then at last it was over. Matthew and I disentangled limbs and got up, legs so dead that I, standing up, reeled and staggered against the paper screen before bowing farewell to the delighted matrons and tiptoeing out to the lobby. Outside, in the soothing sun, Sachiko led our incongruous band to a coffee shop, and as the four of us settled round a circular table, Matthew filled us in on how a two-day trip to Tokyo Disneyland had somehow kept him away for a month. In Tokyo, he explained, he had found everything he wanted: high fashion, neon futurism, even an English-speaking girlfriend. After two weeks, however, of a consuming intensity that had almost frightened him, he had rung her up one day, to find that she had dropped him for a new foreigner.

> —————— ☽ ——————
>
> *The* Japanese cherry tree is cultivated not for its fruit, but for its blossom, which has long been to Japan what the rose is to Western nations....
>
> The Japanese are fond of preserving cherry blossoms in salt and making a kind of tea out of them. The fragrance of the infusion is delicious, but its taste a bitter deception.
>
> ◆
>
> —Basil Hall Chamberlain,
> *Japanese Things: Being Notes*
> *on Various Subjects*
> *Connected with Japan*

"Ah, very beautiful story," said Sachiko dreamily. "Little cherry blossom feeling. One-night dream."

"Yes, yes, precisely," said Matthew agreeably, used by now to the Japanese habit of turning even pain into something lovely, and unaware, perhaps, that she was in effect referring to a one-night stand.

After our coffee was finished, Sachiko dispatched the other two into a taxi bound for a department store, and clomped along the wide boulevard by my side, in tiny footsteps. "I come you room?" she asked. "Are you okay? We little buy cake?" and, stopping at a bakery, we made our way through a riddle of sunny streets, back to my room. There, sitting down, she unclasped her earrings and, laying them tidily on my table, took me by surprise.

"Today," she began, "I wear kimono so you always keep very happy memory of me." I could not fathom what she meant. "You give me much dream, much imagination. I want you write many thing, very beautiful memory of Japan. We together time, very happy, many dream. But then, other life, very difficult. I much much thinking in my heart—then little stomach problem. My heart little sick."

She stopped, and I, accustomed both to the solemnity of her feelings and to their sudden turns, held my breath.

"You have very beautiful bird life," she went on. "Very free, very easy. But my life very different. I tiny, I not have wing. I need more *akirameru*." She stopped and, turning to her crumpled, leather-bound old dictionary, skimmed through the pages and stopped on the word she wanted. "Re-sig-na-tion. Here in Japan, this very important. All person must have this resig—"

"Resignation."

"Re-sig-na-tion. If not have, many problem. Then maybe I must little say goodbye."

Looking back at her, I fumbled for my words. Then, turning to the only piece of paper at hand—the happy orange-and-white bag of the bakery—I sketched a diagram of my heart, and she, a little sadly, nodded over her cake. I then drew another picture, of the three routes open to us.

"Maybe goodbye best," she said. "But please today, you come together my house, play together children?" There was nothing I wanted less to do right now, but I could see that she needed to recast the play, to establish herself again in the mother's role and me as the friend of the family. And so we went back out into the mild spring sun, and on the long train ride across town, I watched her rearrange herself, as I did too, putting on a bright smile and an air of cheerful competence.

Back at home, Yuki and Hiroshi raced out and bounced all over

me, pulling me this way and that, and I began roaring at Hiroshi
like a bear, and lifting Yuki high into the air while she screamed,
and, when they were not looking, wheezing and whistling like an
imagined raccoon. Then Yuki careened off to grab her moth-eaten,
one-eyed orange raccoon. ("Lasker," explained her mother.
"Lasker?" And she sang me the jingle of a TV cartoon, "Rascal
Raccoon.") Then the children, well trained already in how to
entertain all visitors, changed into their best clothes—Yuki into
a pretty frock, Hiroshi donning a red bow tie—and solemnly
took turns playing the piano, feet dangling poignantly only halfway
to the floor. Then all four of us went back to the Nogi Shrine,
in a light spring rain, and played hide-and-seek in the gathering
dark, as we had done on the day we met.

In the dying light, Sachiko bought us all cans of milk tea, and
while the children played with acorns, the two of us padded around
the noiseless shrine, dedicated to the hero of the Russo-Japanese
War, the man who had been the Emperor's headmaster and role
model. The walkways were deserted now in the rain, the wet
ground strewn with petals; the bare branches were black against
graying skies.

"Yesterday," she said dreamily, guiding me to her favorite tree,
"I lie down this bench, and look at sky. Sky very blue; cherry very
pink. Spring wind come down, so soft. I look up, I dream I have
little wing. Bird talking, leaves dancing in spring wind."

She pointed out the different trees to me, told me the stories
that she shared with them, explaining which one was king and
which his ladies-in-waiting. "But today," she went on ruminatively,
"all cherry fall. Little fox wedding day."

"Half rain, half sun, you mean?"

She nodded, and I could see her in a fox wedding mood herself,
caught between conflicting dreams.

In her flat, she cooked a quick dinner and packed the children
off to bed. Then, seated at the small table that took up nearly all of
the poster-filled room, she told me, eyes shining, about all the
hopes she'd ever had, and how they'd disappeared. I looked around
at the pictures of *a-ha,* the grinning sea otter on the ceiling, the

framed photo of her children with the abbot of the temple: this was how the Japanese ended things, I thought, avoiding the embarrassment and mess of sudden death with the clean break of a kind of suicide. Everything brought to a ceremonial close, as shapely as a morning-after poem.

When it came time for me to leave, she brought out a scarf and tied it round my neck to keep me from the cold, and then walked, as usual, to the train station, as on the first day that I'd visited. As the train pulled away, I watched till her small figure was finally out of my sight.

Pico Iyer was born in Oxford in 1957 and was educated at Eton, Oxford, and Harvard. He is an essayist for Time *magazine, a contributing editor at* Condé Nast Traveler, *and the author of several books, including* Video Night in Kathmandu *and* The Lady and the Monk, *from which this was excerpted.*

✦

The Japanese see the tension as one between *honne*, the individual's personal views, and *tatemae*, the views that are demanded by the individual's position in the group. The same difference is expressed in the terms *ninjo*, which translates loosely as "human feelings" or, looser still, as the "dictates of the heart," and *giri*, which is the individual's social obligations.

—Chris Taylor, Robert Strauss, and Tony Wheeler,
Japan - a travel survival kit

* * *

Day in Capri

A traveler learns that keeping a
memory perfect requires a sacrifice.

I WAS WALKING DOWN NAPLES'S PIAZZA DEL MUNICIPIO WHEN A wet head maneuvered under my umbrella. "Lady wanna guy?"

"No, no guide," I told him, glaring until he ducked out. I was in Italy to get over a bad breakup, but I wasn't halfway through my first day when I realized I had made a mistake. Instead of forgetting men, I was warring a new, shameless, rude-resistant breed. It got worse as I moved south. In the train from Venice, I sat next to a well-dressed gentleman who wanted my left breast for his pillow. Then three hooting Neapolitans and a dog on a single Vespa had circled me for blocks as I tried to find my *pensione*. Yesterday my tour guide of Pompeii steered me to ruins which were viewed best, he assured me, from his bedroom. I couldn't even sip a cappuccino in peace. My three weeks were almost up, and I was ready to head home, more disillusioned than when I left.

From the port I could see the island of Capri sunning in the mouth of the bay. The rain didn't (wouldn't, it seemed) dampen it. White-washed houses backed by a green proscenium of vineyards clustered around the harbor and thinned over the two craggy mountain peaks. Capri looked like a place where I could rest. I booked a ticket.

The ferry docked at the Marina Grande. I caught a bus which agonized up the twisting road to the city of Capri in the deep forge between the two mountains. The bus was crammed with women— so they do exist, I thought. They held chickens on their laps and when the bus passed a roadside statue of Mary, the women would shift the squawking orange birds to bless themselves. I was decoding my guidebook's cheap lodgings and decided to find the tourist office in the Piazza Umberto. I hoisted my backpack to my shoulders, barreled between the seats, and set off across the big square lined with oaks. I didn't know yet that my pack's zipper had broken, although I felt the stares of the old men playing chess or drinking grappa on benches in the shade. Later, Massimo would tell me how, from the funicular landing a little farther up the mountain, he looked down to see my determined march as my yellow nightie, a red shower clog, the pairs of blue and white panties fell on the cobblestones. He would say he wanted to run behind me, gathering them like a bouquet.

———)———

*T*he tiny paradise of Capri seems to float in the azure waters of the Bay of Naples. Only four miles long by two miles wide, its name may refer to the Greek word for wild boar, *kapros,* which many think once roamed its craggy granite. Capri became a resort for the powerful as early as 29 B.C., when Augustus began to spend time here between campaigns. Later Roman leaders made it a popular spot for orgies. But it was during the Romantic Period that European writers, poets, and artists crowned Capri as the perfect romantic site, a place of deep colors, fragrant blossoms, and Mediterranean sensuality: a kind of found Eden.

◆

—JBW

Of course, the tourist office was closed. I was leaning against my rezipped pack fretting through my guidebook when a man approached, tall and thin with a mass of brown curls. "Do you need a place to stay?" he asked in English.

"No," I said, without looking up. I knew where this was going.

"Please. That guidebook is no good."

"No," I said again. He paused for a moment, then squatted beside me, took a pencil stub from his pocket, crossed off the first three of the four *pensiones,* and stood up. I felt him standing behind me, then heard him walk slowly away.

The second *pensione* seemed best. I found the bell tower and the narrow blind alley beside it crisscrossed with hanging laundry and heaved my way uphill. I reached the address—now a bicycle rental shop. The first *pensione* was a bakery. Should have listened to the guy in the square, I thought. The owner of the fourth *pensione* showed me to a bright room with white curtains and oleanders in terra cotta pots on the sills. I sat on the bed and it felt good to get the pack off. I napped, dreaming of a face I had come 2,000 miles to forget.

That afternoon, I visited the blue grotto. I hired a rowboat at the Marina Grande, and my guide rowed me around the rocky shoreline and through a tiny opening in the cliff face I hadn't noticed. Inside the huge cave, because of the strange refraction of light, the water glows a silvery sky-blue. Ours was the only boat in the grotto, and as he rowed my guide sang an old ballad for the sheer beauty, I think, of hearing the rolling vowels echo from cave walls which danced with the reflections of waves.

When I got back to my hotel lobby, a woman in a simple white dress was waiting for me. She introduced herself as Giulia, the sister of Massimo.

"Who?"

"The man you met in the Piazza. We knew we could find you here," she said, and we both laughed. They shared the same huge blue eyes, skinny frame, and beautiful English. Giulia asked if I would like to join them for dinner; they knew a place with fresh *foccacia* and a Chianti pressed from the grapes of Capri. Hmmm.... I was a bit lonely, but I wondered if it was a set up, and by this point I had so cultivated my wariness that I couldn't overcome it, couldn't stop asking, "What does he want from me?" So I told Giulia "Maybe next time," knowing my flight left from Naples in two days.

That night, mostly by following the scent of garlic, I found an open-air *trattoria* with bright lanterns hanging from clementines. At one table I saw Massimo and Giulia. He leaned in to hear what she was saying and threw back his head in a laugh that was pleasant and deep. I remembered my abruptness in the Piazza, remembered too that he had smelled of lemons. It occurred to me that in the three weeks I'd been in Italy, I'd gotten drunk with some Americans, exchanged books and addresses with some Canadians, and dined with an Australian couple who was now planning to add my Chicago apartment to their around-the-world itinerary, but I hadn't made friends with any Italians. Meanwhile, the host was escorting me and my dinner companion—a book entitled *Adventures Along the Italian Coast*—to a table for one. "What the hell," I thought, and sat down with Massimo and Giulia.

We ate vine-ripened tomatoes layered with soft moons of buffalo mozzarella, basil leaves, and olive oil so rich it was dark green. "Ah," said Giulia to Massimo, tapping my empty plate, "*buona forchetta!*" A joyous eater. I told them of how my Irish mother loved Italian cuisine and how I got my summer job waiting tables at swank Vincenza's because in the interview I identified twenty-three kinds of pasta. We spoke of cooking then, and Giulia drifted over to a nearby table to greet friends while Massimo and I traded risotto recipes. After dinner over espresso they told me of summers in their uncle's olive grove in Umbria, swaddling the trees' bases in white sheets and not climbing down the trunks until the sheets were heavy with the purple-black fruit. I asked about their family; only their elderly mother was left, so they lived on the island with her. Giulia worked at a gift shop, and Massimo ran the funicular that propelled tourists up the slope of Mt. Tiberio, the southern mountain, "the nobler of the two." We spoke of Segovia and Massimo lost what was left of his shyness and talked about classical guitar. His fingers, I noticed, were long and steady. The things they held—a fork, the stem of his Chianti glass—took on a classical beauty.

As we walked away from the *trattoria,* I asked Massimo if he would play for us. He said yes, and spoke to Giulia in such rapid

Italian I understood little but my name. "What are you saying?" I asked him.

"He says he forgives me," answered Giulia. "Massimo was angry when I told him I had gone to your hotel. He would keep his heart a secret." So it *had* been a set-up, I thought, but Massimo was innocent. He smiled shyly. And when Massimo ducked out of the low door of his home bearing a guitar but no sister, I smiled too.

He drew back vines to reveal a hidden path to the peak of Mt. Tiberio. We hiked under the funicular cables, past the hamlet of fishermen's cottages, past the roses grown on vineyards as a warning because they'll wither early from the virus that kills grapes, past the ruins of one of the twelve villas that Tiberius had built on the mountain. At one point Massimo stopped: "Wait. Dessert." He waded into the brush, returning with honey from a hidden comb. The inside of his wrist was red where he had been stung twice, so I caught his hand and probed the warm skin for a stinger. I didn't want to let it go, so I didn't, and we kept walking.

There was a cool breeze at the top of the mountain, and we sat on the cliff's edge. Far across the bay Vesuvius was a dark shadow, and beneath us lights from the fishermen's boats flickered. Massimo took his guitar from its case and strummed songs he had learned from his grandfather. I watched his strong fingers slide up and down the guitar's neck. There was the sea pounding its rhythm, the taste of salt, the scent of lemon and sagebrush. The stars falling through the curls of his dark hair. He looked at me while he played, and his eyes seemed enormous gilt grottos where rare fish finned down deep, where echoes of love songs curved off the luminous walls. We were kissing then, and Massimo forgot English and crooned soft words. The rocks were just sharp enough under my back, and I kept a sandaled foot over the cliff so I could be close, close enough to the waves' undulant baritone, close enough to it all. *Ti amo.*

The next morning Massimo and I were to meet at the funicular. He'd lift me to the terraced Gardens of Augustus where we'd picnic. He'd feed his *buona forchetta*.

But when I woke with the sea breeze puffing the white gauze curtain into my room like a sail, I didn't want a new day and the chance that we might wreck things. I thought how so much of what is good in this world gets tarnished, qualified, corrected by time. And I wanted that night forever. So I wrapped it all up, bundled the stars and Segovia and lights on the water, lemon, salt kisses, wild sage. I lifted my bag, now latched with Massimo's guitar string. I left.

And even when my bus pulled away from the Piazza and I glimpsed Massimo waiting at the funicular, clacking the handles of his wooden picnic basket, I didn't stop.

This is not a story I tell often. It's like a wish that might disappear if I share it. But sometimes when I'm alone, I unwrap it. I court myself with it. I know one day I'll take a husband and the children that will follow. My husband will be understanding, and I'll tell him of the men I've known, but I'll not mention the man from Capri. My husband will know I own a mystery. He'll love me all the more for it. One day in the drugstore buying children's aspirin, I'll find a bottle of Capri bath oil. It will show a mountain cliff with rocks just sharp enough dropping down to a marina on the sparkling Mediterranean where white boats nose each other in the sun. I'll bathe in that oil only rarely. When I do, my husband will notice through my splash a goodness, something pure in the tub's shallow grotto, as I lie almost close enough to it all.

Beth Ann Fennelly is from Chicago and received her B.A. from the University of Notre Dame. After graduation she taught English in the Czech Republic. Currently she is earning her M.F.A. at the University of Arkansas. She has published poems and essays in The American Scholar, U.S. News and World Report, *and* Best American Poetry 1996.

*

The boatman had deep brown eyes with long lashes. He took me by the hand to steady me onto the small boat, and looking down, I noticed his muscular legs. Sun glimmered on the aquamarine water, and schools of tiny fish spiraled through luminous depths in the caves below. When we returned to the port, the boatman asked, "Why are you staying on the mainland and not here? It's far more beautiful here. Here we have nature, quiet, and the sea, away from the tourists and the chaos." He was right, I felt completely at peace.

But my ferry left in ten minutes and I told him I must be on it. As we turned to go, he looked deeply into me and grew serious. "Go back to your hotel, pack your bags, and come back to the islands on the ferry tomorrow."

"I can't do that," I sputtered. "I have plans with friends."

"The day after tomorrow then," he insisted. "I'll be waiting for you on the dock."

The next day, in spite of myself, I was filled with thoughts of the island and the boatman. I awoke early on Thursday and packed a small overnight bag.

He was waiting on the dock. Our eyes met and he blushed a deep red. He threw his arms around me and shouted, "*Miracolo!* I thought of you constantly but didn't dare to hope you would really come back to the islands and to me."

—Tina Stromsted, "The Italian Boatman"

CAT GONZALEZ

★ ★ ★

The Lucky Thing

A happy couple offer inspiration
with a twist.

THIRTY MINUTES AWAY FROM THE GUADALAJARA AIRPORT, BUT seemingly hundreds of years distant in time, lies the island of Mezcala whose ruins date from the early 19th century. The cobbled roads laid by Mexican insurgents in 1814 make good hiking paths from which to tour the historic area. It would seem a shame to spoil the adventure by describing the ruins. What does bear repeating is the tale of the unusual great-great-grandparents we picked up on the way to the island fortress.

We were in high spirits as we headed east from Chapala following the lake. My sister and I hummed along as my husband Raymundo sang *ranchera* songs from some of the places he'd lived; Zacatecas, Michoacan, and Veracruz. In Tlachichilco we stopped to buy lemonade and a woman with a parasol asked us if we would take her parents to Mezcala. "Always room for two more, especially such a diminutive couple."

With surprising agility this elderly pair snuggled themselves into the Volkswagen between the terrier and my sister. Luisa was about the size of a ten-year-old, and she wore her gray hair in a single braid down her back. Her eyes had a far-away look, as if they gazed backwards almost a century ago. Her husband Manuel

33

wore a *sombrero* with a tassel on the back and a blue shirt that must have been washed at least one hundred times.

"*Ja,*" said Raymundo, "we've got you outnumbered again. Three Mexicans to two *norteamericanas.*" He serenaded us with the song about "bury me with you, if possible in the same coffin" and the old woman harmonized in a surprisingly strong voice.

My sister rolled her eyes at me. Perhaps emboldened by our singing and joking, Manuel began to ask personal questions. "How is it," he ventured, "that you're *norteamericana* and your husband is Mexicano?"

"After being with him for four years, all else pales in comparison," I said in my accented Spanish, and my sister giggled.

"What did she say?" Raymundo of the dark cinnamon skin translated my remark and they both tittered. Luisa fumbled in the string bag tied around her waist and took out some sour capelina fruits gathered from the hills. Manuel made a face and said they were good for your health. We ate as few as courtesy would allow and tried to turn the conversation to the ruins on the island. The old man found the topic of couples infinitely more fascinating, and regaled us with a story of how his wife nursed him back to health when he had typhoid fever. Her knowledge of herbs had saved his life, so now he eats whatever she offers.

Then he continued to quiz my husband. How long have we been married? How on earth did he ever get used to me? Raymundo shook his head and ran his hand over his dark curls. "It wasn't easy." He is a weaver of tales as compelling as his songs, and soon he had the passengers chuckling. He told them that he'd known me for two years before he ever saw me wearing anything besides shorts and t-shirts. "Most unfeminine." Dust clouds enveloped us, burros laden with wood moved quickly out of the road, and a pair of brilliant orioles flew out of the shrubbery.

Luisa spoke in Manuel's ear and they pointed out that I still don't dress in the Mexican custom. The implication is that I'm incurably *norteamericana.* "How about her face?" asked Luisa. "Did you like her face?"

"It was hard to get used to at first," laughed Raymundo, showing white teeth. "Our women make their eyes a work of art. Catherine, no. Unadorned eyes in an almost naked face. After I fell in love with her, I thought her eyes were a work of art just as they are, green as the sea." He sang Prince Tizoc's song about "loving you more than my eyes" and the old couple joined in again.

We stopped at a meadow to share our lemonade and my sister and I noticed how tenderly Manuel helped his wife to alight from the car. We told them they were an inspiration to us. They giggled and admitted that they had a lot of adjusting to do also. Manuel confessed that he wasn't very responsible when he was young. Vermillion flycatchers swooped across Lake Chapala to catch insects and yellow warblers sang love songs. Luisa said that they were only fourteen and fifteen when they married.

As they made small jokes about their years together, I sensed that they endured because they had the will to survive. To survive heartbreak, hard times, the gradual ebbing of physical strength, the rise and fall of sexual desire, the births and deaths of children. As if reading my mind, Manuel said, with no trace of embarrassment, "We still care for each other as much as on the day we were married." And that was 80 years ago, added his wife.

The three of us exchanged surprised glances. We told them we had thought they were at least 10 years younger. Manuel said he wasn't deaf a decade ago.

"But the lucky thing is, I can still see."

In her lilting voice Luisa piped up, "You see, I'm blind, so he's my eyes. But he depends on me. The lucky thing is, I can still hear."

Cat Gonzalez was born in Denver and lives happily in Mexico in the countryside near Guadalajara with two ducks, two pheasants, two dogs, two turtles, and the sweet man she writes of in this essay. By the time you read this, the baby pheasants will be hatched and her book of short stories and essays, Reflections of Mexico in My Eyes, *will be available.*

✴

There is only one terminal dignity: love.

—Helen Hayes

LEE GUTKIND

⋆ * ⋆

Sweet Mystery of Life

A man lost in the forest—and in life—
is saved by heavenly music.

AN ELDERLY MAN WITH A LONG WHITE APRON WRAPPED AROUND
his waist and a light dusting of flour on his fingertips stepped out
of the kitchen and plodded across the room, waving his arms and
talking simultaneously. "Mama won't let me sit and talk until I
finish baking," he said, nodding in the general direction of a
plump, white-haired lady, who was just now gathering checks and
counting change at the register.

"Can you imagine?" he asked, smiling mischievously, pointing
and wagging his finger, while rocking back and forth on his
heels. "We've been married long enough to raise a family, clear
this land, build this restaurant and all the cabins around it with
our own hands and our own timber, and still, even when I want
to have an innocent conversation with a customer, my wife
won't let me."

Scotty was short and wiry with ruddy cheeks and slightly
bugged-out eyes that danced as he talked. Ever since I had pulled
up on my motorcycle, Scotty had directed toward me an erratic
but continuous commentary about the hardships of living with a
demanding, domineering woman like Mama. But even when he
complained most forcefully, Scotty was nearly always smiling.

I looked up at the old man, returned his smile, and then shrugged sympathetically. I had just devoured some of the best Southern fried chicken I had ever eaten, topping it off with rich apple cobbler. This fellow was an artist with a deep fryer and an oven. My fingertips, which I pondered drowsily, glittered with grease. The wet boots I had placed at the edge of the fire had long ago stopped steaming. My leather jacket, hanging nearby, was now nearly dry. Mama, meanwhile, went about her business quickly and efficiently, finishing her count, stuffing money and receipts into an envelope, without paying the least bit of attention to the protests from her husband.

"Do you hear me, Mama?" Scotty called, his bushy brows scrunched up over his eyes.

The woman, slightly taller than Scotty, cocked her head in an amused but rebellious manner. She had heard her husband all right—this was a game they obviously often played—but chose not to acknowledge his complaint.

There were about two dozen tables in this lodge, arranged around a great stone fireplace, which divided the room in two. Over toward the front was a row of display cases filled with luscious-looking pies and pastries—Scotty's specialties—and handmade quilts, crafts, and carvings.

Scotty, who had remained standing by the fire, continued to shake his head and rock back and forth on his heels, watching and mumbling as Mama, the day's receipts in her hand, headed toward a tiny office near the back of the building. "Scotty, we must have tarts for tomorrow. You promised," she said, not unkindly. "You better bake."

"I'm preparing to do just that, Mama," Scotty answered in a singsong, high-pitched whine, followed by a long, drawn-out sigh. "Right after I rest my feet."

He waited patiently until she closed the door behind her, then walked over to my table, moving in an abrupt and almost mechanical way, as if he were in pain, although his face did not show it. He paused, cocked his ear, and waited a little more, listening while she got herself settled. Then he pulled up a chair and sat down.

"You know," he said, in a hushed tone of confidentiality, "I haven't been living up here in the backwoods all my life."

Facing the fire, Scotty sighed, shook off his slippers, and wiggled his old toes at the coals.

Scotty told me about how it was, growing up in Scotland and, as a teenager during World War I, working in the mines for a few dollars a day, ten hours straight, and how, suddenly, he realized he could no longer make himself shimmy into those dark and endless tunnels, no longer face the stifling, claustrophobic danger for one more day.

He gathered up his belongings and went to America, settling in Cleveland, where he eventually found work in the public library. "We were a poor family, with no money or worldly goods, but my mother passed on a treasure of knowledge to me. She taught me how to bake, how to read, how to sing. With those simple gifts, I've been able to earn most everything I ever wanted in my life here in America—and a lot more than I expected." He stretched his short, wiry frame across the table, grasped my arm, and squeezed it. "Let me tell you how."

It was past 10 p.m., early spring in western Pennsylvania. I was the only customer remaining in this rustic old lodge and restaurant in the heart of Cook Forest.

I had never met Scotty and Mama before and, in fact, had no intention of stopping at their lodge. But, after a long and solitary winter, I had opened my eyes one morning and knew it was time to escape. The claustrophobia, frustration, and self-pity that settles in after an awful February in a cold gray city was too much to take. I packed my saddlebags, gassed up my motorcycle, and thundered out of town. I needed to view the world from a different perspective, and to be alone—not just alone in a room of a house or in the corner of a bar, but in a fresh open space. Cook Forest, less than two hours north of Pittsburgh, was perfect for such instant and soothing isolation.

My plan was to camp at a secluded spot I knew along the Clarion, hang out for a few days, and think. But as I paralleled the winding line of the Allegheny River north from Pittsburgh, it had started to rain. I stubbornly continued riding as the rain turned to sleet. Before I knew what was happening, I was lost in the middle of Cook Forest, immersed in the white, blinding blur of snow.

Luckily, I sniffed out the warm, soothing smoke of a wood fire. Slipping and sliding, I followed my nose to Scotty's.

First Scotty told me of his comfortable, albeit lonely life in Cleveland, cataloguing and lending books by day and reading those that looked most interesting until late into the night. But when the Great Depression hit, public services were immediately cut back. Eventually, Scotty lost his job.

With no work and a dwindling supply of dollars, he had no choice but to go to the country to look for a livelihood. "Many of my friends were heading west, but I had often gone camping in Cook Forest during summer vacations, so I decided to go there, deep into the mountains. So," said Scotty, "I started walking."

Many people think we travel to rush out into crowds of people, but most of us travel to travel within. There is no more quiet and central space than the anonymity of being in a foreign place without ties or obligations.

In quiet moments sitting alone at a cafe, looking down on a village from the edge of a cliff, or in the suspended peace of a soaring cathedral, we can pause to look back with objectivity and forward with intelligence and hope. Travel can be a series of these small epiphanies. With distance we can see patterns, themes, and questions our life has posed to us, and sometimes, in a faraway place, the answers come.

◆

—JBW

He paused to light a cigarette, staring out the window and into the snow with distant, fire-reflecting eyes. "Go on," I said.

"Well, it was tough walking," Scotty continued. "Everywhere you went, people were poor. When I was hungry, I picked berries from bushes, green apples out of trees. Where I could, I chopped wood and performed other odd jobs for my dinner." Sometimes he slept in barns or haylofts, other times he concealed himself in the woods, lying down between green sheets of wild rhododendron, on beds of minty fern.

It was a long up and down walk across Ohio and into Pennsylvania, heading southeast.

"By the time I got to the forest, not too far from where we're sitting, it was pitch-black in the dead of night," Scotty said, dragging from his cigarette.

"I walked into the woods and laid my bedroll down. It was comfortable enough, although much too damp. I was in a stand of virgin pine. I remember because the pine needles cushioned the forest more than a foot deep." It was quiet and fairly warm. Scotty couldn't see the moon because the tops of the trees were literally wrapped around one another in an umbrella of darkness.

Lying on the forest floor, Scotty closed his eyes and tried to sleep, but he was worn-out from all his traveling and more than a little scared. Gradually, he drifted into a troubled sleep.

"In the middle of the night, I woke up." Scotty lowered his voice to a whisper and cocked an eyebrow, pausing dramatically in the silent, shadowed room. "I was convinced that I heard the sound of a rich sweet chorus of voices."

"In the woods?" I asked.

"I wasn't sure," Scotty said, pausing briefly once more to tighten the screw of suspense. "So I lay there on my old brown blanket, my eyes tightly closed, my heart thumping, listening until I knew it was true."

"People were singing?"

"It was gospel!" Scotty said.

"But who?"

Scotty slammed his fist down on the table and rolled his eyes in amazement. "Exactly what I wanted to know. Who in their right mind would be singing gospel—or anything else, for that matter— out in the boondocks in the middle of the night?"

Scotty paused to snub out his cigarette. He looked me over

carefully to be sure he was commanding my undivided attention. He didn't have to worry. I was hooked.

"I lay there and I listened," Scotty repeated, still whispering, "but the sound didn't go away." The echoing harmony filtered through the forest like a gentle breeze. "I finally opened my eyes and stood up. I could see the faint flicker of a campfire off in the distance, so I gathered up my bedroll and started walking toward it." He paused momentarily to ponder. "Although I had never considered myself a spiritually lost person, I tell you, right at that moment, I quite literally felt saved."

"It was a midnight gospel service," he announced, his voice filled with wonder. "Even from far away, I could see the congregation, fifty or more, gathered in a circle. I was drawn to them by some mysterious force. I could feel it pulling at me. I began to run," he said, rotating his elbows and knees back and forth slowly, an old man's movement, but with the slightest hint of a steadfast jog. I wondered again, judging by his stiff, awkward motion, if he were in pain. "By the time I made it through the trees, the service was nearly over. But somebody had already caught my eye."

Suddenly, he took two quick steps toward me. Instinctively, I jumped back in surprise.

"A woman." His arm shot up in the air as he raised his voice. "The most glorious and gorgeous woman I had ever laid eyes on in my whole life. I felt the lightning and thunder reverberating from my temples..." He paused to look up at the oak-beam ceiling, hesitated, then cast his eyes down to the floor "...to my toes."

"What did you do?"

"I couldn't help myself," Scotty shook his head ferociously. "I walked right out into the middle of the circle of those worshipers and stared at her." He paused once again, and a golden glow crept across his face.

For a long while, I sat back, smiled, and waited, savoring the sauce of suspense. As a storyteller, Scotty's timing was impeccable. "And then?" I finally said.

"I started singing," Scotty said. He straightened his shoulders and plodded over to the window

"Singing?"

"Ah, Sweet Mystery of Life."

"What?"

"It's a love song," Scotty answered curtly, looking me up and down with disbelief. "It's the most romantic love song ever written." He rattled off a few bars.

> Ah, sweet mystery of life at last I've found you.
> Ah, at last I know the secret of it all.
>
> All the longing, seeking, striving, waiting, yearning
> The burning hopes, joy and idle tears that fall.

"I'm sorry." I shrugged in embarrassment of my ignorance. "It's nice," I added.

"You better believe it."

When his song was over, Scotty walked slowly across the circle, made yellow by the glow of fire, until he stood right in front of his mysterious lady. I could detect a special glint in Scotty's eye, as if that very night was right now repeating itself in this room, as if that wonderful woman was waiting impatiently for him on the other side of the glass.

"Everyone was watching us now, but it didn't matter a bit," Scotty said. "It wouldn't have mattered if I was in the middle of Carnegie Hall with thousands of people watching, because I felt completely alone with her at that moment, and she was obviously completely comfortable with me. When I finally stopped singing, I reached out and offered her my hand."

"And she took it?"

"Of course." He looked at me suspiciously, but continued. "She took my hand," Scotty said, "and then she got to her feet and stared right into my eyes, and I knew—I knew with more certainty than I had ever known anything in my entire life—that this was the woman I loved and would marry."

"And did you?"

He rolled his eyes and winked at me. I was getting anxious to hear the end of the story, but Scotty would not be hurried. It was his story and he would go along at his own pace, whether I liked it or not.

They spent the rest of the night staring into one another's eyes and talking. At daybreak, they walked up to Seneca Rock, a jutting rocky shelf high above the rippling river, to watch the sunrise. Below them, the Clarion rushed on down towards its eventual union with Allegheny, blazing with new morning light.

They ate salmon for breakfast, Scotty said. Right from the can. And they got to know each other, talking quietly, like old friends. He learned that she had organized these midnight gospel services all on her own, that her father was a minister, and that she was here with a girlfriend, on vacation from Ohio. She loved Cook Forest, she told him, and wanted someday to live here.

They were married within the year, found jobs, and were eventually able to save and borrow enough money to purchase fifty acres near Cook Forest. "Our first buildings were surplus army Quonset huts, purchased in South Carolina and hauled north in an old truck I had managed to salvage and piece together."

"Eventually, we tore down the huts and built these nice cabins behind here, each with its own stone fireplace. Then we put up this lodge, with a fancy, well-equipped kitchen." He stomped his foot, as if to emphasize the solidity of his efforts and investment. Then he paused. "It was a thrill at first; it still is, I guess. But like any other business, it is constantly demanding. Something always comes up."

He was standing at the window, staring out into the silver bed of snow, watching the moonlight bathe the distant hills and trees. He stood there for so long, and concentrated with such force, that you could almost hear the jangled music of his mind as he relived the previous forty years of his life.

Then we heard a scrape against the floor from the next room. The door of the tiny office into which Mama had disappeared some time before opened a wee crack. "Scotty? Where are you? What are you doing?"

Scotty turned ever so slowly away from the window, but he did not answer. Instead, he padded back toward my table, shoved his old feet into his slippers, and paused to look at me. Then he turned and headed into the kitchen, pushing his way through the swinging doors.

"Scotty?" Mama called again.

Instantly, pots, pans, dishes, and silverware began to clatter. It was then that he started singing. I knew what the song was going to be before the first word registered. His rich tenor voice filtered into the room, wrapping me in a cloak of reassuring comfort.

Lee Gutkind, editor of the journal Creative Nonfiction, *has performed as a clown for Ringling Brothers, scrubbed with heart and liver transplant surgeons, traveled with a crew of National League baseball umpires, wandered the country on a motorcycle, and experienced psychotherapy with a distressed family—all as research for eight books, including most recently,* A Veterinarian's Touch. *He is a professor of English at the University of Pittsburgh and director of the Mid-Atlantic Creative Nonfiction Writers' Conference at Goucher College in Baltimore.*

★

Music is the best, most beautiful, and most perfect way that we have of expressing a sweet concord of mind to each other.

—Jonathan Edwards (1753)

SUSAN FEINBERG

* * *

Animal Crackers

A jaded traveler makes a promise
she knows she can keep.

I'D BEEN TRAILING HIM FOR NEARLY TWELVE BLOCKS; HE WAS THE first traveler I'd seen since arriving in Punta Arenas that morning. His blonde curls blew wildly in the winter breeze off the Strait of Magellan; he looked like a Malibu surfer boy, but from his clothes I guessed he wasn't American. When he walked in the middle of the road, so would I. When he criss-crossed from one side to other, I followed. Every so often he'd glance back at me, and keep walking. Finally, he turned off the deserted road and strode up a gentle hill and stopped. We'd arrived at a monument.

I approached him as he was reading the inscription on a plaque. He didn't look up. He was beautiful.

"Hola," I said.

"Do you know the time?" he finally replied, in English. Ivan the world traveler didn't wear a watch.

I confessed that I'd been following him for nearly twenty minutes.

"I know," he said.

We laughed.

We were both headed to Tierra del Fuego, or as Ivan called it, the end of the Earth. During winter, not many tourists come to see the craggy island at the tip of South America. Ivan and I decided to become travel companions. The ferry that would take us across the Strait of Magellan to Argentina wasn't leaving for several days so I moved my belongings into his *hospedaje*, the boarding house of Señora Carmen.

Ivan described Señora Carmen in hues of green and yellow. He surmised she had cancer and suspected she was poisoning our food. Her husband, he added, was surely an alcoholic. We tried to eat out as much as possible.

Ivan and I were the same age, twenty-five. He was a French soccer player who'd been traveling in Asia and South America for over a year. We were the only guests in the *hospedaje* and each had our own private dormitory-like room.

In the supermarket Ivan said I sometimes looked at him as if I wanted to kiss him, but I never did. Maybe I was too cold and tired to think about kissing a French boy with wild curls. Maybe there had been too many men too fast. Maybe it was time to stop.

Before Ivan, there'd been Carlos, whom I found living in a tent behind a farmhouse in San Pedro de Atacama, an oasis village in the driest desert in the world. Carlos told me he was a newspaper reporter. Later I learned he was a university student on vacation. In the tent he lectured me about Chilean politics: the country has six different provinces but over half the population is concentrated in Santiago, that life is shit for most people, that the U.S. ignores what it doesn't want to see. I'm sorry, I am, and I kissed him. I didn't want to stop. Politics was forgotten in a pile of clothes. As we said good-bye at the bus terminal, he told me he loved me. That was a week ago. Before Carlos, there was Bill, the Peace Corps volunteer.

Leaving behind men in dusty towns for my next destination had become an unsettling habit in the past four months of traveling. These men seemed to want something from me that I couldn't give, and I tried not to make promises I couldn't keep.

Once we arrived in the Ushuaia, Argentina, the closest town to Tierra del Fuego National Park, Ivan and I got a room together to save money. The outrageous exchange rate in Argentina barely allowed us to eat. The family who owned the house ate steak every afternoon. Meanwhile, Ivan and I pooled our resources to buy bread, cream cheese, and canned fish.

Ivan and I fought. I was a slob. He was a miser. Still, I was falling in love. One afternoon the family left us alone in the house. I was engrossed in my journal. Snow fell wet and silent against the window. Ivan tapped his fingers loudly against the glass. I drank a glass of peach juice and pretended to ignore him.

"Everyone is gone. We will eat. We will eat everything to forget our hunger. Stay in your diary. Stay in your peach juice. Stay in it," he said.

I wrote down his words to remember him later. "Don't be so serious. You can be serious all your life. You have only four days with me. Don't be so serious."

That snowy afternoon I said yes. The wind rocked the storm shutters back and forth, creating dancing shadows on Ivan's face as he leaned against the wooden headboard. I remember his blond curls, motionless beneath the white wall with the crucifix and the painting of a peasant woman with a baby in her arms. Later we hid under the blankets eating cardboard animal crackers. The crumbs rubbed against our bare bodies. We couldn't see the colors or shapes, really, except when the storm shutters blew open allowing light to fill the room. Ivan asked me never to eat animal crackers in this way with another man.

I agreed. It was a promise I could keep.

Susan Feinberg is a freelance writer and reporter. She lives in Brooklyn with her many roommates and their pets.

✳

Since its discovery by Magellan in 1520, Patagonia was known as a country of black fogs and whirlwinds at the end of the habited world. The word "Patagonia," like Mandalay or Timbuctoo, lodged itself in the Western imagination as a metaphor for The Ultimate, the point beyond which one could not go. Indeed, in the opening chapter of *Moby Dick*, Melville uses "Patagonian" as an adjective for the outlandish, the monstrous and fatally attractive.

—Bruce Chatwin, *Patagonia Revisited* by Bruce Chatwin and Paul Theroux

★ ★ ★

Lila's Ballet Shoes

*A small Parisian dances
into a boy's heart.*

THAT WINTER IN PARIS WAS THE LONELIEST OF MY LIFE. I WAS thirteen, a smallish boy with glasses and a cowlick that wouldn't lie down. My father, a U.S. Foreign Service officer, was pleased that he had been assigned to a "plum" post, but that didn't matter to me. Paris might have been Siberia as far as I was concerned.

We lived, my father, my younger sister and brother, and I, in the third story flat of an old apartment house on Avenue Victor Hugo, within sight of the Bois de Boulogne. My mother, an attractive woman frustrated by a passionless, unromantic marriage, had insisted on remaining in the United States to pursue a career in real estate. Thus, the only woman in our home was our rather grumpy, irritable cook, Yvonne.

The four of us arrived in Paris on a sultry, somnolent August day. Soon, the furniture was moved in, Yvonne and a housecleaner were engaged, and by the first of September we were up early and trudging off to school, a *lycee* some blocks away, knapsacks full of paper, pencils, and lunch. My father settled into his job at the embassy, and was seldom home before eight or nine in the evening.

Soon the crisp leaves of October carpeted the paths of the Bois de Boulogne, beneath the blazing arches and vaults of the oaks and beech trees. November brought chill rains and early dusk, and we marched to and from the *lycee* in the dark. My mother's weekly letters, eagerly watched for, were our only solace in a strange and unfamiliar world growing colder and lonelier day by day.

The winter months seemed endless. I struggled hopelessly with my classes at the *lycee,* the intricacies of French, and silently endured the peevish criticism of my teachers. I was perpetually in fear of the taunting, sometimes bullying machismo of a group of boys who were determined to make my life a living hell. They waited for me in the schoolyard at lunch, and after school followed me homeward, sending threats and epithets after my retreating form. I counted the hours, days, and weeks until school was out in June.

Finally the dank, cold days of winter softened with the early hints of spring. Twilight lasted a little longer, and a delicate mauve light pearled the air just before sunrise. Bulbs appeared, and the faintest green haze of buds appeared against the black branches of the Bois de Boulogne.

One day a new family moved into the flat above us. I was standing on our balcony, breathing in the evening air now alive with smells of new life, and looking at the sidewalk below, when a large blob of warm spittle landed directly on the back of my neck. Enraged, thinking it was bird droppings, I whirled to look up, and stared up into two eyes narrowed in mischief, a grinning mouth, and an impish face crowned with a bob of reddish hair.

With a smothered giggle, the face withdrew. I wiped the back of my neck in disgust. Just what I need, I thought, to make my life even sweeter. A little punk from upstairs to torment me.

Armed with an implacable thirst for revenge, I bided my time. The face did not reappear on the balcony above, but sometimes, looking up from the street as I approached the entrance of the apartment, I would see it peering down at me from between the geranium pots.

Her name was Lila, I discovered upon hearing her mother call to her. She was a student of ballet, and left for the dance studio every afternoon after school, dressed in a leotard, a short red woolen cape, and carrying a little bag. A taxi met her at the sidewalk in front of the apartment promptly at four-thirty. With this in mind, I planned my revenge. I collected a saucepan full of dishwater, coffee grounds, egg whites, and food scraps, poising it on the balcony railing above the apartment door. Listening intently, I heard the grating of the guard screen opening, then the door. Racing to the balcony, I checked the position of my brimming saucepan, took aim at the sidewalk below, and held my breath.

Hugely overanxious, bursting with malicious glee, I heard the big iron front door swing open, and I launched my smelly retribution. Too late I heard the doorman intone "*Bonjour, Madame.*" *Madame?* Indeed, for to my horror I watched the plummeting cataract open like a dirty jellyfish and envelope Mme. St. Martin in the puce concoction intended for Lila.

Mme. St. Martin was a large, effusive, middle-aged woman, and was leaving for a soiree dressed in hat and fur-trimmed coat. Her look of utter disbelief, changing to one of savage fury that would have given pause to a charging cape buffalo is forever lasered into my memory. Stepping daintily around the mess, and the bellowing Mme. St. Martin, Lila looked up, waved, stuck out her tongue, and tripped lightly to her taxi.

Two weeks later, after the inquisition of my crime was complete and punishment meted out, liberated from my room I decided to escape to the Bois de Boulogne, now almost canopied in bright green new leaves.

Walking glumly along my favorite path to one of the lakes, a light voice called "hallo," from behind me. It was Lila, her feet booted into a pair of roller skates, a little skirt flouncing around her long, slim dancer's legs, a bright beret pulled down around her ears. She skated gracefully in a long ellipse around me, smiling.

"Is everything OK?," she said, teasingly.

"Not bad, I guess," I replied, gloomily.

"You were very stupid," Lila said, skating languidly a little closer.

"You almost got it," I muttered, incensed.

"Ha, you were too much in a hurry!" she said with a toss of her head, turning to skate backwards a little awkwardly, less steadily.

"Maybe," I replied tersely. "You shouldn't spit where you might step on it."

Lila laughed, a lilting, insouciant laugh. "Oh, OK, I'm sorry." Then she guffawed. "The look on Mme. St. Martin's face! It was wonderful! She will be complaining about you to the whole neighborhood until she dies."

The thought of living beneath the fire-breathing dragon of Mme. St. Martin was almost overwhelming.

"I don't care. I'm going back to America pretty soon," I responded.

"I'm going to America when I'm a ballerina, to dance in New York. I will be famous!" Lila raised her arms and pivoted clumsily in a pirouette, then caught her skate and fell hard.

"Ow, I'm hurt." She rubbed tearfully at the scrapes on her calf and thigh, now oozing tiny red droplets.

"Get up," I said, hauling her up by the armpits. I supported her over to a nearby bench.

"Sit!" I ordered.

Taking out a dirty handkerchief, I washed it in a drinking fountain and daubed at the wounds.

"It stings!" Lila hissed.

Sitting close to her I looked up into a delicate face, not conventionally pretty, but slightly askew, with a long scooped nose sloping upwards, and a bit sideways, like a cockeyed ski jump. Her hair was short, straight, and reddish-blonde, an indeterminate color. It fell in bangs over her forehead and curved around her cheeks like long, stylish wings. Her eyes were small, greenish, and danced and glittered with sarcastic mirth when she spoke, but grew darker, almost hazel, when she was in a rare, serious mood.

"Thank you," she whispered. "I'm really sorry I spit on you." She put her hand on mine.

"It's OK," I said off-handedly, something tight in my chest. It was hard to breathe.

"Forget it. Actually," I gave a sheepish grin, "it felt kind of good, at first. "

Lila laughed gaily, her green eyes glinted, and her small white teeth flashed. She squeezed my hand.

"I like you. Let's be friends." She kissed me light as a feather, brushing her lips on my cheek.

Our adventures together were many and various during those light-hearted, almost carefree spring months. I taught Lila how to throw and catch a baseball, and something about the New York Yankees. She taught me how to fly a kite, to hold myself upright and walk properly, like a dancer, and where the best hidden spots were in the Bois to spy on young lovers, in hopes of seeing them "doing it." Lila also taught me how to smoke, stealing cigarettes from her parents, and we would swagger through alleyways far from home, sharing a baguette and a coke between puffs.

Saturdays after her ballet class, we would go off for long excursions to the Seine, to Montmartre, hoping to get a look into the garish interior of the Crazy Horse Saloon, and up and down the endless Champs Élysées, staring at the fashionable strollers, and marveling at the fabulously expensive shops.

Once, browsing through a bookstall, I saw a poster of a portrait by Modigliani of a young woman. I had seen his portraits before, but now I was transfixed. It was almost Lila. The oval face, the long curving neck, the sloping nose and faintly Oriental eyes, all Lila's.

"Look," I said, pointing, "it's you!"

"Of course it's me," she said nonchalantly. "I was certainly Modigliani's lover in my last lifetime." Lila was most interested in Buddhism, and believed in past lives and reincarnations.

"Well," I said shyly, gazing at her admiringly, "you will be my Modigliani lady, and when I'm a great painter I'll come to New York and paint your picture when you dance at the Metropolitan."

I was not particularly aware of it then, but that was the moment I fell in love with Lila.

My time remaining with her was not long, for soon it was June, and school finally ended. My mother, after all, did come to Paris to attempt a reconciliation with my father, and the family took a long tour through France by car. It was decided that I would return to the States with my mother, to go to private school, while she resolved some business matters and wrapped up her affairs. So in August we left Paris.

As it happened, my mother never returned to Paris to live with my father, brother, and sister. And I never saw Lila again. She did not come to see me off on the train to Le Havre, but we said an awkward, faintly embarrassed goodbye in the hallway in front of my apartment. Lila refused to be sad or sentimental, but remained quintessentially French, her gaiety laced with sarcasm. The only trace of regret I could detect was a slightly forced quality to her jokes. "When I come to New York, you'd better be rich, because I want a limousine, and to be taken to all the famous clubs and expensive restaurants," she admonished me.

"And you promise to give me time to paint your portrait?" I insisted.

"Certainly! But you must take me to Radio City Hall and the Empire State Tower."

"OK. And to the Statue of Liberty and Central Park. We'll roller skate."

"To a New York Yankees baseball game?"

"Promise!"

Then she handed me a rumpled package tied with old ribbon, kissed me quickly on the mouth, and was gone.

The package, which I

A dancer's ballet shoes are very intimate belongings, reflecting the personality of the owner. Pointe shoes have thin leather soles, no heel, a plaster box for the toes, and are covered with pink satin. Ballet shoes do not come in left and right versions, instead, each molds itself to the right or left foot of an individaul dancer as they are worn. Usually a dancer will darn the toes of new shoes herself immediately for better traction. She also sews her own heavy satin ribbons on her shoes at the particular point that works best for her and gives her the best support. A dancer is reluctant to give up a pair of old shoes, no matter how worn, since they have become friends, and new ones are so difficult to break in.

◆

—Lynn Magruder, "Conversations"

opened on the train, contained a pair of her old, worn-out ballet slippers, with long, faded ribbons, and a pack of Lucky Strikes, my favorites. She must have saved up for them.

I think of Lila whenever I see a Modigliani portrait, or "La Sylphide" or "Swan Lake."

I sometimes wondered if she danced in a major hall, or saw a baseball game. I gave up smoking a long time ago, but old Lucky Strike ads bring back a strange yearning. And sometimes I unwrap the dancing shoes, and closing my eyes, I smell the faintest musty aroma of sweat and perfume, like dried roses.

A romantic by nature, Gordon Langdon Magill's imagination was stimulated to write this "recherché du temps perdue" while listening to a favorite ballet suite. As a Foreign Service "brat," frequent world travels gave him a wanderlust that continues unabated today.

★

As a boy, Proust's narrator longs to befriend the beautiful, vivacious Gilberte, whom he has met playing in the Champs-Élysées. Eventually, his wish comes true. Gilberte becomes his friend, and invites him regularly to tea at her house. There she cuts him slices of cake, ministers to his needs, and treats him with great affection.

He is happy, but, soon enough, not as happy as he should be. For so long, the idea of having tea in Gilberte's house was like a vague, chimerical dream, but after quarter of an hour in her drawing room, it is the time before he knew her, before she was cutting him cake and showering him with affection, that starts to grow chimerical and vague.

The outcome can only be a certain blindness to the favors he is enjoying. He will soon forget what there is to be grateful for because the memory of Gilberte-less life will fade, and with it, evidence of what there is to savor.

The reason for this neglect is that, like all of us in the Proustian conception, the narrator is a creature of habit, and therefore always liable to grow contemptuous of what is familiar.

We only really know what is new, what suddenly introduces to our sensibility a change of tone which strikes us, that for which habit has not yet substituted its pale facsimiles.

—Alain de Botton, *How Proust Can Change Your Life: Not a Novel*

$\star \; ^{\star} \; \star$

Twenty-four Hours

A single day makes all the difference.

I SLIDE ONTO THE BENCH OF THE VICTORIA PEAK TRAM, GAZING OUT the window at the concrete giants that mold the city of Hong Kong. It's 11:30 a.m. In exactly 24 hours, I will fly back home to Los Angeles.

I am tired and depressed from the strenuous work of the last three weeks and from being alone. A part of me has secretly hoped that maybe, just maybe, I might meet someone new and exciting on this trip.

I feel someone slide onto the seat next to me. My eyes widen as I take in the sight of the tall, dark-haired man who stares back at me with warm brown eyes. We both burst into laughter. Incongruously, we are both dressed exactly alike: White pants, blue shirts, and white jackets.

"I guess we're the Bobbsey twins," I say as our chuckles dwindle.

"Bobbsey twins?" he asks in a foreign accent I later learn is his native Dutch.

"An American phrase."

"You are an American, then?"

Yes, I tell him and explain how I've come to be in Hong Kong. I babble on and on. Within moments, I'm sure he has a pretty good idea of my state of mind.

"I've spent the last three weeks in China, on business, myself." His name is Peter, and he tells me how difficult his trip had been, the depression he'd found himself in. Although he is glad to be back in his adopted Hong Kong, he cannot seem to shake the blues that engulf him.

We talk as the tram rumbles out of the station and are still chatting as it reaches the bottom of the hill. Rising to depart, people step out into the aisle way, separating us, but we continue to talk over their heads. Then the distance grows and he is at the doorway while I am stuck in the aisle.

"Nice meeting you. Too bad it was not three weeks ago," he calls out as he disappears.

Minutes later I depart from the tram and my new friend is gone. Disappointed, I join the taxi queue. It is then that I feel a hand rest on my shoulder.

"You do have to eat lunch today, do you not?"

I look up to see brown eyes looking down at me.

"I know it's somewhere on my list of things to do today."

Peter's eyes crinkle around the edges as he laughs and grabs my hand, leading me through the throng of people. I step briskly to keep up with his long-legged stride. On the way he asks me about my plans for my last day. I am embarrassed to admit that I have no agenda other than souvenir shopping, especially after I'd complained about not having had the time to see much of the city. He only nods.

The Italian cafe with its red-checked table cloths and candle-filled Chianti bottles is new for me in a city where I'd grown accustomed to Chinese restaurants. We talk non-stop and laugh at each other as we step over each other's words.

"If you'll stop by my office with me so I can check in with my partner, I'll go shopping with you at Stanley Market," Peter offers as we leave the restaurant. "And my partner is having a small dinner party tonight. Will you join me?"

"Why not?" I laugh, filled with a reckless giddiness.

We take the elevator to the seventeenth floor of a monstrous skyscraper. In the silence he leans over and kisses my forehead. As the door opens, a good-natured Englishman appears and the two embrace. After a whispered conversation, Peter leaves the room, singing, in search of an elusive fax.

"You're joining us for dinner?" his partner, Ian, asks me.

"Yes, if that's all right?"

"Couldn't be better," he smiles. "I don't know what you did to that man, but please don't stop." He draws closer and whispers. "He called me when he returned from China last night. At first, I was not sure who it was. He was so down."

Peter returns to the room and we're off. Ian kisses my hand. "Until tonight," he winks. As we leave, Ian asks where we're off to.

"Shopping," answers Peter. As the elevator doors close, I see Ian's mouth drop.

At Stanley, I find the stall where sweaters are sold. Peter haggles with the seller. I want to go back to my hotel to get the sweaters I'd bought before and have him renegotiate the price, but he only laughs.

He decides I need to see more of Hong Kong. We move on to Aberdeen Harbor.

"We'll try to make your last day unforgettable," he says.

Peter negotiates with an elderly Chinese man, Mr. Nguy, who bows and smiles at me, his eyes hidden behind mirrored sunglasses. He motions for us to get into the small boat. I wonder about its seaworthiness.

"Nice looking boat," I say as I inhale the fumes from a fresh coat of varnish.

"*Sampans,*" Peter says.

Mr. Nguy launches the *sampan* with one oar and we head toward the center of the marina.

Aberdeen Harbor is filled with vessels. Black tire inner tubes are strung along the sides of the boats, protecting them from jarring their neighbors. We watch as mothers wearing oversized sun hats shoo young children out of the way so they can hang the family laundry out to dry.

As the sun starts to go down, Peter suggests that we go to his flat to enjoy the sunset. We hail another taxi and head back to Victoria Peak. Peter lives at the top.

His flat is sumptuous and has the best view of Hong Kong that I have witnessed. He opens the sliding glass windows and pulls up a chair for me to perch on and watch the view and hands me a glass of cabernet. I lean back and relax as the cool autumn air and the sound of a piano solo sweeps over me. Silently we watch as the sun's brightness dims and the lights of the city slowly begin to spark up in distant bursts across the harbor below.

We smile at each other, slowly, tentatively. He reaches over to stroke my face.

When his lips touch mine I can taste the faint traces of chocolate from the wine and the breezes of Hong Kong seem to engulf me as his arms slide around me.

"We had better go to dinner," he says after a time.

The dinner party is across the hall at Ian's flat. I meet Jean Claude, Jean Luc, and Lucia. The conversation is lively and spicy, much like the food, although it is difficult to follow from time to time when it changes from English to French to Dutch. Maria, the housekeeper and cook, confuses everyone, save Ian, when she speaks in her native Tagalog.

Dinner is a seven course meal, starting out with the wine. As

> ———— ☽ ————
>
> *I* couldn't take my eyes off the Chinese journalists. One at a time, sometimes two, they walked up to the front desk of the Hong Kong hotel I was visiting. But they didn't just walk in, they *entered*. I was transfixed by their designer suits, no-nonsense haircuts, and expensive Italian shoes. Their computer cases were unscuffed, and their cell phones kept professionally out of view. They all seemed to wear silver oval glasses. Maybe they needed the prescriptions, and maybe they didn't.
>
> They looked intellectual. Distinguished. Complete. I didn't know their names, their dialects, or their business. All I knew was that they were tall, dark, handsome…and Asian.
>
> ◆
>
> —Jennifer Leo,
> "Chinese Like Me"

Maria pours and we taste, I am astounded when all of the men, except our host, complain most solemnly.

"What is this swill you serve us?" asks Peter. He, Jean Claude, and Jean Luc rise from the table and gather all of the glasses and the bottle. They move to the nearby window and pour the wine out, four stories down to the ground. Across the table, Lucia smiles and winks conspiratorially.

"That's it then," says Ian as he turns to Maria. "Now you can bring out the good wine." No one speaks while Maria leaves, then returns with a fresh bottle. We watch as she makes an elaborate display of removing the cork and pours wine all around.

Each of us reach for our glass, taking a tentative sip.

"This is more like it," says Peter.

Ian catches my quizzical gaze.

"I made the bloody awful mistake one time of trying to dupe them in a wine tasting. They have never let me forget it. Now, it does not matter what I serve from the first bottle, they will pour it out the window as a reminder of my little joke."

After dinner we adjourn to the living room for coffee and after-dinner drinks. Peter declares that we should go out dancing.

"But it is two a.m." Lucia's eyes widen.

"That is when this town comes alive," Peter says. "Besides, I promised Cheryl that I would make her last day in Hong Kong one she would never forget. The day is not over yet."

The French beg off due to jet lag and Ian shakes his head. Peter and I walk down the hill in the quiet darkness of the night.

There is a taxi waiting at the bottom of the hill. We drive down the mountain and through the sleepy city streets. As we turn into the Wanchai district, a flood of people fill the streets. Peter leads me to the 97 Club. Despite the line, he is ushered in immediately.

The club is loud and smoky, filled with strobing lights and American '70s disco. Several women come up to greet Peter. He is pleasant but distant, mindful of introducing me. I note that his arm is wrapped firmly around my shoulder at all times. We dance closely and talk through the night.

When we leave the club, the sun is rising.

"I hate airports," Peter tells me as he draws me into his arms, kissing me. We walk the streets as the vendors open up their shop doors and old women set up their wares on the sidewalk. We walk through the park and watch the early morning *tai chi* masters practice their craft. An elderly man strolls past us, carrying his bird in a cage, speaking soothingly to it.

Later, the check-in lines at Kai Tak Airport are long. Families, young lovers, businessmen, and mounds of luggage and large boxes surround us. Words fly randomly through the air; snatches of conversation in English, Chinese, Filipino, and Malaysian float by. Sing-song voices announce boarding calls and gate changes.

Peter stands with one arm around my shoulder, the other holding a newspaper. My turn in the line comes and the attendant hands back my ticket and passport.

"Your flight will board in a few minutes. Please go to immigration now."

We walk away slowly.

"This is as far as I go," Peter says, stopping a distance away from the security machines.

"I can't say good-bye," I tell him, surprised at the strange huskiness in my voice.

"I will not," he says and kisses the top of my forehead.

My breath catches in my throat. I close my eyes, feeling his lips move to each of my cheeks, my chin, my nose. I open my eyes and look up into his. His smile wavers as he pulls me into his arms and kisses me. I am holding onto him so tightly that I think I will crush him, but then I realize that it is he who is holding on so tightly to me.

It is only the sense of people crowding around us that forces us to break apart.

"Until we meet again," he says and kisses me quickly, one final time. "In our world."

We turn away and I move toward immigration. A knot forms in my stomach and I stop. Travelers behind me move around me. I turn around and see Peter across the expanse of the busy terminal in the instant that he turns, his eyes finding mine. He is not smiling. He holds up his hand, still clasping the newspaper and waves.

I look out the window as my plane taxis down the tarmac. My seat-mate has noticed my tears and inquires if I'm all right. Perhaps I did not enjoy my trip to Hong Kong?

"Not at all," I tell him. "I love Hong Kong. It's the most beautiful city in the world."

I look at my watch. 11:30 a.m. Twenty-four hours. A lifetime.

Cheryl Herring is a Californian whose passions include writing and travel.

✶

With the right partner, of course, any restaurant can turn into a bower of romance, with love triumphant despite the presence of peanut shells and sawdust on the floor. Consider for a moment my meal in Hong Kong some years ago with Ms. Right. The setting could not under any circumstance be called romantic: we were seated in a rickety *sampan* in the middle of the Causeway Bay Typhoon shelter just off the main strip on Hong Kong Island. The *sampan* was taking on water at a slow rate kept under control by the boat's owner, a chubby woman in a housecoat who noisily emptied the bilge with a bucket every ten minutes or so.

On this not-very-worthy craft we sat—the two of us and a pair of German tourists who were having a spat and had no interest in talking to us—at a Formica-topped table, with paper towels as our napkins, chipped Melmac as our china and chopsticks with a checkered past as our silver. Our candlelight came from a sputtering Coleman lamp. While we bobbed on this ship of fools, the chubby woman bargained for our meal. She bought us seafood from a market boat and had it cooked by a wok boat as we sipped beers bought from a beverage boat and were serenaded not by Gypsy violinists buy by a trio of women who sang phonetic versions of "You Are My Sunshine" from their sing-song boat.

It sounds colorful at best and dreadful for the most part, but romance is where you find it. We fed each other fried oysters, we licked crab in black-bean sauce from each other's lips, we cooed softly at the exquisite taste of shrimp plunged into boiling water and served instantly, unadulterated by any other flavor. All around us, the lights of Hong Kong sparkled and glowed; in the distance, lightning flashed from a thunderhead over

China. A more romantic experience than that would be hard to imagine. Like the tough weed it can be, love grew and flourished in the midst of all that adversity, nourished by a leaky boat and some terrific clams in spicy garlic sauce.

—Merrill Shindler, "Eating In Ecstasy," *Travel & Leisure*

FRANK X. CASE

★ ★ ★

Equal Pressure

A couple learns a surprising
secret of Mayan culture.

At the window next to my aisle seat on a rising 737 are a handsome young couple escaping the frozen cityscape, seemingly on a honeymoon. The newlyweds whisper contentedly of their future; my thoughts are also of the future, but with a backward glance for perspective.

Across the aisle sleeps my wife of a dozen years. Fit and hearty, if a bit pale, her golden hair falls across her wise face. Calm, reassuring eyes that are now closed in sleep have given comfort to thousands of her patients in family practice medicine. Her large, certain hands that have held newborns and closed lifeless eyes, rest in her lap. We represent a common dilemma; we have grown better and more intertwined with our jobs at the expense of our own connectedness. Cozumel will be a watershed.

We spend the first few days in open-mouthed awe of the wonders of the island. We check off all the usual sights and sounds: wide beaches, buoyant seas, refreshing libations, delicious fish, and the general delight of new places. Still, there is a stilted distance between us. How do two people decompress, both individually and as a couple?

The sound of water as it rushes from the faucet awakens me at

11:00 p.m. on New Year's Eve. Earlier we had eaten lobster and returned to nap in anticipation of a late night.

"C'mon, Dear, let's go," drifts in from the bathroom.

I force myself to recall my earlier conversation with Pepe the bartender. In my mediocre Spanish I had expressed my desire to experience *"Música autentica de Mexico,"* or authentic Mexican music. One more badly dressed, sunburnt tourist doing the Macarena and I would throw up. With enthusiasm he described how *la gente,* the people, would not be at Planet Hollywood on the waterfront but in El Pueblo, the town, to dance and party to the showmanship of Alfredo El Pulpo (The Octopus). I knew little else about this concert but I had a ·good feeling for the advice of my new friend.

We arrive at the Terrazo Lyonais (Lion's Terrace) as Cozumel's only radio station blares, *"cuatro, tres, dos, uno… Feliz Año Nuevo!"* The beer garden sits on a street corner in the *barrio*, lit by a single harsh street light, a good-sized one-story, cinderblock building with a ticket window on one side. At the entrance, two natty bouncers collect the admission fee. The area teems with the activity of any concert: small groups talk easily, young men eye young women and smoke Marlboro Lights, young women pretend not to notice and eye them back. With not a gringo in sight, I swallow hard, step out of the cab and stride purposefully to the ticket window. I forcefully tell my independent, adventurous wife "Stay at my side. Pay attention."

We enter a gymnasium-size hall. At the side of the room and in back, colorful tables with white plastic chairs rise on tiers, and on the far side are more tables on an open air breezy patio. In the middle is a court-sized concrete dance floor. An enormous, unused keyboard platform at the front of the stage nearly obscures the warm-up band.

Although we can hardly see it, we can hear the band, and watch as many couples dance happily. Soon we see my new friend Pepe and his simply elegant wife as they sashay next to us. She wears a white smock with a thick gold band in a geometric pattern that highlights her rich brown skin and her gold inlaid teeth.

Almost all of tonight's revelers are Mayan first and Mexican later. Throughout the night, several people answer me that they do not speak Spanish, only Mayan. The entire room is filled with black-haired Mayans, none over about 5'5". (I am 6'5" and my wife is 5'7".) The Mayan are a handsome people, compact in carriage and demure of personality. They have a habitual greeting of head half-bowed until eye contact is made. Then eyebrows are arched and head raised in acknowledgment. Finally a broad smile. Pepe tells me that Alfredo will not appear until 1:00 a.m., so we grab a table and people-watch.

The men are all dressed similarly in polished boots, pressed jeans, and crisp shirts. The women are in skirts and colorfully embroidered shirts or dresses. All the couples dance in a simple side-step, the sameness of it remarkable. They raise their shoulders rhythmically as they step left, right and back again. Occasionally the men hold their belt buckle in a kind of pose—a Mayan vogue. They then touch-dance with one hand lightly on each other's waist, the other clasped together lightly, as he leads her smartly over the floor, like a *caballero* with a rope lariat. There is another gringo couple who flamboyantly twirl and dip; compared to the locals they look showy and out of place.

A stocky *caballero* approaches our table and politely asks *"¿No hay una problema baile con su esposa?"* My lady is escorted off to dance and I strain eye muscles as I try to inconspicuously monitor them. They return, as he promised, after one dance, and he graciously thanks us and departs. Apparently it is now open season as other, equally *tranquilo* (gentlemanly) would-be dancers approach.

Soon the announcer rumbles the arrival of the headliner. Perhaps a thousand people press forward peacefully for a better look at this Mexican national treasure. To the right are two back-up singers in stiletto heels, sequined bikinis, and elaborately plumed head-dresses. They dance and vamp gracefully in a surprisingly simple but beguiling way. To the left is a male who sings most of the lyrics. El Pulpo appears amidst the dry ice smoke and strobe-light hype.

The Cozumelos stand open-mouthed, eyes transfixed, as the keyboard contraption rises and pivots. The seemingly small man is perched to command the flying bridge, eight keyboards arrayed for optimum reach. The music, as if from an entire mariachi band, soars with a playful sound as cameras flash. The crowd has abandoned their dance in excitement and stares straight ahead.

As a drum machine keeps a syncopated backbeat, he sings simple songs of great love and loss, hard labor and easy smiles, _chupas_ (young girls) and _caballeros_. The audience is mesmerized, yet eventually finds the pulse of the tunes, as dancers turn to face their partners and begin to shuffle gracefully.

Linda and I have a clear line of sight over the heads of the crowd as it undulates in the crowded terrace. We flirt with each other wordlessly and mimic the Mayan shuffle as we giddily hop to the beat. A rare slow ballad begins and the dance floor is suddenly filled with pairs who twirl and spin slowly.

We are a Grateful Dead couple, accustomed to free-form, loose-jointed solo trips. She is a "Dancing Nancy," with perpetual motion but little traditional order to her steps. Also, she does not like to be led. I am more of a gawky, wooden metronome with a side-to-side knock, and an occasional "Wayne's World" air guitar. But we have always envied that classy, effortless dance you see couples

---

Everything we think, feel and do allows us to either join with the universe and fully experience our humanity or distance ourselves from it and protect our egos. From an attitude of mutuality and joining we can fully experience the highest nature of our own being.

The ultimate goal of mutuality is not to find a connection you lost. It is to recognize a connection you've always had. When you see yourself and the world through the eyes of real equality, there is nothing to fear, nothing to prove and nothing more you must be.

◆

—Bruce Derman, Ph.D.
with Michael Hauge,
_We'd Have a Great Relationship
If It Weren't For You:
Regaining Love and Intimacy
Through Mutuality_

do at weddings and here at the Lion's Terrace. We could never pull it off, though. She will not be led and I cannot follow.

She sees me eye the dancers jealously and draws me close to whisper, "One of the *caballeros* showed me earlier." She smiles up to me, "Give me your hand." I do and we embrace lightly as dancers do. She presses firmly against my hand and gives the clue. "Equal pressure." She pushes away into a compact twirl as our hands remain interlocked at the same point in space. Again we meet and complete a classy maneuver. Repeatedly we circle, twirl, and sway, just the two of us alone together amidst hundreds of revelers, bemused by the ease of our newfound grace.

The night hurtles onward with more dances, more stories and goodwill among our newfound friends. El Pulpo continues to energize the crowd even as a 4:00 a.m. cab ride delivers us to our hotel. In the back seat, my wife reaches up to softly kiss my jaw line and whisper a Mexican saying, *"Nuevo Año, nueva vida."*

I pull her closer and take her hand, palm flat as if a pane of glass is between us and answer, "New year, new life."

Two days later at the airport we lounge in the shade on the grass and finish off the last of a Dos XX beer with lime as we await our charter departure. We trade vacation stories with the lovely honeymoon couple we met earlier. When our flight is called we grasp the hands of our partners, and applying equal pressure, step lightly though the airport.

Frank is a recovering National Football League player out of Penn State. He lives with his wife Linda in the foothills of Colorado, where he is now a teacher, writer, storyteller, and bad but enthusiastic dancer. He is currently at work on a coming-of-age novel for teenagers based on a catastrophic Colorado forest fire. This story was the winning entry in the Travelers' Tales Love & Romance Writing Contest.

*

Life has taught us that love does not consist of gazing at each other but in looking together in the same direction.

—Antoine de Saint-Exupéry, *Wind, Sand and Stars,*
translated by Lewis Galantiére

PART TWO

SOME THINGS TO DO

✱

Hotel Paradis-o

A couple goes from "rest-o" to "stay-o"
in a Japanese love hotel.

IT WAS LATE. TOO LATE TO GET BACK TO TOKYO. OUR GUIDEBOOK had no information at all about Shin-Fuji, a small town between Osaka and Tokyo. From the railway station platform there was only one obvious place to stay, a five-story building a few blocks away. The sign on top advertised "Hotel, 6000¥."

When we arrived, there was no one at the front desk. There was no front desk—just photos of the rooms along one wall. Two were illuminated, the rest were dark. We didn't know what to do. There was no one to ask. After four months of honeymoon travel on the road in Asia we were weary. We didn't have the energy to figure out another baffling cross-cultural situation.

A side door opened and an older man and a younger woman came in, all smiles and giddy. Unlike us, they had no luggage and seemed to know the routine. The man quickly withdrew a key from a cubby hole. The adjacent photo instantly went dark. Tittering, the couple disappeared into the elevator.

"What do we do?" my wife said. "There's only one room left."

Before I could answer she was over at the wall. Gingerly, as though extracting the detonator from a bomb, she drew the last key from its slot. Tiny lights embedded in the floor began to flicker, outlining a path down the corridor. From around a corner the glow of a larger light pulsed. We moved cautiously ahead, as though caught in a tractor beam. We looked around. There was no one.

I had no idea what to expect. Even on our budget of $200 a day the astounding cost of everything in Japan had limited us to sex-segregated guest houses and youth hostels. Now, without having checked in, without having spoken to anyone, without having left an imprint of our Visa card, we were about to enter a hotel room. I opened the door.

"Look at this!" Nina said. This room was huge, as big as a typical American hotel room and much bigger than any other place we had stayed in Japan. We exchanged our street shoes for the "house" slippers that waited on the threshold. The larger pair had a groom in a tuxedo embossed on the rubber toe piece. Nina's had a bride in white.

"They must know we're newlyweds," she said, leaping onto the bed. She held up the condoms and the origami lovebirds that had been left on the pillow. "They've thought of everything."

I opened the room service menu. There was no sushi on this menu. But there were a lot of things that looked like sushi. The most outlandish was adorned with small nubs and a collar that resembled an anemone from a Jacques Cousteau special. Apparently it cost 13,000 yen, batteries not included. I reflected on what had happened so far. The May-December couple with no luggage, no front desk, condoms on the pillow, and the very special room service menu. I knew we had stumbled onto something truly unusual. We had checked into our first Japanese love hotel.

We had heard about love hotels. *"Abec hoteru,"* our guidebook called them—discreet, fantasy getaways the Japanese use for afternoon and evening assignations. We had even looked for some, but, assuming they would resemble the tawdry, no-tell motels that line America's secondary thoroughfares, we were unable to find any. Now, without speaking to a person, without seeing a single employee, we were in one.

The room was replete with electronic gadgets straight out of Hugh Hefner's bedroom. There were remotes for everything; the lights, the 440 channels of music, the air-conditioning, the television, the bed.

"What are you doing?" Nina said. She had changed into a *yukata*, one of the razor crisp robes that came with the room.

"Hang on a second," I told her. "I've got to check this stuff out. I mean come on, I have to. I'm a guy."

"If you don't stop right now," she said, "I'm taking a shower."

I could feel the tension rising between us, but I couldn't help myself. The room was like mission control in Houston. Given what the menu had to offer, I *had* to find out what was on cable.

"I'll be there in a second," I told her.

"Some love hotel," she muttered and stalked out.

I toyed with everything. The fridge was a little automat, stocked with sushi and sandwiches just waiting for my 100-yen coins. There was a karaoke machine with dual mikes. The accompanying songbook was the size of the Manhattan directory and had every song of Elton John and Andrew Lloyd Webber, plus thousands of Japanese favorites. In one corner there was a small weight-lifting machine.

"What exactly do the Japanese do in these places?" I wondered.

A curious pneumatic tube system, the kind once used for billing in old-fashioned department stores, snaked out of the wall. I turned on the television. A man was binding up a woman in Saran Wrap. Clearly this was no Motel 6.

***K**issing and love play are alien to the tradition of love-making but there are a growing number of exceptions. It is all neatly summed up in the Japanese saying that "foreigners make love from the waist upwards." The beautiful erotic prints of the eighteenth and nineteenth centuries confirm this attitude. Japanese ladies and gentlemen seldom bothered to undress before getting to it. Part of the explanation could lie in the difficulty of retying the elaborate sash of a woman's kimono.*

◆

—John Lowe, *Into Japan*

"C'mere, c'mere, c'mere," Nina cried from the bathroom, "Read these." She handed me a basket full of complimentary toiletries. On the tiny bag that held a "Hair Band," I read the caption. It seemed familiar; but I couldn't place it: "Let us be lovers, we'll marry our fortunes together. I've got some real estate here in my bag."

"'I've got some real estate here in my bag.' What is that supposed to mean?" I said.

Nina raced back to the bed. "Oh my God," she said, "That's from 'America.' Simon and Garfunkel were here."

I followed her back to bed, ready to resume the romance that had dwindled over the last few days as we pinched pennies on everything.

"What's that?" she said.

"What's what?"

"That," she said pointing to the far wall where a red digital clock was pulsing with the seconds. It read "0:42." We looked at each other. The clock changed to "0:41." It was ticking down.

Suddenly the playfulness that had been building between us was gone. "What do you think this room cost?" Nina said.

"I don't know. The sign said 6000 yen."

"Right," she said, "but do you think that's for an hour or all night?" I felt my chest constrict, and it wasn't from what I'd seen on the television.

We had already seen a $70 cantaloupe and a $100 mushroom for sale and had heard about bars where beer costs $300 a bottle. Before I could complete the thought Nina said, "What if it's 6000 yen an hour?!" It was a great room, but we didn't have $600 to spend for one night. I began to panic. I picked up the phone. A woman answered.

"Hello, do you speak English?" I asked. At first I thought she said, "What do you think of our sushi?" but then I ralized she was speaking Japanese. "How much does this room cost?" I asked anyway, wondering how one counts above 1,000 in Japanese.

Nina handed me a brochure from the Japanese National Tourist Organization. It had all the standard questions and answers needed by tourists written in both English and Japanese. The tourist, me, is supposed to point to the questions and the happy-to-assist Japanese person is supposed to point to the correct answer. It works less well on the telephone.

I opened to the hotel section and said, "*Kone heya wa ikura desu ka?*" which, according to the book, means "How much is this room?" This unleashed an immediate answer I didn't understand at all, except that it sounded like "$1,200 or whatever you have left—whichever is more." Sweat began beading on my forehead.

By now my bride was laughing hysterically. My mind strayed from the *raison d'etre* of love hotels and began to focus on the Japanese penal system. "Maybe we should leave now," I suggested.

"Are you crazy?" Nina said. "It's after midnight. We're going to sleep. I don't care what it costs."

"Right," I thought. "This is why the groom's family pays for the honeymoon." As I put my head down, I saw traveler's checks flying out of my wallet. The digital clock clicked down to "0:08."

"What's that?" Nina said. Someone was knocking at the door. The digital clock pulsed "0:00." In the hallway a dissolute Japanese woman waited. The minute she saw me she began speaking rapidly in Japanese. When she finished I patted myself on the chest with both hands the way Indians used to do in old Westerns and said, "English." Evidently she was unable to pick up the language from this gesture and took off again in Japanese. Somewhere in her stream of words an island rose above the torrent. "Check-out-o" I thought I heard her say.

"Check-out-o?" I asked.

"Check-out-o," she insisted.

Now the picture began to clear. The clock had ticked down. Our time was up. I had heard a "kerplunk" in the pneumatic tube. When I hadn't put in my money this woman was sent out to collect.

"No check-out-o," I said. I put my hands to the side of my head like the woman in the Singapore Airlines ad and repeated, "No check-out-o. Sleep-o."

She started up again in Japanese. I gestured for the woman to come inside the room. She threw her hands up in front of her face and waved them back and forth as though trying to stop a runaway train. She wasn't coming in. Even love hotels have rules.

From the bed Nina called, "Try the book." I retrieved the pamphlet, hoping it might work better face to face than it had over the phone.

In the pamphlet I pointed to "How much does this room cost?" She wrote 6000¥ on her palm. Still, I didn't know if that was per hour, for two hours, for the time we had been there, or what. With book, pen, and a rudimentary written language that consisted of these symbols—¥, ?, → —together with the hours of the day written in the 24-hour clock of the military, I was able to figure out that our first two hours cost 6000¥ and the rest of the night would be another 6000¥. I paid her the money. I wasn't ready for the challenge of the pneumatic tube.

"Only 6000 yen for midnight to 10 a.m.," Nina said. "That's not bad."

It's true we had been spending nearly that amount to stay in separate bunkrooms with Korean school kids on vacation. If love hotels were all like the "Dear Hotel," it looked like the reasonable and romantic way to see Japan.

The next day we were off to Nikko, an alpine town north of Tokyo famous for its temples and natural beauty. "To hell with natural beauty," Nina said. "We've got plenty in California. Let's find another love hotel."

Although well known to the Japanese, the locations of love hotels are not mentioned in guidebooks. After quickly seeing the sights of Nikko, we went to tourist information. An older, genteel Japanese woman stood at the desk.

"You ask her," I said to Nina.

"I'm not asking her," Nina said. "She's like a grandmother."

As we glared at each other, the lady asked in perfect English, "May I help you?"

I looked at this lovely woman who was waiting patiently. I couldn't do it. What would she think of Americans if I asked her about an *abec hoteru*? I gathered my courage. At last I asked, "Is there a bank anywhere near here?"

The clerk at the bank was a young man who also spoke English. After we changed money I gestured that he should come closer. From inches away I whispered, "Can you tell me if there is an *abec hoteru* around here?"

"Abec hoteru?" he restated at full voice, apparently not constrained by any prudish American convention regarding places for sexual trysts. "Just moment please." He then turned to a female teller and began a conversation in Japanese that sounded something like Abbott and Costello's "Who's on first?" routine, with *abec hoteru* running the bases. After much discussion that involved the entire staff of the bank as well as the use of several maps, he directed us to a hotel up the street. When we got there a dozen elderly women were getting off tour buses and checking in. Something had gotten lost in the translation.

"What should we do?" Nina asked.

To get to Nikko we had changed trains in Utsunomiya, a small junction town. The bullet train had sped past a bright neon sign for "The James Dean Hotel." It had to be what we were looking for.

"Let's go back to the James Dean," I suggested.

By the time we returned to Utsunomiya it was already

—— ☽ ——

*O*utside the cities there are also "motero" for the the motorised trade. While Japan does have motels of the kind found in Western countries, the majority are of the variety just described. There is usually no mistaking the two types as the exteriors of love hotels and motels are often the ultimate in bad taste, with garish pink neon signs bordering the roof, flashing signs and outlandish architecture. There is one in the shape of a ship, while another in the Gotanda section of Tokyo is known throughout the country for its pseudo-feudal castle architecture, complete with turrets and other gewgaws.

♦

—Ian McQueen,
Japan - a travel survival kit

past 10 p.m. Nina suggested taking a taxi, but the flag-fall was 600 yen and every mile was about that much again. Getting to the James Dean could cost a fortune. Besides, it seemed to me the hotel was near the station. I figured we could walk. As we learned an hour later, it's difficult to judge distances while on a train going 180 miles per hour.

Pulling our suitcases behind us, we were soon trudging down narrow roads on the outskirts of town. I could see the neon glow on the far horizon. Like desperate gamblers low on gas it drew us on like the distant lights of Las Vegas. We were walking through rice fields and around agricultural warehouses. The roads were empty. But the lights were getting closer. So was an odd, rhythmic sound.

Thhhh-kwack! We heard. *Thhh-kwack! Thhh-kwack!* We turned a corner. In front of a convenience store a man and a woman were hitting golf balls tied to elastic cord. *Thhhh-kwack!* The ball took off, fell to the ground and snapped back to the tee.

We stopped and watched them. They stopped and watched us— two *gaijin* pulling suitcases in the middle of nowhere at midnight. And we thought they were strange. We continued on. They watched us leave. *Thhh-kwack!*

We were absolutely beat when we got to the James Dean. It was in an enclave of love hotels. Next door was the Passion, a metallic, futuristic castle. Down the street was the Chalet, an ersatz Tudor building with turrets worthy of Rapunzel's affection. Each had individual parking spaces for each room. The couple pulls in, closes a curtain behind the car and goes directly inside without being seen by anyone. We circumnavigated the building. All the garage curtains were drawn closed. We had shortchanged the historical wonders of Nikko. We had walked for more than an hour. And now, at midnight, on a Thursday, the James Dean was full.

We wheeled our bags across the street to the Cosmo Part II. Each of us and each of our bags tripped the electronic sensor at the gate. No doubt wondering how four cars could pull in at the same time, the proprietor, an old man in slippers with a cordless phone, shuffled out. From my experience the night before I was now nearly fluent in love hotel Japanese.

"Check-in-o," I said.

"Hai, check-in-o," the old man responded. He then asked, "Rest-o?"

I shook my head no and said, "Stay-o." "Rest-o" is the word for the two-hour tryst enjoyed morning, noon and night by seemingly every person in Utsunomiya and the rest of Japan. "Stay-o," which runs overnight, begins only when most lovers have gone home to spouses or parents. If one can wait around, a stay-o costs much less than a traditional hotel and comes with more exciting fixtures.

The proprietor showed us a graphic display of the rooms. We chose the "disco" room. Our stay-o in rural Utsunomiya would cost 6000 yen.

"It's better than last night," Nina said. The room was twice as spacious as our room at the Dear. Not only did it have everything the Dear had, but it had a sauna, a large selection of adult videotapes and, directly above the bed, the *pièce de resistancé,* the item I had wanted above my bed ever since junior high, a rotating mirrored ball. I started surfing the music system in search of "Disco Inferno."

The phone rang. I picked it up. I heard the old man's voice. "Front-o," he said.

"What do you think he wants?" I asked Nina. I went downstairs.

At the foot of the stairs was a small trap door, the kind used by milkmen for home delivery. The old man's arms were jutting through, a small Coca-Cola bottle in each hand.

"For you," he said in English. "For American friend." It was the most touching thing anyone had done for us in Japan.

After we finished with the bath and the sauna we were ready for bed. "Do you want to see what's on TV?" Nina said softly, raising her eyebrows in a coy, newlywed kind of way. We had never watched any adult anything before. "It could be educational."

I clicked the set on. Evidently the Japanese have a thing for fresh foods because again a man was sealing a woman up with plastic wrap.

"Oh my God. I can't watch this," Nina said. "Turn it off. No, don't turn it off. No, I've got to watch this."

We watched until the woman looked like she would stay fresh until at least tomorrow. The man began to undress. As the camera dropped to follow the action, the anatomically correct, precisely outlined parts of the image became blurred, digitally scrambled. This didn't conceal the faces of the actors but only the areas most people are interested in seeing when watching these films.

The sexual encounter that followed was like watching two pulsing, swirling lava flows merging with one another. Everything was rendered in a wild paisley.

"What is this?" Nina asked. "Are they trying to protect us from something? We're in a love hotel."

"Yes we are," I said, turning on the rotating mirrored ball above the bed. Little ovals of reflected light spun around the room. I drew her near.

"Wait a minute," she interrupted. Don't you think you should…you know, sing some karaoke? Or do some weight lifting? That machine is going to waste." Laughing she added, "Oh, I don't understand this country at all."

The next morning, before leaving, I put 200 yen in the karaoke machine and crooned my own rendition of "You're Just Too Good to Be True." Nina woke up just in time to see me hop on the weight machine for a quick twenty reps. I then brewed two cups of complimentary coffee. Fully pumped up, I pulled the karaoke mike into bed. Nina looked at me and said, "I think it's time for us to leave."

By the time we returned to Tokyo, we were expert love hotel spotters. Near railroad stations they seemed to comprise entire blocks. They dotted residential neighborhoods. How could we have overlooked places with names, English names, like The Happy Heart Hotel, The Once Around, The Sweet Night Inn? Even the Japanese neon signs took on a certain stimulating familiarity. We became fluent in identifying the essential characteristics of love hotels; the wild architecture, the wilder names, the continuous streams of cars and pedestrians, and, always, the sign out front with the prices.

After four months of honeymoon travel by plane, train, car, boat, and motorcycle, it was now time to head home. Ours had been an amazing journey where each day contained an element of the surreal. We had hoped to go on to Europe, but time and budget prevented that. So, in lieu of Paris, we spent our last night in Tokyo at "Le Chic" where all the little sayings on the toiletries were in French. We used the room to its fullest. No gizmo was left untouched. When we were finally exhausted, when we had taken advantage of everything Le Chic had to offer, I dimmed the lights and tucked Nina in. I put a few coins in the karaoke machine and softly began singing *"Chansons d'Amour."* Paris had nothing more to offer.

Robert Strauss is the author of more than two dozen television documentaries and has worked as a management consultant in over fifty countries. His articles have appeared in the Chicago Tribune, Saveur, San Francisco Examiner, *and* West. *When not investigating the highlights of Japanese love hotels he is likely to be at home spending a quiet evening with his wife and their baby daughter. He claims his favorite part of traveling is when the doors to the plane are closed for take-off and everything is out of his hands.*

✳

Besides the lavish square bed decorated in red, black, and white satin like a boxing ring, I counted mirrors everywhere, a pay TV stocked with porn videos, a camera and equipment to make your own tapes for instant replay, a refrigerator full of drinks and a vending machine stocked with condoms in neon rainbow colors, dildos, and French ticklers.

And an open shower/bathroom.

No door.

I was surprised to see that the love hotel was steeped in privacy everywhere except in the room itself. I thought this strange, since the whole concept of the love hotel grew out of the lack of privacy in the typical Japanese house. Imagine, only thin shoji or paper walls separating you from your mother-in-law in the next room.

—Jina Bacarr, "Afternoon in Tokyo"

✦ ✦ ✦

Black Hair and
a Bull's Ear

Be careful what you wish for.

IT WAS MIDNIGHT AT A CROWDED SMALL-TOWN TRAIN STATION IN Spain. I had to interview someone in the north of the country early the next morning. I was tired, cranky, and anticipating the uncomfortable railroad ride toward tomorrow's travails. I was not the mellow, flexible traveler I claimed to be.

Disciplining myself to be observant is important for me to be able to record people, places, things, events. I learned a trick long ago that forces me out of myself and into my surroundings. I pick out someone nearby and study them in detail, unobtrusively. As I sat sulking in the station, I forced myself to concentrate on the person sitting directly in front of me. I started by looking down at the floor. Dark green canvas duffel bag next to someone wearing scuffed, high-top Nikes. Faded jeans with a rip in the knee (hairy, so I hoped it meant the subject of my observation was male). Next to the knee, what looked like a folded-up red tablecloth on the bench next to him. Moving upward, a beat-up, butterscotch leather jacket, light blue shirt. I usually wear sunglasses to hide my curiosity, but it was night, I wasn't in a particularly trendy spot, and didn't want to seem odd. Resorting to the obvious, I asked him the time. He was not hard to enjoy looking at. Black hair and blue-grey eyes, always a dangerous combination as far as my heart's sentimental history is concerned. It was getting later, but some of my crankiness faded. He noticed me looking (so much for subtlety), and made some comment about hoping the train would be on time. Aha, I thought, he wants to talk. His name was Olimpio and he was a bullfighter. In training, he said, but with several important amateur successes and an agent interested in talking about representation. What I took for a tablecloth was really his *muleta*, the red cloth waved in front of the bull to make him angry and charge. The train arrived punctually. We boarded together and had a compartment to ourselves.

We talked all night. Mutual fascination turned into fast friendship. He had never met anyone from New York, let alone an American who spoke his language. I had never met anyone who actually got paid to dress up in one of those fabulous sparkly suit of lights to star in a deadly *taurine pas de deux*.

We were headed to the same city. He was booked into the local bullring. I was going to be around for the next few days, and was thrilled to be invited both to watch him practice and to see the actual event. *Blood and Sand* is high on my list of favorite stories and movies. The idea of acting out a Rita Hayworth and Tyrone Power fantasy was seductive. I bought a red and black lace fan and practiced coquettish moves.

The day of the fight arrived. I sat front row center in the shady side of the ring. This was before the blood and pain of the spectacle had lost its thrill for me, so the peppy pasadoble music and the pageantry of it all was intoxicating. And, oh, the sound of the cape swirling and swishing around my bullfighter *amigo* as he worked on mesmerizing that big, black bull!

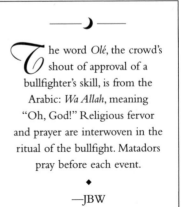

The word *Olé*, the crowd's shout of approval of a bullfighter's skill, is from the Arabic: *Wa Allah*, meaning "Oh, God!" Religious fervor and prayer are interwoven in the ritual of the bullfight. Matadors pray before each event.

♦

—JBW

Olimpio fought well. The crowd shouted for him to be awarded an ear for bravery. The authorities agreed, and he paraded around the ring, holding the ear aloft. When he passed in front of me, he bowed, pressed the ear to his heart, and then presented it to me. The crowd sighed. I suddenly couldn't move, couldn't talk, couldn't breathe. A man sitting next to me held out a handkerchief, wrapped the ear in it, and gave it to me. When the fights were over and we exited the ring, I couldn't throw the thing away in plain sight, so slipped it into my knapsack and headed for the nearby cafe where my *torero* friend and I were to meet.

We were standing at the bar and were just about to toast his success when a beautiful, dark-haired woman with fire in her eyes and what looked like a forked tongue walked up behind Olimpio and said, "You fought bravely today. I guess you didn't see me in the crowd." Uh oh, I thought. Another one who forgot to tell me about his girlfriend. He introduced us, then apologized and told me they were expected for dinner at her parents' house. I wondered why he hadn't dedicated part of the bull to her.

So much for Tyrone Power, my fan technique, and plans for borrowing those tight silver-embroidered leggings. Olimpio did come the next day to see me off at the airport and promised to write. I kissed him goodbye and gave him back the ear.

New York-based writer Mary Ellen Schultz learned how to use a fan while living with her flamenco-dancing aunt in Madrid. She still dreams in Spanish and fantasizes about going back to learn how to dance flamenco, fight bulls, and break hearts (not necessarily in that order).

★

The figure of the nineteenth-century *torero* is identical with that of the romantic hero of fiction and poetry. Born to poverty and obscurity, he transcends his origins through his innate capacity to cope with nature, in the form of the *toro*; he wins popular acclaim by his exploits, which in turn absolve him from conventional social restraints. A natural aristocrat, his wealth and tastes incline him away from his background toward the aristocracy. He is expected to be as potent sexually as he is open-handed with his money. Above all, he escapes the vulgar fate of ordinary men because he is marked for violent death; not the lugubrious death in bed following debilitating illness but a glorious death on the horns of a *toro*. The Spanish needed neither a Wagner nor Bizet, for they had the romantic motif of love-death in their vision of the *torero*. The *torero* achieves the fulfillment of romantic individualism and egotism. If his art is circumscribed by rule and ritual, his success depends upon his ability to improvise through inspiration, and for the romantic, inspiration is virtually all.

—John McCormick and Mario Sevilla Mascareñas,
*The Complete Aficionado: A Comprehensive Survey
of the Art and Technique of Modern Toreo*

✦ ✦ ✦

Wind in the West

A couple finds that the road to
understanding is full of curves.

IT WAS ABOUT DIRT, REALLY. AND WIND BLOWING THROUGH ME, hollowing me out like an old gourd. And about wondering how I could be David's wife and still be myself at the same time. I asked David to come with me for a week on our motorcycles, with no plan, just the road. He said yes, and went out to buy a new BMW touring bike that cost five times what I'd ever spend on a car. David knows how to commit himself. We set a date to leave: September 11, the day before our first wedding anniversary. It seemed appropriate.

The day has finally come.

It's taken us five hours to pack, even though we have only a cubic foot of space each to store all we'll need for a week. Since we don't know where we are going, we prepare for all climates. David has brought four pairs of long underwear. I wear my black leather jacket and pants, bought just for this trip.

We plan to ride south first, maybe as far as Bakersfield. We pass Hollister, then Coalinga, and travel down Route 5 to an anonymous truck stop for gas. We examine the map for a good place to stop for the night. We decide to turn east and look for a hotel in the Sierra foothills. A town called Woody looks promising.

Motorcycling is all about commitment. To turn the bike, you need to lean, and the faster you're going, the more you have to lean. Deaths occur when a biker, usually a beginner, is afraid to commit to the turn. You'll feel as though you're going too fast, freeze up, and forget to lean the bike. Without the lean, you ride straight into on-coming traffic in the opposite lane. If you are so unlucky to meet an obstruction there, it's likely you will die, even with a helmet on. My style is to ride at a calm pace just inside the speed limit. David often rides ahead, out of sight. This suits me just fine on this trip, which, unlike our honey-moon exactly one year be-fore, feels like my personal pilgrimage.

By the time we cross the Central Valley and start to climb the hills, the sun turns the grass a burnt apricot color, then sets, leaving us in total darkness. We pass Woody

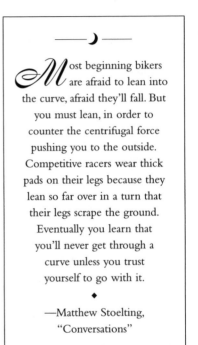

*M*ost beginning bikers are afraid to lean into the curve, afraid they'll fall. But you must lean, in order to counter the centrifugal force pushing you to the outside. Competitive racers wear thick pads on their legs because they lean so far over in a turn that their legs scrape the ground. Eventually you learn that you'll never get through a curve unless you trust yourself to go with it.

♦

—Matthew Stoelting, "Conversations"

without even noticing, up a lonely road that continues to wind more tightly as we climb. The traveler's eternal question—"What am I doing here?" consumes my mind. David is in the lead, so I blame him for our predicament. A neon CAFE sign lights up the road. Salvation.

A group of preteen boys is in the parking lot yelling their heads off and giving each other wedgies. They quiet down as we swing off our motorcycles and walk through their midst to the door of the cafe. Inside, people stare. It's the black leather, I think—it makes people believe you want to beat them up and take their money. The cashier gives us the names and telephone numbers of some homes in the neighborhood that still take in strangers for a fee, and lets David use the telephone.

While he's calling, she offers me a vinyl booth to sit in, and joins me. She is round, with solid legs and quiet hands. She sizes me up slowly.

"Where are you from?" she asks, and I tell her. She looks me over again, then asks me slowly, "Where are you going?" This question is more difficult to answer, but I say we're going to Death Valley. She nods slowly, sage-like, as if she already knew.

"Watch out for the animals," she says. "Free range all around here."

David comes back and tells me that no one wants to put us up for the night. Back on the road, I wonder furiously about how I can watch for animals I'll never see, in the black, on a road impossibly darker than before. I try not to think about it, and just follow David's taillight. My own headlight shows me tree trunks the size of small houses: we're in Sequoia National Forest. Exactly an hour and a half later we reach a crossroads and another sign: MOTEL. We check in, find our room, and make love on a mattress that's covered by plastic underneath the sheets, celebrating the last night of our first year together as husband and wife.

The next morning we make coffee on the portable stove in our room, then drink it outside in paper cups, where the air's so clean it hurts to breathe. "Happy Anniversary," we tell each other.

I can tell that David is filled with a grand contentment. He leans back in the broken lounge chair outside our motel room and looks up at the trees. My own feelings are complex. I'm thinking, the honeymoon must be over now. That all I'll have left to look forward to is staid motherhood, something I've always wanted, something I'd put off so successfully. In a week I'll be 35. This trip feels like my last big adventure.

We get on our bikes and start down a long road where the sequoias suddenly all disappear and we're riding through a forest of parched-looking joshua trees. At Interstate 395, we join a long caravan of RV's, trucks, mobile homes. The crowd on the road surprises me. On maps, this side of the Sierras looks like a true wasteland, with most of the map filled with white areas that say DANGER - NUCLEAR TEST ZONE.

A few miles further north, David and I make a right turn and ride due east, towards Death Valley, leaving the RV caravan behind us, riding alone on a straight road heading up towards the hills. It's 113 degrees Fahrenheit, like breathing oatmeal. In an hour we reach the crest of the first ridge of hills and roll down into the Panamint Valley, where we stop at a tourist trap, drink milkshakes, and write each other love letters to commemorate our paper anniversary. Then up another ridge, another 5000 feet, before the road pours us out into Death Valley, the lowest spot in the continent. I'm struggling on my little bike to keep up with David. I get vertigo trying not to look into the abyss on the side of the road, trying not to think about sliding over the edge.

We stop for gas and a Coke at a green shack on the valley floor. The sun has dipped, and the thermometer outside the store says 105. David is riding in a t-shirt and shorts; I've kept all my protective leather gear on. A woman in shorts and a halter top looks at me in my leather suit, and says brightly, "Aren't you hot?"

"Yes," I say, and we look at each other a moment across a vast chasm of not-understanding. We are no longer of the same species, she and I.

David and I ride on. But not too far. We stop early this day, in Beatty, Nevada, unable to ride by the motel sign that promises POOL - AIRCON - CABLE TV. The pool is ten feet by twenty, icy cold, and just fine. A crowd of Germans do laps. A man named Hermann introduces himself to David heartily, speaking English in a precise way. He is ready to meet some natives, some local color like us.

"Where are you from?" he asks David, who seems not to remember.

The next day is 54 degrees Fahrenheit, 59 degrees cooler than the day before. It's snowing in Colorado, so we nix our idea of visiting friends in Boulder. An old Harley rider once told David about a hot springs in the Great Smokey Valley, 200 miles to the north, and we set out to find it.

It's cold, especially since we're creating our own wind chill factor by hurling our bodies through space at tremendous speeds. A separate gale is sweeping at right angles to the road, making us lean hard into it, just to ride straight. We stop after a few miles and get out all of David's long underwear that seemed so ridiculous the day before. David rides faster in cold weather, whereas I tend to hunker down, hug the gas tank, and ride slow to keep the breeze to a minimum. Soon he pulls away from me and I'm alone, no traffic, nothing but a straight road on toward the vanishing point. I meet him again in Tonopah, memorable for its very tall McDonald's sign visible from seven miles away. We consult the map, then ride north.

The towns from here to Austin are collections of mobile homes, so remote that they don't even bother to put out the "WELCOME TO ANYTOWN/POPULATION 74" signs. We ride past a boy with a trampoline in his front yard, who graces us with a back flip, probably the only audience he's had today. Every few miles a signpost marks a dirt road running at right angles to the highway, always with names like "Birch Creek Way," when there is neither birch nor creek anywhere in sight. Late afternoon, we find the road we're looking for, a rutted track disappearing into the hills. At the end of it, hidden behind a mound, we find a seven-foot corrugated steel tub full of hot, clean spring water.

Here we are in this lovely, lonely spot, a hot spring in the desert, where nothing ever changes. There's a sign next to the tub, courtesy of the Bureau of Land Management, cautioning us to keep children away from open water sources. There's no sound except the water flowing. No wind at all: we've ridden right through it to a quiet place. A few birds circle. We don't speak to one another, we're so tired. But the water is fine.

Later, we ride another 20 miles, into Austin, where a man with ropes for suspenders and a long beard asks us where we're from and what we're doing in town.

"We're on vacation," David says. The man looks nonplussed. Crazy Californians, I can hear him thinking.

✳

The next day we ride north again, following a route that will take us into eastern Oregon. On Route 95 the road is so straight and the land so barren that I can see obstructions from miles away. What looks like a piece of retread in the road sprouts wings and a crow flies out of the way. We travel fast here, faster—90, 95, 110 miles per hour, until I feel like I'll be blown off. I think about risk. Is it riskier to ride motorcycles, or to smoke cigarettes? Riskier to take each day as it comes or to plan ahead and miss some sweet surprise? Is it riskier to fall in love with your husband over and over again, or to settle into being just pals? This trip has isolated us from one another, not brought us closer together. My image of David now is a leather-covered back, riding away from me.

My husband has disappeared once more ahead of me in a cloud of dust.

I stop after awhile, to put on a thicker pair of gloves. I turn the engine off. The solitude is very pure. Only the road reminds me that there are others of my kind. The air is filled with the sound of the wind here. It fills my ears. Plants like hands grow between jagged rocks. The sharp edges of the rocks surprise me. They should have been worn smooth by the wind long ago, but they look as if they were just blown out of the earth. I can hear a car coming from miles away, see a plume of dust on the horizon. The wind moves behind me like a herd of animals.

After a sign that says FINAL WARNING - CONSERVE BRAKES I spill out into Oregon, wet, lush, full of trees.

I meet David again in Lakeview. We've ridden 362 miles today, about 200 miles too far. All we have left is to go home. And whatever it was I came out here to find, I still haven't found it.

David complains about the road the next morning: too crowded, too straight, too far. He tells me this trip makes him feel his loneliness. I've about lost my patience. I ride doggedly, not enjoying it, preoccupied with what's gone wrong. He passes by the huge logging trucks that I'm afraid to pass, feeling the threat of on-

coming cars, not having the guts to move ahead, so I'm stuck behind them for miles breathing diesel fumes. I fume also.

A few miles east of Klamath Falls, riding together again, the road
turns sharply without warning over deep-rutted railway tracks.
David slides over the tracks, skids, makes it. I freeze, miss the turn,
and ride straight into the other lane blind. I'm riding out of control, crossing the opposite lane, where a truck just misses me and I
see David's horrified face through the dust, looking for me, seeing
me safe.

We keep riding as though nothing had happened.

Later, when it's evening, we're together at a place called Big
Bend, where we discover that the resort we'd planned to stay in
is closed for renovations and we'll need to travel seventeen miles
back to the main road, then another twenty to the nearest town,
Burney, to yet another no-star hotel by the side of the road. There
is a forest here of deep, old trees, soft breezes, birds finding their
place for the night. We're standing by a clear stream falling over
rocks. At any other time this place would be breathtakingly
lovely, a sacred spot. We don't even speak, we're so angry at one
another. "I'll wait for you at the bottom of the hill," David says,
and leaves me.

I take my own sweet time going down the hill, tired of trying
to keep up with him. At the bottom we argue explosively.

"You ride like a fucking grandma," he says.

"You're riding too fast for me to keep up," I spit back at him.
We both claim that this stupid trip was the other guy's idea. He
yells at me for riding in front of that truck near Klamath Falls. I cry
like a fool, while the sun goes down and leaves us in the dark.
Logging trucks continue to roll by, making us choke. Our argument feels elemental, like a struggle to the death. Only later do I
understand it was our way of coping with what it would be like to
be permanently separated.

I wake up with David's arms wrapped tightly around me, and
the knowledge that he's held me that way all night. Something has
happened to us, some process David and I built together through

the course of an argument that had nothing to do with the words we said to one another.

Today as we ride, David slows down, I learn to let go a little and trust my skills, and we ride together. We're mindful of each other, respectful of each other's style. The idea of going home, to our home, suddenly fills me with light instead of dread, and the world sings.

David signals and we pull over to a patch of redwoods by the side of the highway, a rest stop where retired couples have taken a break from their vacations to sip lemonade. I say, hello to one woman, and she looks past my shoulder and says nothing. I understand her reluctance when I go to the lady's room, and see a wild woman with a film of sweaty grime on her face, staring back at me out of the sheet of steel put there for a mirror.

Looking into those wild eyes, I suddenly feel like I've arrived somewhere, somewhere that I belong. I decide not to brush my hair. "You're pretty," David says when he sees me again.

We hug the coast and ride south. I feel the temperature drop as we ascend each ridge, then rise again as we reach a valley floor. I feel the sea air rising up to meet me. The road pours itself under me, liquid curves. By the time we pull into our driveway we've ridden 7 miles short of 2,000, a long way to go to find what I had in the beginning. The difference is, I'm no longer driven to find out exactly what's ahead.

David and I take each turn, together. And with David next to me—my dear friend, my love, my husband—I know now where I'm from, where I'm going, and how to watch out for the animals.

Since writing this story, Claire Tristram has celebrated four more anniversaries with husband David, as well as the birth of their daughter, Lucille. Lucy's arrival inspired her travel-loving mom to write Have Kid Will Travel: 101 Survival Strategies for Vacationing with Your Baby.

✳

For my part, I travel not to go anywhere, but to go. I travel for travel's sake. The great affair is to move.

—Robert Louis Stevenson, *Travels with a Donkey* (1878)

★ ★ ★

Wacky Weekend

A couple explores their love by
bringing the world to them.

IT WAS ALL PLANNED. WEEKS OF BROCHURES, PRICE COMPARISONS, schedules, bookings, lists and more lists. Papayas and palm trees...mangoes and moonlight strolls...lobsters, lobsters, lobsters. A long, long weekend on a Caribbean island.

Wonderful!

Then something happened.

Darling, she said (slowly, with feeling—always a danger sign). Isn't it a wee bit expensive for a weekend? After all, as soon as we're unpacked we'll be packing again.

Yes, but...

We won't even have enough time to get a decent tan...

Yes, but...

And they told us it rains every afternoon...

Yes, but...

And didn't they warn us about...

End of discussion.

Instead we created what is bound to become a time-honored tradition: the www. The Wonderful Wacky Weekend. Three days of all the best gourmet foods we've always wanted to try, the best wines, a big box of crazy-priced chocolates, music we've never *really* listened to, fantastic recipes to cook together…and a savings of hundreds to top it off.

We canceled everything and made the living room the focus of our first WWW. But it was the wrong mood: too bright, too cluttered with furniture.

A desert tent, I said.

She agreed.

So a desert tent it was: king-size mattress dragged from the bedroom, pillows and cushions everywhere, blinds down for a soft-filtered, dusky light, candles, incense. The tent itself was a huge Indonesian cloth (a beautiful wedding present, never used) suspended from the ceiling light and tied by red ribbons to the walls. You had to crawl in and out. The space inside curved down and then slightly up at the edges in soft folds—it truly felt like a tent, an Arabian Nights fantasy. The mood inside was exotic and erotic, with purples, indigos and scarlets glowing in gentle light. The two cats loved it.

We stopped work early after Friday lunch and went shopping: a small jar of Beluga Malossol caviar, four superb pâtés (two soft and velvety and two country-chunky), wafer-thin Parma prosciutto, German Westphalian ham, three types of Italian salami, cheeses galore (including a superbly soft Gorgonzola and a wheel of triple-crème Explorateur), a whole gamy pheasant, Scottish smoked salmon, *escargots*, a

―――― ☽ ――――

"At last I found voice," she wrote, "and said, 'I do not want to think it over—I have been thinking it over for six years, ever since I first saw you at Boulogne. I have prayed for you every morning and night, I have followed your career minutely, I have read every word you ever wrote, and I would rather have a crust and a tent with you than be queen of all the world; and so I say, now, Yes! yes! YES!'"

♦

—Isabel Burton, *The Romance of Isabel Lady Burton: The Story of Her Life* by W. H. Wilkins (1897)

box of Dolcetti Delicati, three different types of coffee beans, sheets of dried seaweed for sushi, homemade pastas, five varieties of fresh mushrooms, exotic salad ingredients we'd only read about in magazines, Kalamata Greek olives, pineapples, mangoes, papayas, clusters of fresh asparagus, one whole black truffle cushioned in a glass vial, loaves of fresh Italian and French breads—and a huge lobster, of course.

And the wines! Taittinger and Veuve Clicquot brut champagnes, a Chassagne-Montrachet, a Mayacamas '83 cabernet sauvignon, Duceli-Beaucaillou bordeaux, Barolo Monprivato '83, Morey-St.-Denis Paivelley '85 and three others I'm too modest to mention.

We entered our retreat and carefully laid the delicacies on our glass coffee table (the one with the chip on the corner), disguised with my grandmother's hand-crocheted cloths. We lit new incense sticks, put on a quiet tape of bamboo flute music, took the phone off the hook, locked all the doors, removed all clocks and watches.

At last look it was 6:15 p.m. on Friday evening. Our first WWW was in session.

We had no real idea what we planned to do or what outcomes we expected. We decided to let things happen as they happened, timelessly—to nibble when we felt like nibbling, talk when the mood struck, sleep when we were sleepy.

We began with the Debussy and the caviar—fat bubbles bursting with salt-fishy pungency—washed down with tiny glasses of vodka (the vodka bottle frozen in a solid block of ice with two full-petaled daisies inside the ice—carefully molded inside an empty milk carton).

We read fragments of works we hadn't touched for years: Tolstoy, Steinbeck, Wordsworth, Frost, Hardy, Thoreau (no speed reading permitted, and no Agatha Christies). And then we did something we hadn't done since our VW camper days—we read aloud to one another. *The Old Curiosity Shop* filled our flickering tent with Dickens' outrageous characters and dastardly-intrigues. I read fragments of *The Prophet*, followed by random poems from *The Oxford Treasury* at romantic intervals.

We slept for a while, then woke to the utter silence of night. I cooked a small pasta dish in the early hours before dawn—fettuc-cine with double cream and smoked salmon sprinkled with fresh tarragon. We allowed ourselves one Perugina chocolate kiss each and two balloons of Remy Martin.

Later, unused to the mattressed tent floor, I requested a massage, and soon reciprocated. This led to more passioned moments that reminded us why we'd married each other more than thirty years ago. Sort of honeymoon and first-date sensations all rolling to-gether.

But perhaps our greatest pleasure was in talking. We played memory games to see how intensely we could remember past experiences. We talked about my writing and books, about her human services work. We traded hopes and schemes and "What if" scenarios. We remembered past homes and places we'd lived— our tiny cubist cottage in a remote Canary Island village, our cave-like Yorkshire Dales farm rented from the man who invented "Blue Wensleydale" cheese, our fancy apartment in Tehran when we worked for the Shah of Iran, our camper-home in southern Italy and weeks of exploring the wild places of Oregon's northern coast. We planned new adventures on a big, worn map of the world—a Sahara crossing, Inner Mongolia, a trek in Thailand's Golden Triangle, a journey to the lost Atlantis of the Azores, a beach-bum life in Goa for a few weeks, a trip behind the Himalayas to hidden Ladakh...

We slept again, and then we cooked together—crazy creations in puffy pastry; tiny truffled quiches; English scones (more like real teeth-smashing "rock buns"); rolled phyllo things; liqueur-based dressings for watercress, endive and grape salads; a sinfully rich zabaglione. We even invented a rather unusual fruit punch crammed with fresh pineapple, mango slices, passion fruit and limes and called it the CCC—the Caribbean Compensation Concoction.

ZZ Top and old Chuck Berry tapes would wake us from lethargy, shaking the cottony pyramid of our tent; James Taylor and Jim Croce provided quieter interludes. We even rediscovered the tingle of rough-edged truths in early Bob Dylan songs. Then came the giant symphonies—we listened to all Beethoven's nine in a marathon session broken by reading, more reminiscing and charcoal sketches of one another done by candlelight. We enjoyed a "Mostly Mozart" concert after a particularly intriguing luncheon of wafer-thin filet mignon slices barely warmed in a port and orange-zest sauce with sautéed mixed mushrooms and saffroned couscous.

We got crazier as the weekend progressed. We wrote two short stories together, a few fragments of poems; we invented an odd board game; we designed our "perfect house" using favorite features of the 30-odd different places we'd lived in since our marriage. We made loving phone calls (from inside the tent) to people we missed and felt we'd overlooked.

Somewhere in the middle of Sunday we decided to forget Monday: Our WWW was too precious and enduring an experience to be terminated by the clock. So we made brief calls, and gave ourselves the gift of time.

We were on a soaring high, roller-coasting through emotions, finding new facets of each other. We created menus for future house guests; we designed ridiculous furniture (a diamond-shaped dinner set, new ways to display books); we dreamed up four new businesses. We even wrote a song, using my old, battered guitar for inspiration.

And as Monday merged into Tuesday, our WWW slowly wound down by itself, without anticlimaxes or withdrawal pains. We were satiated—gastronomically, emotionally, spiritually.

So we wrapped up the remnants of cheeses and pâtés, replaced the cushions, lowered the tent, tugged the mattress back to the bedroom. But we kept the lights low, and the candles glowing.

David Yeadon is author/illustrator of over twenty travel books, the most recent being Lost Worlds: Exploring the Earth's Remote Places *and* The Back of Beyond: Travels to the Wild Places of the Earth. *He is a travel feature writer for* National Geographic, National Geographic Traveler, The Washington Post *and numerous other magazines and his work has been featured in many travel anthologies. He lives with his wife and cat on an idyllic lake north of New York City.*

✳

I am a vagabond by trade, one who feels the next trip is always the best trip. So what did I go and do? I fell in love—madly in love—with a man who won't budge, a man committed to taking the road less traveled, both literally and figuratively. In every sense of the word, he is a rock. And like any rock worth its weight, he is solid and strong and steadfast. He is also immovable.

To be fair, he's not completely root bound. He'll take off on business trips if necessary. but will he run off to Las Vegas for a madcap weekend with the woman he loves? Will he spend a quiet week by the lake? Will he go gallery-hopping in SoHo?

Hell no, he won't go.

I fantasize endlessly about what it would be like, although true to my nature, those fantasies are overly romanticized—there is never a squabble between us! In mind's eye, I see us walking hand in hand down the Rue Saint-Louis, licking cones of glace au chocolat. I imagine kissing him under those blue, blue Maui skies. I visualize us swaying to the sounds of a calypso band on a windless Caribbean night. He will have none of it.

Other men in my life would go anywhere. Do anything. They would pack their bags and flee at a moment's notice. Of course, it goes without saying that a talent for packing one's bags at a moment's notice in not always a good trait in a man.

So what to do. Move on? It's crossed my mind. But truth be told, I really don't want to. The object of my affection may be immovable, but he's also funny and smart and passionate and kind. He's taught me how to Cajun dance, introduced me to Buddy Guy's music, analyzed my dreams, offered advice on my investments, and has listened, really listened, when I talk to him.

What he does, of course is open up my world, taking me to places I've never imagined and most certainly never would have found on my own. So we do travel together, in a fashion. Like all trips, some are blissful, some are boring. Many are comfortable, others are fraught with danger. But they all have the stuff of which good adventures are made. I leave the journey a little wiser, about myself and about the ways of the world.

—M. Eileen Brown, "No Travelin' Man"

In a Soldier's Care

A guardian angel with a phrasebook
keeps watch over a traveler.

THE WISH TO HAVE MY LIFE ORCHESTRATED AS IF IT WERE A FILM was fulfilled in Verona, Italy, the summer I turned 21.

I was part of a summer program for young musicians that was held in this city of golden light and arched bridges. We were housed in a magnificent old building with high ceilings and windows so large I could curl up on a windowsill for a nap.

The building's old stones kept the secrets of countless people who had lived in the rooms, but they could not keep out the awareness that for centuries, human dramas had been played out within the walls.

Dedicated to their art, the young musicians in the summer program were up before dawn perfecting their pieces and I awoke to the gentle melodies of Vivaldi, Bach, and Stravinsky.

While I dressed, Lalo played in the background and while eating breakfast, gypsy music urged me to hurry up, that there was much life to be lived.

But it was the melancholy music that best expressed my state of mind. Not a musician myself, I had been invited to the program to study photography and my teacher had never shown up. All the other students were musicians who studied and practiced all day and so most of my time was spent alone. I couldn't speak a word of Italian and wandered the streets with my camera longing for someone to share the discovery of hidden restaurants, unexpected frescos, the brooding statues in the cemeteries and the celestial art in the churches.

After a couple of weeks of wandering down winding streets and weaving in and out of alleys, I had the odd sensation that I was being followed. I'd walk faster, turn a corner and abruptly stop, looking back, hoping to catch someone. There was never anyone in sight. Yet the feeling persisted.

After a few days of this, I took a seat outside a small cafe on a dead end street and decided to sip lemon sodas until I was certain there was no one pursuing me. I passed two hours looking at pictures in an Italian newspaper, writing letters, and photographing children who played nearby. When I had just about given up the notion that I was being followed, a dark, handsome man in a military uniform quietly slipped into the seat beside me. He gestured to my camera. Assuming he wanted his picture taken, I picked it up. He put his hand over mine briefly, shook his head, and pulled an Italian/English dictionary out of his back pocket.

For over an hour, we took turns looking up words and pointing them out to each other, trying to communicate.

He was intrigued that I was an American and wanted to know why I was in Verona. He was a soldier serving his mandatory tour of duty. He took off his hat and showed me a series of lines he'd written under the brim to keep track of how many months he had been in the service. Altogether, he would have to serve fifteen months.

I asked if he had been following me. He leaned forward, took my hand, looked into my eyes. I melted. Would he kiss me? We were total strangers, couldn't even understand each other's language, but we had found each other. Ah, for a student nearby to fill the air with triumphant music.

But there was no kiss. He dropped my hand and went back to the dictionary. "Alone. Dangerous. Bad. Places. Hurt. Protect. Duty." How sweet. He was concerned about me and had decided to be my bodyguard.

I took the dictionary in turn. Pointed out "Thank you. No fear. Safe."

He shook his head, tipped his hat. "No safe," he said.

I pointed to my watch. He nodded. We both rose, and he walked me back to the building in which I was staying.

"Care," he said, and gestured to himself, then to me.

True to his word, he began looking out for me. When I left in the morning, he was outside waiting for me. Sometimes he would walk beside me, sometimes a block or so behind. Sometimes we would have a lemon soda together and he would insist I order them so he could laugh with the waiter over the odd way I pronounced the word "lemon." Sometimes I would think I was alone, but would turn around and find him there. Sometimes he was with another soldier or two, but usually he was alone.

We found out little things about each other. He had a large family, just like me. He wanted to go to college, to do something great with his life, but first he had to get out of the military. He would like to go to the U.S. where mail is delivered at the same time every day. We both loved ice cream and he thought eating pizza with hands was a good idea no matter what everyone else in his country thought.

He told me what was good and not so good to order in restaurants, and took me to places he thought I would want to photograph.

I was no longer lonely and the melancholy music that used to define my life in Italy no longer fit. I begged the music students to play gypsy music and pieces fast and joyful.

The other students noticed that the soldier was often near me, and one of the students followed us to a park and took out his violin and played while my soldier and I ate fruit and freshly baked bread.

Time passed too quickly and there were but a few days left. I wondered if I was nothing more than someone to watch over or if my soldier was falling for me as I was for him. But I was too shy to ask and certainly would never make the first move.

He knew when I would leave, and on my last day asked what we should do that night. I took his dictionary and pointed out words. "Group. Students. Opera. Late."

His face lit up. Perhaps he did not understand. I pointed out more words. "Must go. Not alone. Home. Leave. Early." The word for tomorrow I knew *"Domani."*

He grinned, took my hand, held it for a minute and raised it to his lips. "Good-bye," he said in English. "For now."

That was it, then? He was content to say good-bye, leaving with the suggestions that we might meet again some day? I was devastated.

That night all the students and teachers went to the opera. Ah, how lovely it was, held in an amphitheater over 2,000 years old. The costumes were magnificent. The music almost too beautiful to bear. But I could not lose myself in it when I knew I would not see my soldier again. I tried not to cry, but a tear or two slipped down my cheek.

I felt a hand on my shoulder and looked up. My soldier!

He handed me a rose and motioned for me to follow him. I didn't hesitate. He led me to a higher seat where the breeze moved the music through the air. The opera

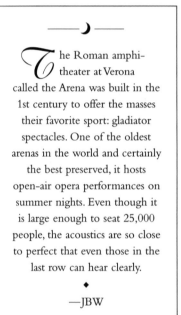

he Roman amphi-theater at Verona called the Arena was built in the 1st century to offer the masses their favorite sport: gladiator spectacles. One of the oldest arenas in the world and certainly the best preserved, it hosts open-air opera performances on summer nights. Even though it is large enough to seat 25,000 people, the acoustics are so close to perfect that even those in the last row can hear clearly.

◆

—JBW

came to life as we sat hand-in-hand, shoulder-to-shoulder. When the final curtain came down and the crowd rose to their feet, he leaned forward and kissed me to the sound of a full-house clapping. The applause, no doubt intended for the opera, was, in my heart, intended solely for my soldier and me.

He slipped a piece of paper into my hand, kissed me again, and walked me back home. He kissed me once more at the door. A long kiss, one that would linger for the rest of my life.

Later that night, when everyone slept, I climbed up on the windowsill and read the note he had given me by moonlight. "Always. Remember. *Domani*. Love."

I have never forgotten, and whenever I hear the sweet notes of a violin, I can feel my soldier following.

Nancy Hill is a writer and photographer living in Portland, Oregon, dreaming of adventure while living days of practicality. But change is always just around the corner.

★

A kiss is a lovely trick designed by nature to stop speech when words become superfluous.

—Ingrid Bergman, *Viva*

ARTHUR DAWSON

⋆ ⋆ ⋆

Desperately Seeking
Protection

*A couple gets creative when
phrasebooks fail.*

THREE MONTHS INTO OUR TRIP AROUND THE WORLD, MY WIFE
and I ran out of condoms. Jill checked every word she could think
of in our Spanish/English dictionary. No luck. I was on my own.

"*¿Tiene...prophylacticos?*" I asked the clerk in the *farmacia,* my
voice carrying an extra question mark for the word I'd just invented. To my surprise, he smiled knowingly and reached under
the counter. "Prophylactic" was an old friend; even as a teenager
I could say it to a white-coated pharmacist, without batting an eye.
The word was wonderful—it produced boxes of condoms with a
minimum of embarrassment.

I'd forgotten I was in Quito, Ecuador. The clerk was only the
first in a crowd of people waiting to be intimately involved with
my purchase. After I chose which kind I wanted, a second man
delivered the *prophylacticos* to a woman standing at a low table,
who began wrapping them neatly in white paper. Meanwhile, I
was pointed over to the cashier, who greeted me with a puzzled
expression.

"Four boxes of prophylactics!" the first clerk shouted across the
store, turning the heads of the half dozen other customers.
Resisting the urge to bolt, I paid the cashier two hundred sucres

and waited for the condoms, thinking my ordeal was over. Instead, I was handed a piece of paper and steered to yet another clerk, who took my receipt and studied it carefully. After several tries he finally located the correct package on the counter and put the goods into my waiting hands. By the time I managed to slip self-consciously out the door, everyone in the *farmacia* knew exactly what I was carrying.

By the time we reached Brazil, six months and four countries later, I was a seasoned purchaser of *prophylacticos,* almost as comfortable buying condoms as I was ordering beer. Switching from Spanish to Portuguese didn't seem like a big deal. After all, the authors of my Portuguese/English dictionary assured me it contained all the vocabulary required "to cope in everyday situations." With their book in my hands I was "well armed to confront foreign travel with confidence," a regular Indiana Jones of linguistics.

With the word *prophylactico* resting nonchalantly on the tip of my tongue, I strolled into a *farmacia* in Rio. Although I had a hard time understanding Brazilians, they could decipher my Spanish with little difficulty; the two languages are closely related.

Procuring condoms in sensuous, sexy Brazil ought to be a cinch. The man behind the counter looked up from his newspaper.

"*¿Tem prophylacticos?*" I asked. No response. A bed-sheet could have registered the same blank reaction.

"Eh?"

"*¿Tem...condom?*" I said, twisting the English word into a semblance of Latin pronunciation. Another vacant stare.

> *L*ife is a foreign language. All men mispronounce it.
>
> ◆
>
> —Christopher Morley,
> *Thunder on the Left* (1925)

"*¿Contraceptivos?*" Nothing. Time to consult the book.

A word of advice to the fornicating traveler: it seems that the editor of many pocket-size foreign dictionaries is a 93-year-old spinster in a long-sleeved black dress who draws lines of ink through any word she finds offensive. Under her autocratic rule, the entire region from the belly button to the knees remains a verbal dark continent, shrouded in mystery. Only the buttocks rise through the obscuring mists, like nineteenth century rumors of the Mountains of the Moon. As for the other organs—there are no other organs.

My search was fruitless. I'd have to work around this. "The organ in front of my buttocks needs a bag so my wife doesn't have a baby." Even blanker looks. I pointed an index finger at my crotch. "I need a bag for *esperma,*" I said, Latinizing another English word. He wasn't getting it. Time to start drawing.

Pulling paper and pencil from my daypack, I sketched a circle with a dark ring around the edge, then drew an arrow to the right, illustrating how it looked unrolled. Picking up my drawing, the clerk stepped out from behind the counter and waved me to follow him. Finally we were getting somewhere.

Stopping in front of a shelf, he bent down. *"¿Este?"* he asked, holding up a hot water bottle.

"No," I smiled. *"Obrigado."*

I found Jill, who'd made herself conveniently scarce during the negotiations, and we left the store. It was a balmy Saturday night in Rio, the streets full of couples holding hands, and in quiet corners, kissing passionately. There had to be contraceptives around here somewhere. Again and again, at several more *farmacias,* I pulled out my sketch, tried to explain what I wanted, and gestured lewdly, but the responses were equally disappointing.

"Maybe we should just give up. Looks like we're not meant to make love in Brazil," Jill sighed.

"Let's try one more," I said.

A middle-aged woman greeted us at the back of a long, narrow store. "I don't speak Portuguese very well," I apologized in the language. "We don't want to have a baby."

Her eyes lit up, her hands skittered into a drawer, and in a moment she'd piled a dozen boxes in front of us. Condoms!

"What kind do you want?"

It was hard to tell much from the packages, which had pictures

of beaches and sunsets and couples embracing in misty gardens.
There was only one way to find out which brand was best.

"We'll take one of each."

With a little giggle, the woman pulled out a big sheet of paper
to wrap the twelve boxes. "What're these called?" I asked.

"Preservativos."

"Preservativos," I tested my pronunciation.

"Sim, preservativos."

With raised eyebrows and a grin she wished us a very good
night. Bidding her the same, I tucked the package under my arm,
and carried our treasure off into the steamy Brazilian night.

In India we didn't have to go searching for condoms; they came
looking for us. We were sitting in the office of a Gandhian ashram
in Bodhgaya, talking with an energetic grey-haired man named
Gauri, when the conversation turned towards marriage, families,
and children. Gauri had twenty kids.

"So you are married?" Gauri asked.

"Yes, six years and very happy," said Jill, patting my hand.

"And you have no children?"

"Not yet. It is very difficult to travel with kids," I said. "They
don't fit very well into backpacks."

Gauri chuckled. "So you must use Nirodh."

"What's Nirodh?" I asked.

"You know... Nirodh," he said, repeating the only word he knew.

"What does it look like?" asked Jill.

"It looks like...Nirodh."

"Is it for a man or a woman?"

"It is for the man. Here, I will show you." Gauri opened a metal
cabinet against the opposite wall and returned with a handful of
red, blue, and white packages, all strung together like sausages. It
was a roll of condoms, about twenty of them. Printed across the
wrappers in English and Sanskrit was Nirodh, while smaller letters
proclaimed: "Not for Sale," "Free Supply," and "For one use only."
They were official government condoms, part of India's population
control program.

"May I open one up?" I asked Gauri.

"Certainly. The government gives them out freely."

Inside I found a condom thick enough to double as an inner tube on an Indian bike.

"So Nirodh is what you use?" Gauri was still wondering.

"Yeah."

"May I see what kind of Nirodh you have in America?" Gauri had an amazing talent for delving into the most intimate subject with childlike innocence and curiosity. We'd known each other less than twenty minutes.

"...sure. I'll go get one." I brought one made in Kenya down from our room. We'd stocked up there before coming to India.

"May I open it?"

"Go right ahead."

Tearing through the wrapper, Gauri pulled out the condom and stretched it between his fingers, testing its thickness.

"I think this is much superior to ours."

"It's much thinner," I agreed.

"Better for a man's pleasure," he said, handing it back.

"It's yours," I told him.

"Oh thank you very much. Those Nirodh are for you."

"Thanks," I said without enthusiasm. I supposed they'd be good for emergencies.

Gauri was more grateful than I realized. When he discovered we still had four months of travel ahead, his forehead knotted with concern. "You need more Nirodh. That is not enough," he shook his head at the twenty packets on the table. Rising from his chair, he walked back to the cabinet. This time when Gauri returned, his hands were overflowing with condoms; they filled his palms and stuck out through the cracks between his fingers. He dumped them on the table.

"Do you think this will be enough?" At least six dozen condoms were now piled in front of me.

"Oh yes," I answered, holding back a laugh. "This will be plenty."

"I can get you more, I just need to go to the clinic," he offered, still worried. In his eyes 70 condoms were a meager supply; it wasn't surprising that he'd fathered twenty children.

"Oh no, this is fine Gauri."

"You are certain? You do not want to run out."

"No, no. This is much more than we need." What was I going to do with handfuls of Indian condoms? Make slingshots?

"If you need more you can go to any government clinic and get them."

"We'll do that Gauri. Thanks."

A few days later I did my part for India's population control program by leaving most of the Nirodh in a hotel room drawer as complimentary gifts for ill-prepared guests.

After successfully crossing the prophylactic wastelands of India and Nepal, we reached Bangkok. Two days later, before I'd learned enough Thai to say hello and thank you, Jill and I polished off the last of our Kenyan condoms. Thai is a daunting, tonal language where the pitch of your voice can completely change the meaning of a word. Even reading from a phrase book, I often said the right word the wrong way, though in this case I wouldn't have to worry about that—once again neither "condom" nor any of its synonyms appeared in our dictionary. So unarmed with even a guess at the name of what I was looking for, I set out on one final condom hunt in a foreign land.

On Patphong Road, the center of Bangkok's massage parlor and girlie show industry, I squeezed through the evening crowd, past vendors selling pirated cassettes of western pop music, Rolex watch imitations, and copies of designer clothing. Tantalizing glimpses of Thai women, naked and dancing beneath banks of colored lights, flashed through open doorways while strip joint hucksters grabbed my arm, enticing me with printed menus of the lewd acts their girls did on stage. One offered, "She can write your name holding a pen in her…"

Leaving him behind, I entered the fluorescent calm of a drugstore. I had no plan of action, no idea what I was going to do next. While the man at the counter waited on another customer, I considered my strategy. Should I draw a picture? Point at my crotch? Make obscene gestures? Then something by the cash register caught my eye; variety packs of condoms—six different kinds for only 80 baht. Some were decorated with feathers, others festooned with long, rubbery protrusions that jiggled and bounced. One had folds and bumps on the tip. All of them looked like they'd been designed for extraterrestrial anatomies, or as headgear for Carnival. And yes, next to these were boxes of normal, everyday condoms.

The other shopper walked towards the door, I gestured to the clerk and raised one finger. Our communication was perfect; he rang up the sale, took my money, stuffed the condoms in a paper bag and handed them over. They lasted all the way home to California.

Six months after returning to the States, we got a letter from Gauri, who wrote, "Still I am remembering all the discussions that we have done in the office. Thanks dear friends. I hope the thing I have given you might have been finished by now."

I am holding on to three or four of Gauri's Nirodh, just for emergencies.

Arthur Dawson is the author of A Passport From the Elements, *which chronicles a three-year journey he and his wife made around the world, traveling by sailboat, elephant, dugout canoe, steam train, and at least one bus with no brakes. Since their return home in 1989, he's been a little more stationary, teaching poetry to elementary school children and writing in a studio he built near Jack London's former ranch in Glen Ellen, California. No longer "seeking protection," the Dawsons just had their first child.*

*

There is nothing like desire for preventing the thing one says from bearing any resemblance to what one has in mind.

—Marcel Proust, *Guermantes Way* (1921)

MARY GAFFNEY

* * *

Transformation in Venice

A new husband finds
his romantic heart.

THE WEDDING HAD GONE PERFECTLY. I WAS SLENDER AND RADIANT in white. My three sisters were beautiful bridesmaids carrying yellow roses. Both of our families were present, and they got along. The church was picturesque. The cake had three tiers. We cut the first piece together and fed each other. We changed into traveling clothes and left for the airport in a shower of rice.

Our honeymoon was the first trip to Europe for both of us. We were so exhausted from the wedding festivities and jet lag, that we slept through our time in Madrid. Later, when people heard we missed the Prado Museum and other sights, they'd snicker. They thought they knew what we were doing in bed, but they were wrong.

We should have extended our stay, but we had prepaid reservations farther down the road. We climbed into a rental car, and drove straight into honeymoon hell. By the time we'd finished with Spain, we knew that we didn't enjoy traveling together. That was an ominous discovery, for what is life but the journey between birth and death? And what is your spouse if not your traveling companion on that big trip?

Our travel styles were totally different. I wanted to get up early, especially if it was a travel day. Driving during daylight, we could see the country. Lee wanted to sleep late and then drive 120 miles per hour to make up for lost time. We had *many* prepaid reservations, so we were frequently racing to the next stop, usually before we'd really seen the last stop. No matter how fast he drove, we never seemed to make it before dark. Between him sleeping late and driving after dark, I was missing Europe.

Day or night, Lee's driving terrified me. Of course, I'd ridden with him before, but that was in the United States where we have speed limits. "Stop wringing your hands and biting your lips," he said. "You look like you're scared to death."

"I *am*," I said. He didn't slow down. Obviously, he didn't really love me.

It occurred to me in Paris that I could go sightseeing by myself, but I felt guilty leaving Lee. He was feeling ill. He got sick again in Germany and Switzerland. He didn't get sick in Luxembourg, probably because we weren't there long enough, only overnight. I wondered why the marriage vows say "in sickness and in health?" Does anyone have a *problem* with health? They should just ask if you promise to love them in sickness. Even then, we'd imagine something dramatic: a tragic accident or terminal illness. We wouldn't think about hives, hay fever, eczema, asthma, poison oak, cold sores, bad teeth, flu, sensitive stomachs, headaches, hypochondria, phobias, neurosis, limp penises, lack of stamina, poor muscle tone. It's amazing how much minor conditions can interfere with a honeymoon. And Lee was young, supposedly in the prime of life. I felt discouraged. "Can't you feel bad while sightseeing the same as while lying in bed?" I asked.

"You're the most unsympathetic person in the world," he said. I felt like a monster. He should have married a nicer person, a nurse perhaps. He should have married...someone else.

I woke up in the morning feeling sensuous and aroused, but Lee was no more interested in waking up to make love than he was to go sightseeing. Young husbands are supposed to be insatiable sex animals. Instead it was me. Lee was easily satisfied; I was never satisfied. My sexy black lace lingerie scared him. My dissatisfaction scared him. I should have married a braver person, a healthier, a lustier man. I should have married...someone else.

By the time we finished the tortuous twists and turns of Switzerland's St. Gotthard's Pass, we were nearly catatonic. Fortunately, we were also in Italy. We turned the car in at a rental agency on the outskirts of Venice and caught a water taxi at the piazzale Roma. As the boat pulled out into the canal, Lee put an arm around me and pulled me close. I snuggled in even closer. Venice got us out of the car and into each others arms. Suddenly our honeymoon changed from a high speed road trip to a slow, in-depth exploration of a new city and a new way of life. Our honeymoon began.

It was as if we were floating into a good dream together. This was the Venice we'd seen in museum paintings and reproductions, the Venice of Marco Polo, Thomas Mann, Evelyn Waugh. Our hotel, the Europa and Regina, consisted of two former palaces on the Grand Canal, described by Goethe as "the most beautiful street in the world." The floors of the hotel were polished marble. Sparkling crystal chandeliers lit the opulent public rooms. Our own room was only slightly less elegant, and we had a view of the Grand Canal. I could see Venice without leaving our room. Lee could sleep in peace.

I slipped out of bed early our first morning to see a new day begin on the Grand Canal. As I sat by our window, mesmerized by the scene below, I was startled by Lee's voice.

He said, "You look beautiful. Don't move. I want to do a sketch of you sitting right there." He began to draw.

> "*D*id you or didn't you?" I began asking every married person I met. Not the most scientific method, yet revealing. Out of twenty-five couples only five said they had, and even those seemed to have done it more out of obligation than ardor. Laugh we might, but deep down we still feel we're just supposed to have sex on our wedding nights. It's not rational. It's ritual.
>
> ◆
>
> —Jill Eisenstadt, "The Virgin Bride," *The New York Times Magazine*

I said, "I can't believe you're awake so early."

"My sleeping pills are at the bottom of the Grand Canal by now," he said. "They did help me with the time change and noisy hotels, but then I couldn't wake up in the morning."

"I noticed."

"I've been a jerk, haven't I?" he said.

"Kind of."

"It doesn't mean I don't love you. You know how insecure I can be, and here I am on my honeymoon having sleep problems and health problems and going from one country to another where I can't talk the talk. I've felt like an idiot, but Venice has revived me."

"Does that mean you learned Italian in your sleep last night?"

He laughed. "Venice is so *visual*. Maybe it's because I'm an artist, but it speaks to me in a language I understand."

Venice awoke the romantic in Lee and provided him with a grand stage on which to both display and indulge his assets and interests. He was an artist and an art lover, a wine connoisseur, a gourmet, a shopper, a clothes horse, a hedonist. Venice reminded us both that he was not an ordinary man.

Staying in a hotel that used to be a palace made him feel like a king, and he treated me like his queen. We had pale brown cappuccino at an outdoor table on Piazza San Marco, and he presented me with a tiny green velvet box. Inside was a pair of dangly gold earrings shaped like miniature gondolas. I loved the earrings, the attention, my husband.

Lee bought a suit and wore it to Harry's Bar. We dined on superb Venetian fish soup and scampi Thermidor with rice pilaf. He said, "If Hemingway were here tonight, he'd try to take you away from me."

"I wouldn't go," I said.

Lee looked so dashing and European in the Continental cut suit that it seemed natural for him to speak a new language, the Venetian language of love.

We walked and walked, holding hands, not knowing where we were, not caring. We got lost, and it was fun. Pigeons serenaded us as we marveled at the magnificent eleventh-century Basilica of

San Marco and the intricate exterior of the Doges' Palace. We ate
at a little cafe that wasn't mentioned in our guidebook, and the
Chianti and *fegato alla Veneziana* were excellent. Lee held the glass
of deep red wine toward me and said, "Here's to the woman I
love." We took a gondola back to the hotel, and as the black vessel
slipped through the water, Lee kissed me. We made love that
night. "Do you still have that skimpy black underwear?" he asked.
I nodded yes. "I'd like for you to wear it tomorrow."

On our return from Burano Island, we passed narrow canals
lined on either side with buildings that hugged up to each other.
Their reflections trembled on the water toward their opposites, as
if they could merge while yet remaining separate, like lovers.

Our son was born nine months later. We thought seriously
about naming him Venice.

Mary Gaffney is a writer who lives in Northern California.

★

Venice was the late Walt Disney's favorite city. With its scenic canals,
ornate bridges, and grandiose *palazzi* and *piazzi*, it is easy to see why
Venice grabbed his heart. Not only is it stunningly beautiful, but the
whole tourist section of the city has an amusement park feel to it. It's
almost as if what you're seeing is too magnificent, too stunning to be real.
                                        —Doug Morris, *Italy Guide*

LUCY McCAULEY

* * *

Return to Donostia

*A visitor looks back before looking
forward with new hope.*

I AM IN SAN SEBASTIÁN AGAIN, IN SPAIN'S BASQUE COUNTRY, UP
north. The Basques call this city Donostia, a name I prefer because
it sounds like the song that it is. Listen: wind feathering through
fingers of tamarisk trees, whistling between gnarled fists of plane
trees. Donostia. Wind kissing waves in the bay then trilling over
white froth and sand as the rain begins, mixing with the sea like a
symphony, percussion and strings.

Concha Bay is like this: a circle, nearly complete, a ring with a
small break where sea rushes in. Evening arrives and the bay moves
from turquoise to navy. The rain comes in sheets, muting the sea
to deep gray; then as suddenly the clouds part, unveiling golden
rays that play across cloudy-blue waves. At the far end of the bay, a
bump of an island blends into Mount Igüeldo behind it, one indis-
tinguishable from the other from where I stand at a sea wall near
the fishermen's quarter. Moving left around the circle of bay, buildings appear, white against green, then the hazy triangle of a distant
mountain.

A small beach, Ondarreta, turns into Concha Beach, a semicircle of sand where waves become foam and boys kick a soccer ball
despite the showers that start and stop again. On the promenade

above the beach, people step to the dance of the *paseo,* this one clasping a child's hand, that one leaning on a cane, this one holding onto a lover.

Then comes a small harbor where boats dock, and the sea wall that I lean against, my palms flat against cold stone. Behind me rises another mountain, Urgull. At its peak a statue of Christ in white stone, enormous and glowing in floodlights, stands watch. From the base of the mountain below begins a wall of fish houses extending all the way to the bay's end. Clothes hang from second and third floor lines: bedsheets, boxer shorts, slips. On the ground floors of these houses you can get cold beer and calamares and sit at an outdoor table to watch the water and the mountains change color.

When I was last in Donostia, I sat on the sea wall I stand by now. There is a photograph: a red bandanna around my neck, the seasky-mountains behind me, the blue and gray of a cloudy sunset. I wear the bandanna with a navy sweater and the white pants of summer (it was June). My shoes were flats that took two weeks to break in, and in the picture you can see the bandaids on my ankles. It was ten years ago; I was just 25, my knees drawn up, arms wrapped around them, me smiling at my husband taking the picture.

There is a street that runs from the old quarter to the newer city. Standing in it you can see from end to end, and at each rises a cathedral. The one in the city looms high, with spires. The other is the simpler, smaller Basilica de Santa María.

I visited there today. Something about the place seems gentle, a Basilica meant to embrace and hold rather than to frighten, as so many cathedrals do with their gargoyles and faces twisted in stone. Inside, orchestral music resounds off the high, crisscrossing ceiling, swells like the sea. It is Beethoven and it is piped in, but no matter. The cathedral is dark except for sunlight falling through windows high on each side, brightening then darkening as the rays intensify and fade, converging in a crescendo with the music over the walls, the columns, the arching stone. At the altar, no crosses or Virgins sit in gilded splendor, just a painting of St. Sebastián being martyred, a single spotlight illuminating his loin cloth, brilliant red.

I walked through the cathedral today thinking about the sea wall and the photograph. Once, after we'd separated, he asked me to stop by while he was away and feed the cat we'd kept together. Inside, I was tentative entering the rooms where we'd lived for three years, wanting to look around and not wanting to. I did both, I suppose: I looked through a kind of haze, as if cataracts covered my eyes. But in one corner of the room I saw the photograph. He'd enlarged and framed it, and I wondered then if he'd asked me to come just to see what he'd done.

In the cathedral, I thought of the June ten years ago, my smile in the photograph, the breezy warmth of summer, the days to which we thought we were headed. It is September now, rather than June. And there is no one with whom to eat calamares, sit in silent conspiracy at an outdoor table in the fishermen's quarter still unchanged from a decade ago. And it is chilly and raining rather than warm. But it is not unpleasant. As I approach this early fall of my life, things are different, but not unpleasant. I do have questions; I wonder: Am I happier? What has happened in ten years? Nothing, I think. Everything.

———) ———

*T*he stonework streets in the old section of town were wet, the cold accentuated by the dense shadows cast by ancient tall buildings. We wandered through these narrow antique corridors, amazed by the architecture, the strangeness of the Basque language on the signs, looking for warmth. All of a sudden we turned a corner and the iconic architecture of a cathedral completely filled the narrow frame at the end of the street. It was like coming out of a dark tunnel into the expansive light of day. We forgot the cold. Suddenly we could understand the implicit importance of the church to the Basque people. It was as if we were lost, and seeing it were found. We looked up and there it was.

◆

—Judy Rose, "Memories of San Sebastian"

In the cathedral, a place my ex-husband and I never saw together, I wept at the sound of Beethoven echoing through the columns and at the sight of a large cluster of votive candles glowing red like a bonfire. I wept at the sunlight, the way it streamed through simple, white-glass windows and struck the stone floor, warmed the top of my head and then my face when I turned it up.

A cloud passed and the windows darkened. I had no answers: to why I had been to this city ten years before with someone I thought I'd be with forever, and why I was here today alone. Still, when I sat in a pew, and knelt on the pad beneath, something I have never done in all the years I've entered churches, I bowed my head and the tears came while I knelt in that beautiful, shadowy-light place enveloped by music. And after I'd cried into my hands, I looked up and the light again rained in from the windows, and I knew something I had not known when I'd walked inside: That my loves had been real, that my good-byes had been necessary. That life would make things right.

Lucy McCauley's travel writing has appeared in such publications as The Atlantic Monthly, Harvard Review, *and the Travelers' Tales books* A Woman's World *and* San Francisco. *Based in Cambridge, Massachusetts, she is the editor of* Travelers' Tales: Spain *and* Travelers' Tales: Women in the Wild.

✶

Many talk of love at first sight. But few can claim to complete loss of love at an effable instant when one suddenly becomes indifferent to that object of one's not-so-obscure desire.

It happened to me one cool, foggy night on a Berkeley-to-San Francisco bus. I was sitting next to the woman I had been trying to woo. We were going to an old college friend's party.

If women were once told that the way to a man's heart is through his stomach, then men still are led to believe that you can win a woman's affections if you can make her laugh. So I was telling her a funny story involving a goat. I delivered the punch line. No laughter. Not even a crease of a smile. I "explained" the joke, already an admission of failure to communicate. She lit up and said, "Oh a *goat*! I thought it involved a *coat*!"

I looked out the bus window. A patch of floating dark cloud obscured the moon—and at that instant, it happened! I felt free.

After months of indelicate, pimply obsession, I suddenly felt mysteriously liberated because all my passion for her vanished. And I still don't know why. Because the "I" in me did not decide not to love her anymore. At that ineffable moment the veil of "*maya*" dropped-and I felt only an extraordinary sense of liberation, equanimity, and sweet joy.

-Rajendra S. Khadka, "Advice to the Lovelorn"

⋆ ⋆ ⋆

Pizza in Papeete

A flirtation with a beautiful young
islander teaches a traveler about
Tahiti and himself.

"I MEET YOU LATER AT THE PEARL SHOP," THE GIRL SAID. HER accent was a vanilla-expresso-ginger blend of English-French-Tahitian, her smile coconut-white in a pretty brown face.

"You know the place?…near the yacht harbor? My cousin works there. You can meet her. She is beautiful!"

We were on the afterdeck of the square-rigged ship that is a replica of HMS *Bounty*. A French TV version of the famous mutiny story was being filmed. Now the day's shooting was finished and we were sailing into Tahiti's Matavai Bay at sunset—the very place Captain Bligh had anchored the original *Bounty* more than 200 years ago.

Everything that had happened today seemed a too-exquisite coincidence—all the elements of a South Seas adventure were unexpectedly in place: a ship under sail, an exotic port, a friendly island girl—and me, the visiting white man.

"Can we have pizza tonight?" Janou asked with easy familiarity. It was as if we had known each other for a long, comfortable time.

"Pizza? I thought you were Tahitian!"

"Tahitians love pizza!" Her smile was pure mischief.

I was allowing myself to succumb to the same fantasy that had seduced the *Bounty's* crew. But then, I thought, I was not the first writer to be so tempted. Had not Melville and Maugham and Rupert Brooke and Pierre Loti and Robert Louis Stevenson all written of the sexuality, if not the loves, they found in Tahiti?

And Gauguin, of course, don't forget Gauguin!

We had met only this morning, Janou and I, amidst all the clutter of movie making on the *Bounty's* deck. We shared coffee and a baguette during a break. She was one of several "native girl" extras who would spend most of the day toplessly-nude while cameras rolled. No one had introduced us, it wasn't necessary. No man and woman who want to know each

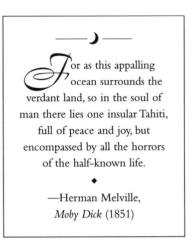

For as this appalling ocean surrounds the verdant land, so in the soul of man there lies one insular Tahiti, full of peace and joy, but encompassed by all the horrors of the half-known life.

◆

—Herman Melville, *Moby Dick* (1851)

other better need an introduction in Tahiti—never did, never will. The code of the hibiscus blossom over one ear still tells all: right side, married; left side, looking. It is introduction enough.

In the soft light of dusk, the girl adjusted her small brown body within a lime-and-blue *pareau* that was tied modestly under her arms; she tugged the thin, sarong-like sheath of cloth around by its single knot, retying it higher and tighter. A child wrapped in a bathtowel could not have seemed more innocent. Janou was in her twenties, less than half my age.

"You will remember where to find me? At the shop where they sell black pearls?" she repeated. I said yes, I knew the place—and yes, we would have a date and yes I would buy her pizza for dinner.

"You won't stand me down?" she said, making a small, pouting mouth that dissolved again into a smile.

"Up," I corrected, "not down."

"Yes," she said. "Seven-thirty."

"If you're not there, I'll ask your cousin!"

The gentle sea hissed beneath the *Bounty's* moving hull. Beyond a fringe of surf, the green velvet island was sculpted by dark valleys.

We met on time at the pearl shop. My "native girl" from the *Bounty* had changed into a long, flower-print dress with puff sleeves, almost a missionary style. She wore a tiare of flowers around her head.

"You must have a flower too," Janou said, pinching a blossom from a bush in front of the store. "Which ear?" she asked, her eyes dancing with flirtation.

"Left," I said, turning my head that way, but slanting my gaze back onto her face. "As if you didn't know, you wench!"

"Winch? What is she?"

"Never mind. You're beautiful…"

Our date began with a whooping, jay-walking run through the harbor-front traffic to the long Papeete pier. Inter-island boats and a large cruise ship were docked. Janou wanted me to meet some of her fiends, she said; they would come here soon. We sat on bent-wire stools at one of the food trucks that park on the pier, drank cold Hinano beer from cans and watched the towering white cruise ship become a twinkling wedding cake against the tropic darkness. Scents of wok cooking swirled in the evening air. Mynah birds chattered in trees. A warm, night breeze came down from the island's hilly interior, carrying a promise of rain.

Soon enough, some of Janou's friends came strolling by—or skidded to a stop on mopeds. Everyone in Tahiti knows everyone else it seems, but they laugh when they find each other as if any chance meeting were the greatest surprise and coincidence. Imagine finding you here, Janou! And drinking beer with this nice looking man whom you have not yet introduced!

A radio in one of the food stalls was broadcasting the world news of the day in melodious French. No one was listening.

I soon came to the conclusion that Janou must be related to almost everyone on the island. Before long, all her young cousins and friends became a happy multitude, snacking, laughing, thumping out percussion rhythms on any surface that would echo—and whispering. I supposed, from their glances, that the whispers were about me. Who is this latest man from the outside world whom our Janou has taken a shine to? Not that any relationship would necessarily be important beyond tonight or tomorrow in Papeete. Fresh romance is as common as fresh flowers in Tahiti. Affairs last a week (a French friend told me); marriages perhaps a year.

Under the artificial moonlight of the pier lamps, Janou seemed prettier than half nude on the ship. She slipped one hugging arm around my waist, almost tilting me from my stool. To her friends she seemed to be saying, Look at him!...Look at this new friend I found on the *Bounty*! She counted all my French francs when I paid for beer, peered curiously at my American credit cards and teased me about being "old and rich" (which, coming from her, made me feel young and poor).

We talked about her movie. It seemed Janou did not know the history of the mutiny or really care much about it. She remembered only that the tale has to do with Tahiti and that Marlon Brando was once somehow connected with it. Captain Cook? Fletcher Christian? Captain Bligh? Just names...when are we going to eat pizza?

Did she mind being photographed all day with so little on, I asked? "You know I have long hair," she replied with a shy smile—which turned to a very un-shy giggle. Quickly reaching her hands behind her head, she divided her long, black mane, pulled two shining, molton rivers of hair over her shoulders and spread them across the front of her dress. "See?" she said. "This way, I am not a naked savage! What does it matter anyway?" Janou asked, turning unexpectedly philosophical. "Everyone on Tahiti wear the *pareau*, no? What does it hide? Only an idea, yes? Does a piece of cotton make so much different?"

"Well, yes," I said. "It does...and then again, no, it doesn't. It depends," I tried to explain, fumbling, "on how one wears the *pareau*." Janou's friends laughed at my awkward descriptions. A number of them were drinking beer with us now, hanging around the food trucks, their bare feet moving almost imperceptibly as if in response to some inner drums. The rhythms of a wildly erotic dance called the *tamure* are the heartbeat of the island.

"Where are you from?" one of the cousins asked me. "What do you do?"

How could such questions be answered in any sensible way here, in the South Seas? How could a young Tahitian, who knows absolutely how to build a canoe from a solid log, imagine a city of seven million Americans who have never even carved a piece of wood? How can a girl who uses only coconut oil on her skin and hair imagine the cosmetics department at Sak's?

When I said I was a writer, everyone laughed at that too. No, Janou said, do not believe him, he is joking. That I could be a writer was apparently not possible. Nordhoff and Hall were dead, after all. There were no more writers in Janou's world, Tahiti had been written out long ago. There were no more world-class mutinies either, I thought, only those on film.

And none of Gauguin's horses running on a pink sand beach.

It seemed, after some discussion, that I would be obliged to have an identity of some sort after all. What was I doing on the *Bounty* today anyway? Why was I in Tahiti?

"You are from the *Liberte*?" Janou asked, pointing at the cruise ship.

"No," I said, "not from the ship—well, yes, I had been on the ship, but I wasn't a tourist."

"Then you are the captain!" she decided with a happy shriek. Then as we sat on the pier, she told every new arrival that I was the captain of *Liberte*. "You see!" she said, pinching the gray hair of my sideburns, "he is old enough to be captain!"

Intimations of age can give me a pang if they come with rejection. In this floating, ageless moment in Tahiti, a girl's approving acknowledgment of that "touch of gray" in my sideburns made me feel only triumph over life's odds.

Janou said she had a large family and I must meet them all—tomorrow and the day after. Soon, at any rate. I promised to do this, of course. "Where do they live?" I asked.

"Oh, all over. Some on this island, some away…but when do we eat pizza?"

"Now," I said, "if you wish; pizza now. *Avanti* to pizza!"

The last beers were tilted up and drained, mopeds started in a cloud of sweet blue smoke, goodbyes were waved, hugs exchanged. The party on the pier was over for tonight. Janou had disbanded her court. As if by some common consent, they all went their way and left us abruptly alone.

Under the dark, leafy canopy of old tamanu trees, the island girl and the ship's captain walked along Boulevard Pomare looking for pizza. We held hands; a liquid palette of colors spilling from neon signs washed over our faces: gold, green, violet, red. Some of the combinations might have pleased Gauguin himself, I thought.

"Do you fall in love with me tonight?" Janou asked, taking me totally by surprise with the question—and its ambiguity. The scent of plumeria drifted from her tiare. Surely there was, in that moment, a temptation to make a quick, impulsive answer. Romance had seemed so near and accessible all day; would it now arrive? Before I could decide between my head and my heart, Janou had put another question.

"You love Tahiti?"

"Yes," I said, and then, quietly, I added another "yes." There had been two questions, after all. Janou didn't notice.

"Then why do you go away tomorrow?" she asked mock-sad.

Though the Lafayette Nightclub is gone from Arue and Quinn's Tahitian Hut no longer graces Papeete's waterfront, Tahiti remains a delightful, enchanting place. In the late afternoon, as Tahitian crews practice canoe racing in the lagoon and Moorea gains a pink hue, the romance surfaces. If you steer clear of the traffic jams and congestion in commercial Papeete and avoid the tourist ghettos west of the city, you can get a taste of the magic Gauguin encountered.

◆

—David Stanley,
South Pacific Handbook

Out of some remote mental chamber I recalled that I had told Janou I was flying to Rangiroa, a distant atoll. It was a place I wanted to see. I explained that it was just for a day or two.

Reassured, she hugged my arm, but the only words she spoke were about pizza. "Pescadou is the best place," she said, pointing. "It is just there on the Rue Javouhey." I could already smell the oregano.

The restaurant was crowded, noisy, smoky, its tables covered in red checks, Chianti bottles hanging in rafia jackets. There were old tourists and young locals. I hoped my gray sideburns did not label me a tourist; I wanted Janou's presence to make me seem local.

We ordered: pizza with anchovies? Yes; mushrooms? Of course: sausage? Why not? It was a night for everything, including a decent French wine.

Our waitress had hand-lettered her phone number on the front of her t-shirt. We teased her, how's business? She teased back. Tahiti! No wonder there had been a mutiny. No wonder Gauguin had painted the island women, one after another after another, compulsively trying to make the world understand the beauty and sensuality he had found.

After dinner we walked along the quai, looking at splendid yachts from all the continents—visitors from New York, Sydney, Rio, Southampton, even Basle at the heart of Europe. I asked where Janou lived and she named a village. "Not far," she said. "I go there in Le Truck," which is what Papeete's homemade public buses are called.

A little beyond the bright center of town, Janou tugged me toward a particular doorway. A face framed in a small window looked out, studying us briefly. Then the door opened.

"You may not like this place," she said, "but please come with me. It is not at all Tahitian."

The Paradise discotheque was a throbbing cavern of thunder and darkness where shafts of laser-violet light indiscriminately pierced walls and people, where icy strobe flashes turned faces to frozen masks of pain, fear, and joy.

"Do you like to dance?"

"Not here," I said almost too quickly, "not this." I felt awkward—and a sudden stinging flash of deja vu: the Sixties, the Beatles, my children's guitars and drums. (Where was Janou then? First grade?) Disco was not my generation, I rationalized, but I knew that was an excuse and I felt old for making it. Janou didn't seem to care. The pounding music animated her face (when I could see it) and made her seem a lovely savage again.

We found two chairs with a tiny, round table between them. A few tourists from the cruise ship sat nearby; waiters carrying trays of drinks maneuvered between embracing couples. Lighters flared and the ripe stink of Gauloise cigarettes evoked France. An animated cartoon was being projected over and through the dancers and onto a battered screen: Pluto and Donald Duck engaged in a manic chase on and off the wall and across the surfaces of rocking bodies.

Janou was soon spotted by more of her friends. A young man took her away to dance. His Polynesian features were finely drawn. He moved as if he had log drums in his soul and steel in his sinews. Janou followed him as she could, hobbled some by her long dress. In one moment she swept by our table and dropped the tiare of flowers in my lap. Later, she emerged from the ladies' room free of her missionary dress and re-wrapped in a bright new *pareau*. Then her hair came free and swirled under the colored lights.

When the music slowed, Janou would come back to me and sip her drink. She introduced Pierre, whose café-au-lait skin was shining with sweat. Then, when the heavy blood-thumping beat resumed, the two of them returned to the floor, a pair of young gymnasts, catching all eyes with their skill and beauty, commanding more and more space as other dancers stopped to watch.

I enjoyed being a spectator, but not being in the way. After a time, I drained my glass and looked at my watch. What a day it had been anyway, I thought—beginning with Captain Bligh on the high seas and ending in this contemporary version of Gauguin's world of passion, color and sexuality.

"You are tired, my captain?" Janou asked. She was taking a break, holding Pierre's hand; they were out of breath with each other.

"No," I said. "Not tired." I could have said that I was really full of happiness.

"You love Tahiti?"

"I've answered that…"

"You love me?"

"I answered that, too, Janou…"

"You don't need to take me home, you know," she said.

"I know," I said, acknowledging Pierre.

"Thank you for pizza," Janou said.

"Thank you for Tahiti," I said.

An earthquake of sound rumbled from the throbbing speakers and I did not hear her reply. She swirled off with her young man, her body moving freely within the new *pareau*.

I paid the check then and, as I left, took one flower from Janou's tiare.

Charles N. Barnard's work has been appearing in major U.S. magazines for 48 years and he says he's still trying to get it right.

★

I wasn't the first American to fall in love in Tahiti, and surely I won't be the last. She saw me off at the airport, the young woman I fell in love with, and handed me a small tiare bud as we kissed and said good-bye. As is the custom, I put the flower behind my ear and wore it that way all the way home, on the long flight to New York.

Did I fall in love with one Tahitian woman or all of them? I'm still not sure. This seems to happen to all men who visit the island. Herman Melville, Robert Lewis Stevenson, Somerset Maugham, James Michener and those far less articulate found them irresistible as well.

I never heard from her again, and after several months, I stopped writing. I was hurt, but not surprised. A friend on the island had warned me that Tahitian women rarely look back. With an almost childlike perspective, they only live in the present—only now—which might be one of the secrets of their overwhelming appeal. My friend said it was also a kind of insulation for them against generations of broken promises, of people who went there, fell in love and never had the courage to go back.

—Ron Butler, "Tahiti Casts a Romantic Spell on Visitor"

PART THREE

GOING YOUR OWN WAY

PAT HANNA KUEHL

* * *

The Sand Dollar Theory

A beloved spouse keeps on keeping on.

MY GERMAN HUSBAND CLAIMED HE WAS BORN UNDER A wandering star. He was born and grew up in Bavaria, moved to Canada to become fluent in English (for better engineering assignments in Africa), eventually moved to Denver as chief engineer for a firm that built dams in the Far East.

Max was off to the Philippines, Hong Kong, Indonesia, Turkey, or wherever at the ring of the telephone. Herr Kuehl was the ultimate frequent traveler. I met him in St. Croix when we both were there on a Denver travel club trip. When I asked why anyone who traveled so much would join a travel club, he said he was home so seldom he had few opportunities to meet single women. I could understand that. As a reporter on a morning newspaper, working until 10 p.m., I had my own problems maintaining a social life.

He called me the next time he was in town and we clicked. At first it seemed terribly romantic, getting phone calls from the Philippines or Indonesia, letters from Korea and Hong Kong, gifts from Turkey and all of the above. Meeting his plane when he finally got home was a joyous occasion to be toasted with champagne and a late candlelit dinner.

When, a few weeks later, it was time to take him back to the airport for another long separation, I felt like Bergman saying goodbye to Bogart in *Casablanca*. With tears in my eyes, I returned to my desk and resumed my all-consuming battle with deadlines.

It was still early in the relationship when we flew to Mexico for a week's vacation. It was glorious! I loved Max, loved Mazatlan, loved walking the beach for miles, watching schools of dolphins cavorting in the surf.

We made a big thing about gathering sand dollars. I'd spot one, then lose it when an incoming wave washed it away before I could pick it up. But Max rarely missed. His long arm would sweep down to the sand and pluck the treasure just before the water reached it.

"Let that be a lesson to you," he said. "Grab happiness when you see it before something washes it away."

When we came upon a construction site where workmen were preparing the foundation for beachside condominiums, we stopped to investigate. From my first glimpse of the model plans, I knew it was time to put the Sand Dollar Theory into practice. I would own one of those beach condos in Mazatlan.

Max thought I was crazy, of course. I didn't care. I was going to put down my down payment. He could do as he liked—he'd be off somewhere exotic anyhow. But I would have my own piece of paradise on the Pacific.

All joy...emphasizes our pilgrim status; always reminds, beckons, awakens desire. Our best havings are wantings.

◆

—C. S. Lewis

Two weeks later, he called from Honolulu en route to Manila. OK, he'd be my partner in the condo. He wired his part of the payment, we each signed the contract with the builder, and thus began more than a year of coping with construction problems, Mexican style. There were multiple calls, letters and weekend visits to Mazatlan to find a wood carver to make our furniture (none of that factory stuff for us), select upholstery, draperies, linens, kitchen equipment, argue with the builder about quality standards.

Max, the German engineer, had big problems with the Mexican approach to building specifications and deadlines. My job was to soothe the rumpled spirits left in his wake while he calmed down on the beach, gazing out over his beloved ocean.

It was a wild year but finally our unit was ready for us to move in and we could sit on our own patio, sip our margaritas, and watch the sun sink into the Pacific while the sky turned glorious hues of peach and intense blue. The show just got better at nightfall when the zigzag line of lights on shrimp boats fishing off shore bobbed like diamonds dangling over black velvet.

In the midst of it all we got married. Sharing a Denver address wasn't nearly as challenging as building the beach unit in Mexico. But the best parts of our life together were there in Mazatlan, on R&R visits after Max's returns from his dam assignments *"in der chungel."* (He only *thought* he had lost that German accent.)

Max had just returned from a stint in Lebanon (in the fall of 1980 when bombs were going off like firecrackers in Beirut) when we made our last trip to Mazatlan. The Beirut stop had followed a month on the dam site in Jakarta so he was exhausted and badly needed those sessions of basking in the sun and our long walks on the beach.

On one such hike he admitted the years of long jet journeys and roughing it in backward countries were beginning to take their toll—that he would have to start thinking about settling down. He hated the thought. I was delighted. I was tired of homecoming honeymoons. I wanted an everyday marriage.

It was the first day of Thanksgiving Week and we joked about the snow back in Denver as we stretched our *serapes* on the sun-bleached sand. I sat down and opened my paperback thriller while my husband trotted down to the water's edge, then waded out to where the whitecaps started to break. I looked up from my book from time to time to watch him body surfing like a teenager. Sometimes he seemed to disappear, the waves claiming him like those sand dollars. I was relieved when he finally came back to shore and walked towards me, beaming as he dried off with his towel.

"The water's wonderful!" he said an instant before he collapsed on the sand like a fallen redwood. His heart had stopped. He had left me again, this time for good.

Our last drive through the streets of Mazatlan was in a rickety ambulance wailing its way to a tiny emergency aid station where Max was pronounced dead. That lovely stretch of Escondido Beach where we had felt most alive had become mined with bittersweet memories. It was comforting to know we had gathered our sand dollars while we could.

We had agreed long before that we both preferred cremation. Max had specified his ashes were to go into water, completing the cycle of his life-long fascination with hydraulics. "Just flush me down the toilet and I'll make my own way," he had quipped.

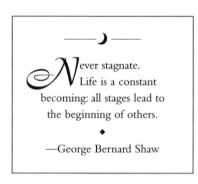

Never stagnate.
Life is a constant becoming: all stages lead to the beginning of others.

◆

—George Bernard Shaw

My first thought was to have the service in Mazatlan and leave his ashes where we'd been the happiest, but arranging cremation is extremely difficult in Mexico. I decided the body would return with me on the plane to Denver where cremation would be no problem.

But what to do with his ashes? Still deep in grief and perhaps thinking none too clearly, I asked one of Max's business associates to take the ashes to the Philippines and put them in the water at the Upper Luzon dam Max had designed and where he had supervised construction. After all, that was the project he had considered his major achievement.

The engineer obliged in taking Max to Manila but then, instead of quietly dumping the ashes into the dam, he mentioned my request to Filipino government officials. After much discussion and miles of red tape, the politicos withheld permission, probably suspecting some ulterior motive for the act. The by-the-book engineer returned to Denver at the end of his business in the Philippines and I received a telephone call saying my husband was back in his office six months after he'd died.

When friends and I finally took Max's remains up to a Colorado mountain lake (no, we didn't ask permission), it was an eerie experience with a blazing peach and blue sunset, not unlike those in Mazatlan, breaking through what had been a steel gray sky. When a younger engineer emptied the container over the lake, the ashes poured out like an Olympic diver plunging into the depths.

After a few tears all around, we started laughing. Max had finally gotten his wish—and who but Herr Kuehl could have racked up flights from Mexico to Denver to Manila, then back to Denver six months after he'd checked out of this life? I figured he was up there riding his wandering star and it was time for me to get back to collecting sand dollars.

Pat Hanna Kuehl is following her wandering star as a freelance travel writer after 25 years as a staff writer for the Rocky Mountain News *in Denver.*

✳

I think that life would suddenly seem wonderful to us if we were threatened to die as you say. Just think of how many projects, travels, love affairs, studies, it—our life—hides from us, made invisible by our laziness which, certain of a future, delays them incessantly.

But let all this threaten to become impossible for ever, how beautiful it would become again! Ah! if only the cataclysm doesn't happen this time, we won't miss visiting the new galleries of the Louvre, throwing ourselves at the feet of Miss X, making a trip to India.

The cataclysm doesn't happen, we don't do any of it, because we find ourselves back in the heart of normal life, where negligence deadens desire. And yet we shouldn't have needed the cataclysm to live life today. It would have been enough to think that we are humans, and that death may come this evening.

—Marcel Proust, quoted in How Proust Can Change
Your Life: Not a Novel by Alain de Botton

BETH CLARK

* * *

Tropical Temptations

Whose life is it anyway?

"GET A GRIP," I TOLD MYSELF. "THIS ISN'T REAL LIFE." THERE I was, on a moonlit dock in Tahiti, staring up at the stars with Hiro, a wild-haired, tattooed man who, a few hours earlier, had been beating drums, juggling knives and poking flaming torches down his throat. We were surrounded by the beauty of deep lagoons, volcanic mountains and a brilliant sky, but I could not take my eyes off him.

Maybe it was his hard-muscled, sun-bronzed body, swathed only in a loincloth. Or perhaps I was just mesmerized by his sweet, sensual nature, and his enigmatic mix of primitive and worldly attitude. Yes, he was covered with Maori warrior tattoos, but he could also speak seven languages. His English was rhythmic, poetic, especially when he sang to me.

Whatever it was, this man made my heart jump. I was obsessed with Hiro's voice, Hiro's face, Hiro's whole exotic existence. I was so thoroughly enchanted that I almost forgot something important:

I'm married. Happily married for four years, to a wonderful guy who happened to be 3,600 miles away.

So, fighting my magnificent obsession, I left the moonlit dock and returned to my bungalow, without Hiro. Alone.

The wind whipped the curtains around as I lay in bed, unable to sleep. The strength of my feelings for Hiro frightened me, mocked the stability I had assumed in my life. The more I tried to convince myself that my attraction was not important, the more I realized that it was.

I knew, intellectually, that I was being seduced as much by the tropics as by Hiro—stunned by the beauty, lulled by the warmth of the winds and the people, dazzled by new experiences. Like Paul Gauguin one hundred years before, I was fleeing civilization, if only for two weeks. The freedom, the isolation from the world, was intoxicating.

Yet I felt vulnerable, and I didn't like that. I had spent my twenties learning how to trust myself—my emotions and my instincts—in complex situations. And marriage had given me continuing lessons about a completely new level of faith, the trust that endures through success and failure, boredom and frenzy.

Ironically, coming from a secure relationship may have made me more susceptible to Hiro. In my single years. I entered everything—chance acquaintances, dating and work relationships—with a wary eye, as if I were walking alone on a dimly lit street.

But now, after years in this marriage, I had fallen into an illusion of security, that feeling of being safely sheltered inside a warm house on a stormy night. On an emotional level, all things—family, friends, work—are secondary to that cocoon of two.

I felt immune to the charms of other men, especially someone who wore palm fronds around his ankles and flowers behind his ear. So when I struck up a casual friendship with Hiro, I may have let myself get closer to him than I would have had I been single. He was shy, nonthreatening; there was no need to put up walls.

My friends and I had all been intrigued by Hiro from the moment we saw him standing, so dignified, with just a cotton *pareo* tied around his waist. We admired his strong presence, his nonchalant comfort within his own skin. I got a closer look later, when I asked him to help me remove a small piece of coral lodged in my heel. As he cradled my foot. I began laughing, partly because I am ticklish, partly because his raw magnetism made me nervous.

The next few days offered a series of increasingly intimate, yet innocent, encounters. Life seemed to conspire to throw us together—on the paths, at the beach, near the lagoon—and we always stopped to talk. My friends took notice of my growing attraction: when Hiro hopped in the van we were taking into town, they nudged me and giggled.

Over the course of the tour, Hiro taught me Tahitian words, songs, and customs: He crushed a brilliant red ginger blossom in my palm to show me how ancient Tahitians cleaned their hands. He even tried to teach me some dances, though my stiffness defied instruction. "You should maybe practice shaking your derriere," he advised tactfully.

Hiro took us snorkeling on his favorite reef, where he dove for clams then held them, wiggling, to my lips for a snack. We then submerged again, holding on to each other for balance, to watch a show of vibrant fish attracted to the shells.

When I was thirsty, Hiro climbed a 50-foot palm to pick a coconut, hacking it open with a machete so that I could drink its fresh milk. Its green sweetness was comforting, eerily familiar, reminding me of the sugarcane that I relished in the summers of my childhood. It was then that I first shocked myself by thinking, I don't want to leave.

That day, Hiro and I sat talking as he wove me a leafy crown. He gently placed it on my head and said, "Tonight, you wear this." I nodded. Then he drew himself up tall, locking his dark eyes with mine. "And you will dance with me!"

My skin tingled from that electric jolt that he caused. I tried to ignore it. "Oh, but you know I hardly dance," I murmured.

He simply looked at me, at my face with no makeup and my wet hair plastered to my head and my extra fifteen pounds, the ones Sam teases me about, and whispered, "You are beautiful."

Suddenly, I identified with all those millions of people who slip off their wedding rings and pretend to be single, all those poor torn souls who break up their lives and the lives of those around them.

I looked down at my left hand and beat a hasty retreat back to my friend's cabin. We tittered over his "Me Tarzan, You Jane"—

style request for a dance. But I didn't tell her about Hiro's compliment, maybe because it frightened me. Now a wind had changed: when I danced with Hiro, when I sat with him on the dock in the moonlight, I felt the danger, the threat to my well-planned life.

Each new encounter with Hiro hooked me deeper into our drama. We had run into each other so often because, Hiro confessed, he had followed me, silently, from the very first day. Even the van ride into town had been a ruse to get to know me better.

I generally avoid temptation unless I can't resist it.

♦

—Mae West

"You know, I'm married," I told him, but he just smiled and answered, "We are just friends." Then he asked if Sam was a jealous man. "I don't give him reason to be," I answered crisply.

In just days, Hiro had transformed me into a giggly, giddy, even moody teenager—me, a 32-year-old woman who gardens, and owns a washer-and-dryer and a retirement fund.

My feelings for Hiro reminded me of my teenage years in part because they were confusing, hard to understand. I searched for a way to label them. It was a longing too strong for friendship, too new to be love, too honorable to signal hot, passionate lust.

Okay, so maybe I lusted just a little. My companions teased me unmercifully about being hypnotized by the swirling tattoos on Hiro's dancing backside.

Sometimes I tried to explain my attraction. "But I never even liked tattoos before!" I would wail.

Ours would stay a delicate relationship, framed by time and place and the fact of my marriage. Even touching his hair, as I did once, seemed aggressive. In fact, I think we both were shocked when I gave him a quick kiss on the cheek at one parting.

And then suddenly, a shock of recognition came to my rescue: I had...a crush! I had a crush on Hiro! Now I smiled in the dark, remembering a little boy long ago in junior high who made my knees shake when he sauntered by.

Nearly all my crushes were fleeting, forgettable. Usually, I just suffered through them silently, waiting for the magic to dispel itself. The few times I acted on my feelings, the relationships didn't work: the reality of the man couldn't keep pace with the heady fantasy.

This crush made me question myself, my marriage, my life. Was I happy? Were we happy? Could I chuck it all and live in a thatched hut?

Labeling my feelings "a crush" made them less scary. But it was still impossible to say *au revoir* to Hiro when it was time to leave. We continued to talk by phone as I traveled on to other islands. Once, I wished aloud for some fresh coconut milk.

"I will send you coconuts, today, on the airplane!" Hiro said in a deep, urgent voice.

"But Hiro, I couldn't open them, I don't have a machete."

"No machete?" he asked sadly.

In the long pause that followed, it seemed that the world rushed in to fill the space between us. Later, I smiled at the silly exchange, but at the time it broke my heart.

I realized that this feverish crush, too, would pass with time. But I also realized that I should never expect to have complete control over my emotions, just my choices. When I married Sam, I didn't vow not to get wild crushes, I just promised not to do anything about them. It was important to walk a fine line: to enjoy my crush but get over it, somehow, without crushing that part of myself that is passionate.

I was fortunate that Hiro was not a coworker, or friend, or neighbor. I had become addicted to those heart-pounding moments around Hiro when I could feel my eyes glow, my skin grow warmer. I knew firsthand that a crush, being both physical and emotional, can make you literally feel like a new person.

So it was with some trepidation that this new person returned home to the same husband, eyes still bright, heart still beating a little faster.

At first, I wanted to tell Sam all about Hiro. Friends cautioned me against it. "Those male egos are too fragile," warned one.

But the more I held back telling him, the more guilty I felt. When Sam borrowed my car, I snatched out the cassette I had listened to repeatedly—one of Hiro singing to me. My photos came back and I breezed through the dozens of Hiro with little explanation.

It put me in a foul mood, holding in my little secret. Finally, I couldn't stand it any longer. One evening, as we walked our dog around the neighborhood, I broke the news: I had a strong crush on that handsome tattooed man starring in the photos.

Sam started laughing. "Okay, does this mean I can go get a crush on some topless dancer now?" I could have killed him. This was serious! But laughing with him did make me lighten up a little.

And that was that, until later in the week, when we were standing in our kitchen with some friends, and Sam told them, "Yeah, B.C. ran off to Tahiti and fell in love with some dancer."

"No," I said a little sadly, "It was just a little vacation crush." And somehow, at that time, the moonlit dock seemed a million lost miles away. Only the lesson remained: I can never really control my heart. Thank heaven.

Beth Clark is a writer living in Los Angeles.

✳

I was comfortably married, obsessively responsible, my yearnings properly repressed when a friend asked if I would like to go to Egypt. The improbability of such a trip prompted a surprising desire in me, stirred a restlessness that I hadn't known existed.

Wallace Stegner wrote about an internal sprite he called a "sensuous little savage." The moment I stepped off the plane in Cairo, I'm convinced that mine awakened. I felt as if some wild little zygote, some diaphanous spirit, was fluttering and unfolding inside me.

As we headed for the ferry, an astoundingly handsome man called out to us to hire his *felluca*, a romantic sail-driven boat that looks as if it were invented to beautify the Nile. He was right out of a harlequin novel—the flowing white *galabiyya*, sparkling brown eyes, tall lithe body, and obvious passion for, at the moment, our business.

Ahmed turned his attention on me. And from the moment he did, I realized he was the brown-skinned incarnate of my first lover, a man who had been killed when I was seventeen. Within a few minutes, repressed tendrils of longing became a siren song. I was aware of the absurdity of my situation—a 43-year-old woman in one of the most beautiful places on earth, the breeze of the Nile filling the sails, and the delirium of an Egyptian spell, a man young enough to be my son and handsome enough to melt the heart of the sphinx flirting with me—and I felt a helpless, unburdening laughter welling.

We were more than continents apart; there were entire worlds of conversation and innuendo that we could never share. Yet our bodies were irrepressibly drawn together though Ahmed sat three safe feet across from me. The cobalt backdrop of the river seemed to press toward me the whiteness of his teeth and garments, and the mahogany of his skin. I began to feel exhausted by the intensity of the attraction.

I tried to explain to Barbara what was happening to me. I felt like an undertow victim. I felt like I needed to come up for air. We reached the inadequate conclusion that pheromones are a powerful thing.

—Lisa Bay, "In the Eyes of Ahmed"

MEREDITH MARAN

✦ ✦ ✦

First Date with Ann

Love is never what it seems.

I'M BARELY AWAKE WHEN THE CLENCHED FIST IN MY ABDOMEN sends me an unmistakable two-word message: bladder infection. "Fuck!" I swear aloud, naming at once my reaction, the cause of my condition, and the activity I'm afraid this condition will preclude.

I planned to become a lesbian today, and while I'm pretty sure lesbians don't call what they—we—do "fucking," it's what I've always called sex and will, until someone teaches me something better. Which is what I was hoping a semistranger named Ann would do, about five hours from now.

Sitting on the toilet dribbling pee and wincing at the all-too-familiar searing sensation that follows, I curse my ill-fated decision to give sex with Rich one last try. Was it two nights ago, or three? I can't remember…as usual. Which is one good reason that my ten-year, two-child, one mortgage, two-car, one-checkbook marriage is ending. I'm counting on Ann to give me another one (good reason, not marriage. That fantasy will come later).

"Not bloody likely," I fret, noting the bright drops of blood in the toilet. Is that a smidgen of relief I feel at the thought that medical restriction might come between me and my long-antici-pated new sexual identity? I grab the bottle of sulfa pills out of the

145

medicine cabinet, promising myself, as I've done each morning since my husband left our home six weeks ago, to scrub out the razor hairs and dried-on shaving cream blobs once and for all.

Before I can set off for my rendezvous with destiny, I've got to get the kids to nursery school. Tying their sneakers is so painful I'm wondering how I can possibly pull off a tryst. I explain to their teacher that Peter and Jesse's dad will be picking them up tonight, limp stiff-legged out to my car, and struggle to stand up straight—so to speak—long enough to pump a tankful of gas.

So far, I admit to myself as I head north out of San Jose, the big day isn't going terribly well.

By the time the San Francisco skyline comes into view, the drug has kicked in. So has the high anxiety. Ending a marriage is one thing. People do that every day. Becoming a lesbian is another. People only do that every day on *Donahue*.

I barely know this woman. We spent three days together, along with twenty thousand other people at a publishing convention in Dallas, eleven months and one marital separation ago. I thought she was a boy until I saw her name on the book she was at the convention to promote: *One Teenager in Ten: Writings by Gay and Lesbian Youth*. She thought I was a married straight woman until she caught the lusty look in my eye. Until she read the poem I sent her as soon as she got home to Boston and I got home to San Jose—ambiguous in intention, but undeniably horny in inspiration. We exchanged equally ambiguous letters and phone calls throughout the next year. When Ann called to say she was coming to visit her brother in California we began a series of awkward negotiations to determine the nature of our impending liaison.

"I'll stay with my friends in San Francisco. You and I could meet for lunch…if you have time," she offered.

"You could stay with Rich and me; we could all hang out together," I countered.

"I could just come meet the kids," Ann responded, beating a hasty retreat around the bush.

And then, six weeks before Ann's scheduled arrival, four years' worth of marriage counseling came to an end and Rich moved out. Days after his departure I called my one lesbian friend, a therapist, and asked her where someone would go if someone wanted to have an affair with someone of the same gender who was coming for a visit from an unnamed East Coast city. And someone's house wasn't a possibility because it was where someone's husband would stay with someone's children while someone went off for the weekend to have sex with someone she'd never had sex with before (who happened to be a woman).

"It's about time," applauded my advisor, who'd had not-entirely-covert designs on me herself. "Go to a gay resort on the Russian River. Try Fife's or The Woods. And tell *someone* I hope everything...*everyone* comes out great." She was still chuckling as I hung up the phone.

I called Fife's. "I'd like to reserve a room for two..." So far, so good. I was pretty sure the guy on the other end couldn't tell I wasn't really gay. Yet. "...with twin beds."

Long silence. "Twin beds?" he repeated, incredulously. Clearly, this wasn't a request he got often. "All we've got are queens," he'd answered imperiously, sounding very much like one, even to my uninitiated ears.

"Well, it's for me and a *friend*," I stammered, "and we don't really want to sleep in one bed..."

"Hold a sec," my tormentor snapped. I heard his muffled voice, then another man's. Then laughter.

"Turns out we have a couple of twins we can roll into a cabin," he said. I hoped fleetingly that he meant twin *beds*, and that I wouldn't be charged extra for a ménage-à-twins. This was going to be enough of a challenge with just Ann and me in the room.

"I'll take it. Thanks," I said, and promptly broke into a full body sweat.

But all that was weeks ago. Before I'd prepared my still-husband, my best friend, my uncomprehending two- and three-year-old sons, and my journal for my upcoming journey to The Other Side. And before I'd managed to get this goddamn bladder infection.

And now, bladder infection and last-minute terrors notwith-standing, I'm on my way. Slowly. I'm having to stop every few minutes to pee, and the truth is, heterosexual marriage—especially the kind I had, in which sexual encounters were easily prevented by bladder infections, nonspecific apathy, or imperceptible shifts in the atmospheric pressure—is looking pretty appealing. I'm not sure what's *less* appealing right now: the thought of letting the seam of my jeans, let alone a new lover, touch my lower chakra—or the thought of embarking on yet another new phase of my 34-year-old life.

I pull up in front of the house where I'm to meet Ann, and practice my Lamaze breathing. It doesn't do a bit more for me now than it did when I was screaming for mercy in labor. I knock on the door, and the woman I've imagined myself in bed with for the past eleven months answers it.

She's very small. She's smiling. I think of a photo of herself she'd sent me, ten years old, with braids down to her waist. I wish she still had those braids. I wish *I* had those braids. We hug stiffly, un-embracingly. I realize she is exactly the same size as I am. My bladder aches, my heart pounds, my brain's taken the last train out of town. "Hi," we both say. "So you were really there all that time," I say. She nods and smiles again. When she's not touching me, she seems so small.

Ann slings her knapsack over her shoulder and we get in the car. "I've never been to the Russian River," she says. Having spent seventeen years as a heterosexual woman grappling with the ethics and feasibility of faking orgasms, I am faced—and so early in my career as a lesbian—with deciding whether or not to fake previous homosexual experience. "Me neither," I say.

> *I* have walked myself into a less safe life. I walk on unsafe streets and in unsafe jungles. My heart has walked me into dangerous loving along the way, loving that has made me use everything I know.
>
> Mostly I walk to get to where I want to be.
>
> I hope I can keep walking until I die. I'd like to be climbing a mountain when that happens.
>
> ◆
>
> —Judith McDaniel,
> *Sanctuary: A Journey*

Fortunately, Ann initiates small talk as we head across San Francisco. I, meanwhile, have been overcome by acute respiratory distress. My lungs seem to have collapsed, and I'm desperately trying to suck some air without making my condition—this new condition—apparent to my unsuspecting suitor…suitress?

The next words I speak are to an Alhambra Water delivery truck driver, twenty minutes later, when I finally get enough oxygen to my brain to realize that somehow the car I'm driving is heading south—back to San Jose, and away from the Russian River.

"How do I get to the Golden Gate Bridge?" I manage to squeak out. The truck driver glances at my license plates; he seems surprised to see that the car isn't a rental. "Do you have a map?" he asks. I glance at Ann to see if the weekend is over yet. She seems quite unconcerned. I realize then that she and I are very much unalike. By this time, I would've asked, snidely, just how long she'd lived in the Bay Area (twenty years, in my case). I would've asked, ever so patiently, if she wanted me to drive. I would've told her to let me off at the nearest lesbian bar so I could find myself some competent, *real* lesbian worth spending a weekend with.

"I'm getting to see more of the city than I'd thought I would," Ann says, with no detectable sarcasm. I apologize, she shakes her head and smiles, and we fall silent. Once we've left the city and are zooming up the right freeway in the right direction, I steal a surreptitious peek at her chest. Pay dirt! Her pale blue button-down shirt is gapped between the middle two buttons, providing me a clear view of her braless, petite, but undeniably female breasts. I allow myself a moment of disappointment—they're not quite the voluptuous kind I'd dreamed of—before acknowledging that, like her body, her breasts are about the same size as mine.

We arrive at Fife's. I park the car. Together, silently, we approach the registration desk. It is not just my heart and bladder that are pounding now. My fingernails are pounding. My eyelashes are pounding. I say my name to the man behind the desk.

"Ah, yes!" he exclaims loudly enough for all the real gay people in the fifty-acre resort to hear. "The ladies with the *twin beds!*"

Without looking at Ann, I snatch the keys from his hand and slink back to the car.

"I just thought…," I mutter in Ann's direction as we approach Cabin 7. "It's okay, Meredith," she says, her smile a bit stretched now. "Whatever you want to do is fine."

What I want to do, I realize as we let ourselves into Cabin 7, is lie down. With Ann. I don't care about the food I've left to spoil in the car or what my husband will think or all the years I've spent longing for sex with a woman, or even the resounding pain in my bladder. I don't know what I want to do, once we're lying down together. I just want to do it. Just like I wanted to with John Melnikoff in fourth grade. Just like I wanted to with Paul when I first saw him hawking his underground newspapers outside our high school. Just like I wanted to, at one time, with my clearly soon-to-be-ex-husband.

The most unexpected thing about this feeling is that it's so utterly familiar. I always thought lust would feel different when it wasn't heterosexual.

I really do want to have sex with this person, I realize to my own great surprise. I really do want to have sex with this woman.

But not just yet. Before I can cross the line that I have approached and avoided for thirty years or so, I must avoid it awhile longer. I say I need a nap. Ann says she'll go for a walk. I declare that I'm not really tired. I jump up and suggest a walk together. Ann and I walk along the narrow sandy path to the river, and there, on the rocky riverbank, I am overwhelmed again by the magnetic pull of gravity, or lust. So I do. Lie down. On my back, with my too-small breasts and my fantasies pointed at the sky. Because I simply cannot stand up when I am this close to Ann, this close to my dream.

She stands with her left foot brushing my right thigh, skipping flat rocks across the slow-moving muddy river. She places three sun-warmed stones carefully on my stomach. She might as well have reached down and caressed my clit. I'm sure she can hear the gathering and dripping of juices between my legs. I wonder if this is lesbian flirting. If she feels what I feel. If she would believe that I feel what she feels.

We go to a restaurant for dinner. She eats a burger; I toy with my tortellini. "I thought most lesbians were vegetarians," I comment. She winces but says patiently, "I'm not."

It's getting dark out. Ann orders a beer. "Are you an alcoholic?" I ask. (I restrain myself from confiding that I've read that many gay people are.) She asks why I'm asking. I ask how old she was when her father died. She asks if I'm nervous about going back to our cabin,

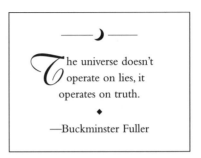

The universe doesn't operate on lies, it operates on truth.

◆

—Buckminster Fuller

about going to bed. I nod. She says, again, "Meredith, we don't have to do anything you don't want to do." We go to the cabin. What *do* I want to do?

I unpack the nightgown I've purchased for this occasion—a flannel one, to prove my intimate knowledge of lesbians' affinity for flannel. I go into the bathroom to put it on, peeling the sopping, sticky underpants off my inflamed genitals. When I come out Ann is in one of the twin beds, wearing a white cotton t-shirt. I wonder if that means I won't get any points for the flannel. I wonder what else, if anything, she's wearing.

I climb into the empty twin bed. I'm shaking; my teeth are chattering. I think of my husband, my children. I close my eyes and see a movie of me getting up, getting into bed with Ann, her arms folding around me, her fingers doing things between my legs no man could ever know to do, my hands squeezing her breasts, her nipples against my nipples. If I ever had a bladder infection, I can't remember it now. If I ever thought I was kidding about this lesbian thing, I was wrong.

I kick the blanket off my legs, leap up, and slide into bed with Ann. She puts her arms around me and breathes deeply. I am quaking inside and outside. She says, even now, "It's okay, Meredith. We can just hold each other."

My body has a need that's burning a hole through the mattress.

My brain is hanging on for dear life to what remains of my hetero-sexuality. Ann strokes my arms with her soft, small, hairless hands. I think of the night, just a few short weeks ago, when Rich and I told our sons we were separating. I think of how Peter asks every day when Daddy and I are going to live together again. Ann's hand brushes past my breast. My cunt clutches. I pull away slightly.

Eventually Ann falls asleep. I listen to her kitty snores and think of the nights I've spent kicking Rich so he'll stop snoring, snores that shook the bed and made sleeping together intolerable and finally impossible. Snores that made me wake up angrier even than I'd fallen asleep.

Ann's digital watch beeps on the hour. After the fourth beep I slip out from between her arms, pull on my clothes, and walk into the dark night. The air is scented with jasmine, like the jasmine Rich planted along the fence of our home in San Jose. There's a phone booth outside the hotel office, with a night light that guides me to it. I dial my home number, where my husband and children sleep.

Before it rings, I hang up. What will I say? "This is your last chance to save me from this," I imagine myself saying to Rich. "Please…save me from this."

I know he can't. I know I can't. I know that "lesbian" isn't really the right word, that my need to separate my life from Rich's and my need to feel Ann's hands and mouth on me are two different needs with two different sources. I know that I have lusted after men, and that I now lust after a woman who sleeps just a few yards from where I stand. I go to where she is.

Meredith Maran started her journalistic career as co-publisher of the nation's first high school underground newspaper at the "prestigious" Bronx High School of Science (circa '67). Since then she has lived life as a back-to-the-land hippie in Taos, a union organizer on Bay Area assembly lines, a suburban wife and mother, an urban lesbian mother, a freelance journalist for magazines ranging from Brides *to* Mother Jones; *from* Parenting *to* New Age Journal, *and as a consultant to a host of socially responsible companies. This story was excerpted from her book* What It's Like to Live Now. *She lives in Oakland, California.*

✳

Stripped of leaves, stripped of love, I run my hands over my single wound and remember how one man was like a light going up inside me, not flesh. Wind comes like horn blasts: the whole mountain range is gathered in one breath. Leaves keep coming off trees as if circulating through a fountain; steep groves of aspens flow.

I search for the possible in the impossible. Nothing. Then I try for the opposite, but the yellow leaves in trees—shaped like mouths—just laugh. Tell me, how can I shut out the longing to comprehend?

—Gretel Ehrlich, *Islands, The Universe, Home*

LAWRENCE MILLMAN

*　*　*

A Walk on the Wild Side

A famous custom catches a traveler—
and his heart—unawares.

ON PREVIOUS VISITS I HAD FALLEN CRAZILY IN LOVE WITH THIS capacious island called Greenland, shaped like a colossal stockinged foot, with a land area four times the size of France and a population slightly smaller than Wauwatosa, Wisconsin. I had fallen in love with its high-flying natives, a race of people who call themselves Inuit (Real People) or Kalladlit (Real, Real People), but never Eskimos, which is a Cree Indian term of disdain meaning "eaters of raw fish" (Frenchmen don't like being called "eaters of garlicky snails," either). I had even fallen in love—for a night—with a young woman who possessed by far the finest pair of eyes I'd ever seen, thus confirming an old northern seafarer's adage that the only two beings in all the world with human eyes are seals and Greenland girls.

I'm not usually inclined to betray an intimacy, but I feel obliged to say a few words about this last-named love because it was as much a cultural liaison as an amatory one:

I had gone to the tiny East Greenland village of Igateq to meet an old man named Salluq, reputedly the last impenitent heathen (others had converted to Christianity by the late 1920s) in the country. Unfortunately Salluq was sailing from Igateq to

Angmagssalik with a cargo of sealskins just as I was sailing from Angmagssalik to Igateq. We never met. And now I found myself stuck in Igateq. The village was draped along a rocky eminence whose hard-used beauty lay wild around it like contours on a map (the perfect place, I thought, for a last heathen). I pitched my tent in the lee of this eminence and settled in for the evening. I was just making a good gut-cauterizing pot of coffee when a young woman suddenly appeared beside me. According to the explorer Knud Rasmussen, Inuit women move with the silence of the ages, and that's exactly how this woman had moved—I hadn't even heard a crunch of silt and gravel to indicate her approach. She was just there, as if by magic. Now she smiled, I smiled. She smiled again, saying: "*Kusunsuaa unsukkapiq?*" (Do you have a nice penis?) I was a little taken aback, as this wasn't the sort of question I was accustomed to in my country. Here, the woman explained, "a nice penis" meant I didn't have gonorrhea. I said my penis was fine, yet I must admit I had no idea what her mission was. Perhaps she was the village nurse carrying out some sort of medical survey.

The woman departed and an hour or so later came back with her husband, a man whose neat tapered body seemed ideally designed to fit into a kayak. He grinned and whacked me on the back, spilling half my cup of coffee. *Ela!* he exclaimed, My little wife fancies you. Glad to know it, I mumbled, still a bit confused, wondering why she fancied a fleabag camper like myself. And, he added, I would be honored if she and you had sexual intercourse tonight. At which point I nearly spilled all the rest of my coffee, too. *Tonight?* I said, buying time to think it over. He nodded pleasantly and whacked me on the back again. I peered up at his little wife, then back at him, and—being young, adventurous, and perhaps even a little naïve—agreed to take him up on his very generous offer.

And so I was introduced to the Inuit custom of wife swapping in its modern incarnation. In the old days the custom satisfied bodily desire even as it kept the wolf from the door. If a man loaned out his wife, he could expect to get meat from her lover once his own cache of meat was gone; the resulting tie was as deep as a kinship tie, and lovers who didn't share their meat often died under very mysterious circumstances. Today, however, there's no need to share one's comestibles—a person can always drop by the Royal Greenlandic Trading Post and purchase a few tins of South African pilchards or a plasticized smear of Danish ham. Yet Greenlanders remain free and easy with each other's charms, as if their mind-set had not quite caught up with the times: I was being *given* a wife with no strings attached. Whether it was because I appeared to be lonely or the woman simply liked my looks, I never found out.

We went back to their two-room shack and I spent the night with the woman Katrina's brown, wondrous eyes gazing up at me and her smooth flesh blended into mine. It was the sort of night when every part of your body has a sense of belonging to every other part as well as to the naked globes and grasses of the carnal Universe itself. But what I most remember about that night was the husband seated at a table in the next room, cheerfully cutting cards, CLACK! CLACK! CLACK! Over and over again. Next morning he thanked me for my visit and gave me a send-off in the form of a succulent haunch of seal.

I returned to my tent and didn't see either of them again. Several days later I was in an outboard heading back to Angmagssalik when the man at the throttle turned to me and inquired whether Katrina made love softly, in the Greenlandic manner, or noisily, in the manner of Europeans. I hesitated and then said: In the Greenlandic manner.

Lawrence Millman has developed a lifelong love of Greenland and is author of Last Places, a Journey in the North.

★

But Eskimo love for—or rather devotion to—each other has very little to do with sex. It is considered rather ludicrous if a man can find pleasure in only one woman; as for the woman, it is considered a great honor if she is desired by many men and can give them pleasure. For this reason, Eskimos have never understood why white people put so much significance on their so-called *wifetrading*.

More important in understanding the Eskimos' sexual ethic is their point of view that sexual desire is entirely natural and normal, something like the desire for food and sleep.

Visiting a wife behind her husband's back just isn't done. It should be clearly understood that, in each case of wife trading or wife borrowing, it is strictly an arrangement made between the men. The wives have little or nothing to say in the matter. The man who dares to visit a woman without her husband's express consent not only delivers a mortal insult to the husband, he also becomes an eyesore to his tribesmen, being guilty of a serious breach of all good rules.

But, conversely, it could also be a dangerous insult to a man to refuse to partake of his wife's embraces when he had clearly indicated that it was permitted. It was like saying that what the house had to offer was not good enough.

—Peter Freuchen, *Peter Freuchen's Book of the Eskimos*

GLENN A. LEICHMAN

★ ★ ★

Growing Up in Nepal

*A trekker finds the hardest climb
is into adulthood.*

"I'M PREGNANT," TERRY SAID. "I CAN'T BELIEVE IT. THE TEST CAME back positive."

I couldn't believe it either. We were sitting on the lawn in the garden outside the hospital in Kathmandu, surrounded by scarlet bougainvillea flowers. Bright sunlight reflected off the snow-capped peaks; it also lit up her smiling face, highlighting her tanned cheeks made thin and spare from a year and a half of traveling in Asia. She had long chestnut hair, streaked blond by the sun, which fell down onto the shoulders of her red dress. She had made the dress herself from cloth purchased at the camel fair in Rajasthan. She loved to sink her hands into the deep pockets, and to run them over the embroidered red and yellow flowers, each with a small mirror in its center. Her bare arms were firm, and she was strong and fit from all of the walking we had been doing.

I thought we were on our way up towards Tibet and I wasn't prepared for this news about an impending birth. I was so consumed by my own narrow vision that I hadn't taken her desire to get pregnant seriously. None of my friends had ever been pregnant and I had no concept of how a prospective father was supposed to act or feel.

"Are you sure? I mean, is the test conclusive, or is it just a maybe?"

"Nope. The baby is due next June. Aren't you thrilled?" Terry looked over at me. Her dark eyebrows arched up in question and her face became a mask of uncertainty. She obviously hoped I would be happy, but her expression showed that she was unsure how I would respond.

"That's great, just great." My voice cracked with emotion, like an adolescent. I wasn't certain that it was my time to have children; I wasn't even certain that there would ever be a time for me to be a parent. Like many of my generation, I was afraid of having a baby, worried that it would force me to settle down and grow up.

I was dressed in a pair of khaki shorts, a blue vest with no shirt, and a pair of Indian sandals. With long blond hair which reached down to my shoulders, a gold earring and a coral necklace, I must have appeared much younger than my 30 years. But just at that moment my carefree smile had evaporated; I felt old and heavy with worry. I looked away from her momentarily, to try to hide my feelings.

"You don't sound all that excited about this baby," she said. "I was hoping you would want to be a father."

"I just wasn't ready for this news and don't know how to react," I replied weakly. "I was really looking forward to taking you trekking."

"I don't want to go trekking," she said.

"Why not? Because you're pregnant?" I asked, still not really understanding her state of mind.

"No. It's not because I'm pregnant," she said, sighing, "but because I'm tired—tired of trekking up mountains into god-forsaken places. I want to sleep in a bed with clean sheets, with no bed bugs or dirt."

"Okay, listen," I said, trying to win her approval. "After this trek we'll get a room in Kathmandu with clean sheets and blankets. And we'll go out to dinner and eat something special, like tandoori chicken."

"No, you still don't get it," she answered, clearly frustrated. "I'm tired of traveling, of being homeless, of having no family or friends nearby. I want to settle down somewhere and raise a family. But I don't want to raise this child alone."

I could tell she was exhausted and out of sorts. I hoped her spirits would improve after we took a break. She usually bounced back from these low moments and often surprised me with her rekindled enthusiasm.

I had met Terry six years ago; I thought she was my perfect soulmate, the person who would wander the globe with me and share a lifetime of travel. We met in a small French restaurant in Kensington called The Ark. She was rolling up a cigarette and drinking a pint of beer. Dressed all in black with oversized earrings, she was the very essence of the bohemian artist that I had always longed for. I thought she was beautiful and exciting. Later, when we had already become lovers, she told me she had been attracted to my smile and graceful manner. I was a young professor of psychology. She thought I was bold and full of confidence—just the person who would take her places she had only before imagined.

But even in her worst nightmares she hadn't imagined *this*. She was pregnant in Kathmandu, one of the filthiest cities in the world, where there were streets called Pig Alley and Freak Street. She had no place to live and no job. I had not yet grasped the significance of what was happening, and she wasn't certain that I ever would.

We had never talked about family life. Neither of us had any idea how much having a baby would change our lives. I knew I should have felt ecstatic, but I didn't; I hated to hurt her by letting my ambivalence show.

"What do you think you'll be doing when you turn fifty?" Terry asked, surprising me with this sudden change of direction.

"I don't know. Why?"

"I was just wondering if you've given any thought to how you want to live the rest of your life."

"You know," I replied, "I haven't wanted to think past this trip around the world. I've always felt that if I looked after today, then tomorrow would look after itself. But whatever happens I just hope that my spirit remains alive—like that old English guy we saw in Agra. He was, what, sixty-seven years old, and there he was, riding a bicycle around India. Do you remember him?"

"Yes, I remember him well," she replied. "I also remember another man I met in Goa, before you got there. He had spent the past twenty years as a travel bum, and now at fifty, was slowly waking up to the fact that the party was over. He told me he would gladly have traded all of his travel memories for a family. I just hope that you don't end up like that."

A week after that pregnancy test we arrived on a slow bus in Pokhara, and set out to find a house to rent. Terry's nesting instinct arrived early; after her extended travels she felt overdue for a rest. We found a house, about a mile from town right next to the lake, with doorways made for people about half our size—each one was four feet high. The walls, light brown in color, were covered with a fresh coat of cow dung. The landlord explained that this was the local method, used instead of paint or plaster.

We lived upstairs, right over a *chai* (tea) shop run by a Nepali woman who looked as old as the house. Although we didn't have far to go to get our morning tea, we had to put up with the smoke from her fire which wafted right through our house whenever she was cooking.

One morning over tea I casually asked Terry, for about the hundredth time, if she was ready to go trekking.

"You know," she answered, "I just don't feel well enough to go anywhere. Maybe you should go by yourself."

"I'd hate to leave you here all alone."

"Then maybe you shouldn't go." But the look she gave me was not inviting.

Terry was finding it difficult to separate her morning sickness from her annoyance with me. She showed no interest in looking at the map of the trail up the Kali Gandaki River. I knew there was nothing she wanted to do less right now than trek up and down these steep mountains.

"If I don't leave in the next couple of days, the permit will expire," I cajoled.

"Do whatever you want," she snapped back.

I was determined to go on one last trek before I left Nepal. Attempting to reach a compromise, I decided to go out for just a week. The next morning I hurriedly departed and literally ran up and down the steps which have been cut into the Himalayan mountains by the thousands of Nepali and Tibetan people who have traversed these paths.

It made no sense at all to race through this staggering scenery; I was hurrying beneath some of the most famous snow-capped mountains in the world—such as Annapurna and Dhaulgiri—which reached up to the clouds 26,000 feet high. Tibetan travelers wandered by, bowing deeply and greeting me curiously, unused to seeing anyone in such a rush. I paid little attention to them, lost in my own unconscious desire to beat the clock. I thought I was racing against the permit expiration date; it wasn't until years later that I realized that it was growing up I was running away from.

On the second day out I walked up over 6,000 steps, out of the bright sun and into the mist of the rhododendron forest, and then ran down the other side. When I finally arrived in Tatopani I discovered much to my chagrin that I could no longer walk down-

---

> —)—
>
> By the time we reached Tatopani we were soaked and chilled to the bone. The storm was finally letting up and the thought of more water was just about more than I could handle. But something inside said, "You've got to do it." It was that inner voice that periodically tries to move me out of lethargy to an experience that's always worthwhile. In this case it was the hot spring at the river a short walk from our guest house, and when I slipped out of my drenched clothes, into swimming trunks, and into the pool, all my cares floated away. I didn't even mind that Raj was getting all of the attention from the flirtatious Nepali woman running the place. I was just happy to be warm.
>
> ◆
>
> —Larry Habegger, "Pilgrimage to Muktinath"

hill. The pounding I had forced my body to endure had caused serious damage to my knees.

I abandoned my plans to go any further. I spent the next week at a Nepali guest house eating pumpkin pie and soaking in the natural hot springs, but my knees felt no better. I had now been gone longer than Terry and I had agreed, and I was certain that she would be worried about me. Determined to get back to her, I took my red flannel pajamas and wrapped each knee tightly—and set off. Unable to bend either knee, I looked like Frankenstein lumbering along the trail.

It took three days to get back to Terry—three days filled with agonized walking. Each day lasted twelve hours—twelve hours of slow, tortuous stumping. While I was struggling to make my legs work, my mind was full of worry about my future. How could I be certain that Terry would still be waiting for me? When I left, I was so ambivalent about wanting a child that perhaps Terry had given up and gone home. I was desperate to get back to her, to tell her how much I loved her. While I had been soaking my knees I had done a lot of soul searching. I had remembered the morning we conceived this baby, in a Buddhist guest house in New Delhi. Was it possible that Buddha was offering us a gift, an unexpected opportunity for enlightenment?

Finally, as I peg-legged my way through the rice paddies near the lake, I saw Terry waiting for me in the distance. She looked so beautiful; her familiar smile was a tonic for my frazzled nerves. Tears flooded my eyes; I felt a miracle had occurred and I had been saved. She raced across the field to meet me. We stood there in the rice paddies, holding on to each other tightly, as if by our embrace we could restore the world to perfect harmony.

"I thought you might never come back," she said at last.

"Where would I go?" I asked incredulously.

"I don't know. Anywhere to get away from me. When you left I was sure that you had decided that you didn't want to be a father—or at least the father of my child."

"When I set off, I was really disappointed. I wanted to show you the snow-covered peaks, to stand beside you beneath the highest mountains in the world. I waited for you as long as I could, but I just had to go. But I never thought of not returning."

"Every night I dreamt I was wandering in the snow covered mountains, lost in the mist," she said. "I kept calling your name, but I couldn't find you. I kept waking up shaking and frightened. When you weren't there in bed next to me I got scared."

"I'm so sorry. I never meant to make you worry. When my knees gave out, it was all I could do to get back to you. I just wanted to make one last run at the high country."

We were forced to spend the next two weeks in the house with the four foot doors in Pokhara while I rehabilitated my knees. As the weather was getting colder and the season was approaching winter, more and more people were leaving the houses by the lake. On Thanksgiving, we invited our only remaining neighbors, a young couple from Paris, to share a meal with us. As a special treat, I cooked up a batch of psychedelic magic mushrooms, which only Gill and I ate. Terry was vehemently opposed to eating the mushrooms, but I shrugged her off, insisting that this was an experience I just had to share with Gill.

At first we both felt exhilarated and talked heartily, our faces quite animated, alternating between my broken French and Gill's pidgin English. Gill had a small goatee, long black hair tied in a pony-tail, and wore a large gold earring in each ear. I thought he looked like a pirate, and enjoyed hanging out with him. A jovial young man of 23, he usually roared with laughter, throwing his head back and howling like a wolf. But on this day Gill found little to laugh about for we had eaten too many mushrooms, and soon both Gill and I were pulled into our own private hallucinations, unable to converse in either French or English. Gill grabbed his girlfriend and fled for home.

I sat in silence, all alone on the verandah over the *chai* shop, leaning uncertainly on a tottering, lopsided, homemade table. My red pajama trousers were brown with dirt stains; smoke from the fire below billowed across my face. Overhead, chickens scampered along the roof, peck-peck-pecking and scratching as they ran.

Through bleary eyes I gazed out at the rice paddies in the distance and noticed that they had begun to ooze and melt, the illusion the effect of the mushrooms. Resting my head in my hands, I sat there lifelessly, pondering my plight. I was no longer the rebellious young professor of psychology struggling to break away. I had destroyed all vestiges of that former life and had now achieved a level of nomadic alienation previously unknown to me. Even Gill, the pirate, had abandoned me.

I roused myself from my reverie. I stood and left the verandah in search of Terry. Gill's sudden departure made Terry's offer of a lifetime of companionship even more striking. I found her in the kitchen, carefully placing our food in a huge biscuit tin. Rats had been eating our food at night and this was her attempt to foil them.

She looked up at my crestfallen face, the one she told me I wore when I felt beaten by the world. She said she could rarely resist

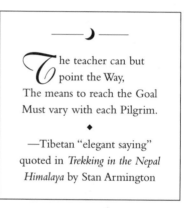

The teacher can but point the Way,
The means to reach the Goal
Must vary with each Pilgrim.

◆

—Tibetan "elegant saying" quoted in *Trekking in the Nepal Himalaya* by Stan Armington

loving me at those times, no matter how angry she was. She was a woman with deep loyalties. Once she fell it would take a lot to get her to fall out of love. I just hoped I hadn't pushed her too far

I looked at her closely. In my hallucinatory state she began to look like her mother. Her hair turned from brown to gray and deep lines appeared in her face. I began to hear her mother's voice. She was telling me that I was an irresponsible bum, not good enough for her daughter. How could I have behaved so poorly on this Thanksgiving Day, especially when her daughter was pregnant? My mouth opened reflexively, and an answer died on my lips. I closed my eyes and shook my head, trying to rid myself of these images. When I opened them Terry was there again.

"I think it's time to leave Nepal," I said. I swept my arm around in an arc, encompassing the whole of our existence, and continued.

"I need to get away from here, from this filth, from these rats, from all of this."

"Here, give me a hand with these rocks," she replied stoically. "I think if we stack them on top of the tin we can keep the rats away tonight."

The next morning I found my passport lying on the floor— chewed in half by the frustrated rats, who could not gain access to their food. We stood in the kitchen, staring at my mangled passport. Teeth marks were visible around the rough edges, and the pages were still damp with rat saliva. We both felt nauseated and sick.

"It's definitely time to leave," she said.

We quickly packed up our few possessions and left the house, stooping over as we walked through the low door for the last time. We said good-bye to the *chai* lady and walked down the dusty road and boarded the bus back to Kathmandu.

Terry sat quietly on the bus, her hands resting on her belly. Every so often she would rub her hands across her stomach; she appeared more aware of the new life she carried inside of her than the scenery passing by outside. I too saw little outside myself. I still felt exhausted and shaken. I didn't have the strength to lift my head and so I sat there, my head tilted back and my eyes closed, shrouded in silence. We didn't speak until we were over half way back to Kathmandu.

The bus had made a rest stop and everyone had gotten off to buy *chai, samosa,* and *papadam.* As we were sipping our tea, Terry asked me where I wanted to go to have the baby.

"I've been thinking that we need to go somewhere more civilized for the birth," I ventured.

She looked over at me and smiled. "I was hoping you would suggest returning to the west. I would really like to go back to London. It would be comforting to be surrounded by all our friends and by familiar places." Her face fell flat when she heard my suggestion.

"Actually, I had a different idea. I was thinking it would be exciting to go to Sapporo, on the island of Hokkaido, in the north of Japan. We can rent a small house there and get ready for the baby. I'm sure I can find a job teaching English and you could do lots of paintings. Maybe you could even sell some. What do you think?"

"Let's get back on the bus," she answered tersely. "I think the driver is ready to go. We'll talk about it later." I knew we would continue this discussion for days. In the end, I knew she would return to London to have the baby. I just hoped that I would want to go with her when the time came.

I did go with her. And years later, when we were both nearing 50, I would look back at this time of travel and sigh. I would wonder what had happened to that young, free-floating couple. Somewhere along the way I would become the responsible son-in-law her parents wanted, and she would turn into the caring daughter-in-law my aging father needed. Her career as an artist would flourish and I would make a living out of listening to people's stories. Sometimes I would even write my own. It was as if our destiny to settle had always been fixed, and no matter how hard I tried I couldn't run away from it.

One evening we went to a dinner party hosted by a couple who had just returned from traveling around the world. Later, as we were lying in bed, she asked me about it.

"I watched you during dinner tonight. You had that faraway look in your eyes again, the one that usually means you have gone out on the road to Tibet once more. Do you ever regret coming back from that last trek?"

I looked over at her. I noticed the fine lines around the corners of her eyes and the gray streaks in her hair. She was no longer the young woman I had traveled around the world with, but I still found her as beautiful as I had that first night at the Ark. Her eyes still sparkled when she looked over at me, and I could see the shy little girl expression I had always loved. It made me want to wrap my arms around her to protect her from the world.

My eyes welled up with tears. "Those memories will keep my spirit strong the rest of my life," I said, tenderly. "They will always be with me, just as I hope you will be." She reached out a hand to gently caress my cheek. I knew that she felt it in her heart long before she felt my lips touching hers.

Glenn A. Leichman lives with his wife and three children in Seattle, Washington. He and Terry recently celebrated their twenty-fifth anniversary together. This past April he took his thirteen-year-old daughter and her friend to India where they went trekking in Sikkim and Nepal. He is hard at work on a book of stories about his world adventures.

★

All of us wanderers are made like this. A good part of our wandering and homelessness is love, eroticism. The romanticism of wandering, at least half of it, is nothing else but a kind of eagerness for adventure. But the other half is another eagerness—an unconscious drive to transfigure and dissolve the erotic.

We wanderers are very cunning—we develop those feelings which are impossible to fulfill; and the love which actually should belong to a woman, we lightly scatter among small towns and mountains, lakes and valleys, children by the side of the road, beggars on the bridge, cows in the pasture, birds and butterflies. We separate love from its object, love alone is enough for us, in the same way that, in wandering, we don't look for a goal, we only look for the happiness of wandering, only the wandering.

—Hermann Hesse, *Wandering: Notes and Sketches* (1920)

* * *

Death of the Mother

*A private joining intensifies as a country's
political fabric comes apart.*

THE DRIVER KEPT HIS HAND ON THE HORN. HE DROVE LIKE A demon, careering at high speeds around cycle rickshaws, ox carts, bicycles, pedestrians, the occasional motor rickshaws, or car. His assistant kept his head poked out the passenger window. His full-time job was to holler abuse at slower traffic in warning of the approaching juggernaut. In India, a truck is power. It stops for nothing, only veers to the side if a greater vehicle, say a packed bus, is bearing down on it, even then swerving only at the last second to avoid a head-on collision. We sped through the countryside back to Patna in an hour and a half, three hours less than the journey out to Vaishali had taken. Crossing over the kilometre-wide Ganges at the Patna bridge, the driver cursed and scowled as we found ourselves wedged into a traffic jam. We stopped moving altogether. After about fifteen minutes, Sabina and I decided it would be better for us to get out and walk. A concrete stairway from the side of the bridge led us down into an industrial section of the city.

The crowd seemed menacingly frenetic after the serenity of Vaishali. Thousands of people filled the streets, rushing in different directions, as if the communal heartbeat of the city had received a syringe full of adrenaline. Rickshaw drivers, their double seats empty, ignored our attempts to flag them down. When at last we cornered one, he told us he didn't know where the Patna Tourist Guest House was. Instead, he dropped us at the train station, but not the one we knew. For the first time we realized we were on the far eastern side of town, ten or so kilometres from our hotel. Dusk was coming. By this time, people should have been returning to their homes and hovels. Instead the streets grew more and more crowded. We saw a newspaper shop swarming with Biharis shouting and struggling for a paper as if they were starving men fighting for rice. Smoke filled the air. Not the acrid curry-and-buffalo-chip scented smoke of cooking fires: it had a chemical odour, like burning paint.

Our eyes filled with dust and stung from the smoke. We were exhausted and filthy. Sabina looked drained, her face coated with dirt from the harrowing truck ride. A dozen lepers sitting in a row at the front of the station began wailing for alms when they saw us. We fled, unable to deal with the artificial urgency of their chorus. Though it would be expensive, we decided to take a motor rickshaw back to the security of our guest house, but couldn't find a single one at the station. We ended up with another pedal-rickshaw driver who told us he could drop us at a motor-rickshaw stand. His eyes were bulging, his motions jerky and erratic as he pulled away from the station.

The area we cycled through seemed desperately poor. Shacks of tin sheeting and canvas lined the roadside. The few women we saw on the streets hurried by with pots and baskets balanced on their hips. Our driver pedalled madly as if afraid to stop, then jammed on the brakes and turned the vehicle around where a crowd had blocked the road ahead. A shop was on fire. Black smoke billowed form the windows and bright red flames licked upwards into the purple sky. The driver turned his head around and yelled something to us in Hindi.

"What does he say?" I tugged at Sabina's sleeve.

"I don't know, something about Indira Gandhi."

She shook her head at him.

The driver reached into the breast pocket of his tattered shirt and brought out a piece of folded newspaper, which he handed to her. It was written in Hindi. Sabina carefully pronounced the phonetic script, squinting at it in the half-light.

"Indira Gandhi...something...I don't know. Why is he giving me this?" She smiled at him and thanked him for showing it to her, offering it back.

The driver turned again, no longer watching where he was driving. He pointed his index finger at her, thumb raised in the air, and jabbed it at her.

"Ki, Ki!" he said ferociously.

She gripped the paper again, pressed it close to her eyes.

"Mein Gott!" she whispered, the blood draining from her face. "They've killed Indira Gandhi. I can read it now. It says here, three Sikhs shot her."

The driver dropped us at an auto-rickshaw stand, where we were piled into the rear with six others heading for Gandhi Maidan near the western train station. It was dark now. The surging crowds had formed themselves into marching armies, chanting anti-Sikh slogans in unison. Again and again the driver had to turn his vehicle around in search of detours to avoid the angry mobs.

"Ah, Indira, I have lost my own mother!" the elderly man crammed next to me cried in his grief.

From the crest of a small hill, I looked back on the eastern half of the city and glimpsed three or four fires burning in the distance. The next day's papers revealed that 47 people had been killed in Bihar State, though unofficial estimates put the number above 50 in Patna alone. In Delhi, 115 had died during the night. Scooters and buses were set on fire. Shops of Sikhs had been looted and set ablaze. So easily marked by their long beards and turbans, the men were beaten, murdered, the women raped. Nine Sikhs were pulled off a train by gunmen and shot on their way to Delhi. From all across the country Sikhs abandoned their homes and struck out for the Punjab, fearing that Hindu and Sikh would never live together in peace again.

The driver seemed lost in the confusion. He turned down blind alleys and unlit back streets. One of the passengers shouted something towards the front.

"Stay on the main road. This is a bad area," Sabina translated for me.

It took another two hours to cross town to Gandhi Maidan, the wide circular park named in honour of Mahatma Gandhi. We found a rickshaw driver willing to take us the last three kilometres to the guest house. Sabina pumped the pedalling Bihari for more information on the assassination. He merely wobbled his head indifferently.

"What, your leader has been murdered, and you don't care?" she said.

"We are poor people here in Bihar," he replied. "What does it matter to us who lives and who dies at the top?"

The tourist guest house was located in the centre of a government office district. The streets were nearly deserted, in eerie contrast to the raging crowd in the east end of town. A shoot-on-sight curfew had been imposed on Patna, we later learned, and it seemed the government offices were the first places the police had moved in to protect. A mournful young man with dark circles under his eyes unlocked the front door of the guest house and told us he had no vacancies.

"But you must have a place for us," said Sabina, marching into the lobby and dropping her bag on the carpet. "Where else are we to go?"

"No room."

"Look, you can't be full," I said. "This place was almost deserted just three days ago. You have a single room?"

Shake of the head.

"Anything?"

Two waiters from the guest house restaurant came out. They had served us dinner every night of our stay and took apparent delight in our under-the-table hand-holding. I hailed them, making deliberately friendly conversation, just to prove to the front desk clerk we had indeed stayed in the guest house before. This would have made no difference had the rooms been full, but I had learned to discard logic in dealing with Indian paper shufflers.

"Well, there is a room," the clerk blurted out suddenly. "But it's got no bed sheets."

"I have a sheet in my bag. We'll take it," I said.

"And no pillowcases."

I marvelled that the man was prepared to turn us out into the insanity of the night rather give us a room with no pillowcases. Most likely, he too was terrified by the assassination. Two more tourists in the hotel would only complicate a life that had already turned frighteningly unpredictable. The clerk simply wanted us to go away. But by proving we were old customers, I had, so it seemed, obliged him to accept us as if we were family. From a cabinet behind the front desk, he suddenly produced a pair of clean linen sheets and handed them across the counter to me without a word. An hour later, pillowcases were sent up to the room.

We spent the night in shock and exhaustion, unable even to touch or hold hands, and I grieved silently that all too soon I would lose her. In the morning the streets were deathly quiet. The hotel restaurant was out of everything but rice, sugar and butter, which made a strange breakfast. We scoured the morning papers for details of the assassination. The killers were Sikh members of Mrs. Gandhi's personal guards. It was betrayal as well as murder. A twenty-four hour shoot-on-sight curfew was in force throughout Patna in an effort to control mob violence and the torching of Sikh shops and homes. Sikh families had gathered in their community temples for protection, surrounded by police patrols. The iron gates of the hotel remained locked. The desk clerks requested that we not go outside the building. Several guests of the hotel told us we would not be permitted to ride the trains even if we were able to make it to the station.

"But are the trains still running?" Sabina asked, her *memsahib* voice sharp.

"Yes, of course. But why take a chance?" advised the betel-chewing politician, still ensconced in his plush seat in the lobby. He was perhaps the sole aspect of Patna that remained unchanged. "You want to risk your life for what? To rush to New Delhi where the violence is worse? No." He turned to me. "Sir, you should not permit your wife to make such a dangerous journey!"

I nodded grimly. "But she's not an Indian wife. I can't tell her what to do."

The politician scowled. Sabina vacillated and at length decided to wait another day. She could catch a very early train and still make it to the airport in time to meet her friend. Through the afternoon we wrote letters and embraced lightly.

Rested, we were able to begin to say goodbye. We went to the roof to watch the sunset. Cooking fires smouldered in the alleyways near the hotel. The families who lived in canvas shelters on the streets had no way to abide by the curfew order, so the armed soldiers at the nearby intersection ignored them. Cows and goats still wandered freely across the main thoroughfares. The gaudy pink, orange and purple Day-Glo paint sprayed across their bony flanks seemed incongruously festive. The blaze of the setting sun appeared equally indifferent to the nation's loss. The god continued to bestow its blessings just as the Vaishali's villagers had beseeched of it only forth-eight hours previously. The pink ellipse widened as it sank through the haze of cooking fires. We followed its stately decline until it hid behind a huge government complex in the next block. A moment later Venus emerged, a single white light in the fading sky.

"Let's lie naked together," said Sabina, touching my arm.

Back in our room, curled together like spoons, only half-undressed, we rocked slightly on our bed until I gently climaxed. Then we stripped away the rest of our clothes. She kissed me and pulled me down on top of her. The strange energy began rising within me once again. Now aware of its course, I began at once to breathe deeply, moving with its flow and giving myself over to it.

"Christ, let it break me now," I prayed silently.

Yet the image that arose was that of the great stone lingam thrusting up out of the earth, and then of Shiva dancing on burning corpses. It was Shiva I yielded to, and I felt the god's blessing blow through me like wind rattling through a half-open window. It tore like a whirlwind. I struggled to keep my breath slow, afraid that if all control was lost, I'd be destroyed. Arms, legs, hands and feet filled with electric fire. My head burned with it. I hyperventilated, then passed through into a calm and tingling awareness, an eye in the centre of the storm. Dimly I sensed Sabina next to me, breathing with the same rapid rhythm. She held my limp penis tightly between her legs. The energy had not yet reached it, but was moving. Her arms caressed my back, stroking me as if to guide the power downward past my belly to my loins. She groaned. Spasms shook her hips. She grabbed the hair of my head and pulled my face hard against her cheek. I quickened, then fought for control of the rhythm.

Sweat drenched us both. How long had it been? An hour? Two? I had no way to measure. Sabina climaxed a second time and sent a jolt through me that triggered my own orgasm. I came without ejaculating, my penis barely stiff. Instead a current shot inside through my body, shaking it violently. My legs arched high behind my back like a scorpion. I reared and became the motion, the rhythm itself. Still the power burned and gathered within, the charge building like lightning, ready to crack me open as it shot inside her. Slowly it forged itself while we rocked faster and faster. Energy throbbed between my thighs. I could feel myself stretching, growing hard against Sabina's skin. My shaft felt like a mould being filled with incandescent metal. Consciousness flickered briefly, rose like a whale surfacing for air before a dive to the black ocean floor. I released a silent prayer.

"O God, split me open, destroy me. This very act, now, I give to you."

From the midst of the heat and fire and pounding of blood came a familiar cool voice inside my head that said, "Then stop."

"What are you saying?"

"Stop."

Shiva, Christ, Buddha, Mara, my own delusion, I didn't know the source of the voice, but I felt afraid of it, for a second hated it and what it was saying. I tried to lose myself again in the fire. But the voice held me.

"Stop."

It drew me back to full consciousness, gave me clear-headed choice. Slowly I eased back on the rhythm, let the current gradually dissolve between us. Some twenty minutes later I lifted my head shakily from her shoulder and looked into the blue of her eyes.

"Can you read my mind?" I asked.

"I don't know."

"But do you know what happened?"

"I think I feel something is changing…Tell me."

"I hope you feel it. Because I think if we continue this to where it could go, to whatever sex is at the end of this, it will bond us deeply. Too deeply for what either of us want or need right now. It would have dissolved us. So…"

"I'm afraid."

"Don't. There's no reason. Oh, Sabina, it's good to be alive with you."

"I had two orgasms. Without contact, without touching, with you limp between my legs. How is it possible?"

"I had an orgasm without an ejaculation or an erection. How is that possible?"

"I felt my breasts fill with milk—no, how could it be?"

"I know. I feel you would have gotten pregnant no matter how many pills you'd taken, if we had continued to the end."

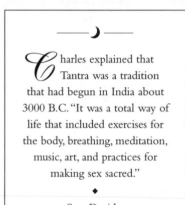

*C*harles explained that Tantra was a tradition that had begun in India about 3000 B.C. "It was a total way of life that included exercises for the body, breathing, meditation, music, art, and practices for making sex sacred."

◆

—Sara Davidson,
"The Politically Incorrect Orgasm," *Mirabella*

I rolled on my side as if to get up, then looked down on her wet, open body. Quickly I rolled back and embraced her again.

"I know," she said, holding me. "It seems so empty."

I cried a bit. She stroked my hair.

At four in the morning we rose. Sabina packed and I carried her bag downstairs. We walked undisturbed through the cool night to the train station. The sleeping bodies of passengers and station beggars covered the floor of the dark waiting room. Their white clothing gave off a ghostly glow. They lay motionless, as if victims of some deadly sleeping gas. The train was two hours late. Standing in the midst of the bodies, like archeologists in a giant communal tomb, Sabina and I went through the painful banalities of exchanging addresses, in case our rendezvous in Bodhgaya did not work out. I laughed feebly at the thought that I should have no expectations for the future. My heart was dead set on meeting her again. The train came. I boarded with her.

"Take good care of you in Nepal," she said like an elder sister.

"Nepal's a lot less dangerous than New Delhi these days. I'll be glad to get out of India. Crazy days ahead."

She nodded. A whistle blew. The train lurched. I leaned forward to kiss her goodbye. Mindful of the two dark-skinned men eyeing us across the compartment, Sabina offered me her cheek.

Tim Ward is a Canadian journalist who spent six years in the Orient. He is the author of What the Buddha Never Taught, The Great Dragon's Fleas, *and* Arousing the Goddess, *from which this story was excerpted. He lives in Maryland.*

*

The Kama-sutra is probably the most famous poem ever written on the finer points of lovemaking, and the erotic temple sculptures at Khajuraho still startle Westerners. The Indian gods copulate blissfully across the pages of the great epics, and every schoolchild knows the love story of the god Krishna and the beautiful milkmaid Radha. She was no worshiping doormat but rather a proud, passionate woman who cried out to Krishna that "my beautiful loins are a deep cavern to take the thrusts of love." Those words were written in the twelfth century, in an erotic, lyrical love poem called the Gitagovinda that is still performed and sung throughout India.

—Elisabeth Bumiller, *May You Be the Mother of a Hundred Sons: A Journey Among the Women of India*

✦ ✦ ✦

The Love Boat

Integrity takes no vacation.

As a researcher who has spent the last twenty years communicating with animals through music, I've gotten used to fielding all sorts of queries from people who want to know exactly what it is that I do. And so I am not surprised when, the day before I'm scheduled to leave for my latest and most intriguing oceanic expedition, I am approached by my friend Kirk, who runs the local music store. As I pick out some guitar strings, Kirk wants to know where I'm headed. "The Canary Islands," I tell him. "We'll be working with pilot whales. Maybe sperm whales if we get lucky."

"What's going on?" he wants to know. "Who's the sponsor?"

As much as I'd like to, I realize I can't duck the questions. "I'll be working with a German alternative community called ZEGG," I explain. "They just built this big boat to do dolphin research, and they invited me aboard for two weeks to show them how I do it. Maybe you've heard of them. They promote free love."

"Spermatozoa whales, huh?" says Kirk, grinning like the Cheshire cat as he hands me the bag of strings. "Sounds like sex, dolphins, and rock 'n' roll." He raises an eyebrow and starts searching my face. "Hey, what does your wife think about your spending two weeks aboard this love boat?"

I'm not sure I like where this conversation is headed, so I grab the strings, bid him *adios,* and head out the door.

Later that evening as I'm preparing to restring my guitar, I feel a strange object bulging through the paper bag. Inside, I spot a gift from Kirk that verifies my growing suspicion that—no matter how much I try to downplay it—this issue of free love is simply not going to go away. Kirk knows I'm a happily married guy. Yet there, among the strings, he has placed a condom.

One week later, on board the *Kairos.* It's eighty degrees today, not a cloud in the afternoon sky. The 14,000 ft. volcano of Teide looms heavy on the northeastern horizon, twenty miles away on the island of Tenerife. Twenty-four people are sitting in a circle on the ship's aft deck, all Germans but for one Swiss, one Swede, and three Americans. It is our group's first day together, and we are passing a "talking stick," each taking a turn to say why we joined this workshop in interspecies communication.

Several people describe their feelings about this morning's close encounter with pilot whales. In hindsight, attracting the whales to our music seemed almost too easy. I had simply plugged my guitar into the ship's sophisticated sound system and begun playing, while others joined in on bass, synthesizer, a drum machine, and any of several rattles and tambourines. We eventually got into a hypnotic groove on the reggae tune "No Woman, No Cry." At that point the sound engineer started transmitting the song through the boat's underwater speaker system. The pilot whales arrived within half an hour. They remained close to the boat for nearly another hour as we recorded the encounter on audio and videotape.

Now one young man at our meeting wants to know what it all means. Did the music really attract the whales? Did we communicate with them? He passes the stick to me.

"Yes, I think we did," I answer. "Did you notice that we were playing reggae? I've found that it's probably better than any other kind of music for whale communication. When you get it right, these huge holes open up in the rhythm. If you keep the groove steady, the whales sometimes understand those holes as an invitation." I hold up my hand to shield my face from the hot sun. "The reggae rhythm is very sophisticated. It doesn't permit much room for cheating. If everyone is in the groove, you simply hear it. Did you hear those few moments when the whales vocalized only in the holes? I've experienced it many times, with many different species of whales and dolphins—but I never get used to it."

The boat's research director, Johannes "Batisse" Ablinger, asks for the talking stick. "I think it's important to open a communication channel between humans and cetaceans. It teaches us something new about the communication that is going on all the time between humans." He pauses a moment to examine the feathers and the beads that dangle off the stick. Then he smiles gently at each person in turn around the circle. "I believe that studying dolphins also fits our philosophy of free love. Dolphins and whales have lived harmoniously with one another for millions of years. Human beings have a lot to learn about loving one another in community by learning to communicate with dolphins."

I was not surprised to hear such thoughts from a member of ZEGG (Zentrum für Experimentelle Gesellschafts Gestaltung, translated as the Center for Experimental Cultural Design). After all, the group operates one of the fastest growing alternative learning centers in Europe and is known for its unconventional ideas. Based out of headquarters once used to train East German secret police, ZEGG boasts some one hundred residents involved in education, alternative energy, and citizen-diplomacy projects in places as disparate as Africa and the former Soviet Union.

Though free love is not the only hat on the ZEGG hat rack, it is the best known and certainly the most scandalous hat. But what does it mean, free love? "Free love," writes ZEGG advocate Amelie Weimar, "is a way of life in which the sexual and loving attention from one person to another will not cause fear, jealousy, or violence in anyone else." Another ZEGG author, Sabine Lichtenfels, writes forcefully that "more people die each year from unresolved sexuality than die in car accidents." One bumper sticker I saw may sum it up: A FREE SOCIETY NEEDS FREE LOVE.

And free love, the group believes, requires powerful women.

Lichtenfels, among others, has argued that if civilization is ever to forge a new societal paradigm free of war, jealousy, and resources depletion the women of the world must lead the way. The concept of the holy prostitute—she who opens both her legs and her heart to heal men of their warring ways—is taken very seriously by the women who join this community. Free love, it is also believed, can mitigate the sexual jealousy that has historically led to the servitude of women.

The group has been compared to the Rajneesh community, and there are similarities, though ZEGG has no guru or paramilitary paranoia. One quality both communities share is a sure knack for bringing to fruition projects their members believe to be culturally significant—no matter how outlandish these projects might seem to outsiders. A convenient example: the *Kairos* itself. The seed money for this unique research vessel—with its onboard recording studio, underwater speaker system, and hydrophones (to receive underwater sounds) was raised in one inspired night of fundraising in 1992, and by the spring of 1993 the boat had been designed and built.

The talking stick continues clockwise around the circle. Three people in a row offer variations on the theme of having first admired whales while watching them on TV nature documentaries. Joining this workshop now offers them an opportunity to finally see whales in the flesh.

The next man changes the subject. He discusses the dissolution of a recent love affair in all its tooth-pulling agony. He shrugs his shoulders and then concludes by wishing that he might rub the lamp of our workshop circle and order up a woman to spend time with during his week on the boat. Several people nod their support, as if saluting the timeworn idea of a consciousness-raising workshop doing double time as a singles bar.

The man's wish finally gives voice to a subject that has subtly captivated the boat all morning long, although it has yet to be formally discussed. Next in line, the *Kairos* cook, donning a winsome smile, expresses great joy that there are so many new men on board with whom she can make love. She in turn hands the stick to the next woman, who nods her head first at the man and then at the woman as if seconding both of their emotions. The stick is passed again. Its current bearer is a young man who looks as if he wouldn't mind mounting the cook right then and there. He smiles, sighs theatrically, then expresses a thought I will hear many more times in the course of this voyage.

"This must be paradise."

He's got a point. Here we are, sailing in splendid weather off the northwest coast of Africa. The ocean is warm; the food is exceptional. Most of our fellow travelers are either musicians or healers, so the boat is constantly filled with the sounds of joyous music and the contented *oohs* and *aahs* of people sitting astride other people and poking their thumbs or kneading their fingers into various vertebrae and muscles. As time has passed clothing has become optional. And, of course, sex is available for anyone wishing to play.

I do not deny that the boat is a stimulating place. But paradise? I'm not so sure. I find myself feeling gratitude that public sex has been relegated to the open foredeck. I don't want to see people making love, so most of the time I find myself avoiding an entire third of the boat. I feel even more uneasy acknowledging that I'm living in a community where sex is politics. I sometimes feel like a recruit from the loyal opposition, a card-carrying member of the monogamy party.

Bald eagles mate for life. Elks and sea lions form harems. Honeybees practice polyandry. Most songbirds mate monogamously, but only on a yearly basis. Many dolphin species spend their entire lives with their mothers, only leaving their pod to go off for a day or a week to practice free love in some other mother's pod. Some observers believe that dolphins are unique among animals because they "enjoy" sex for its own sake, not merely for the evolutionary advantage it imparts. I prefer to place such assertions amidst all the other baggage that accompanies the dolphin myth. Who knows. Maybe millipedes enjoy sex the most. Think of all the possibilities.

Now, after a week aboard the *Kairos,* I realize that I am a disciple of eagles rather than dolphins. I'm a traditionalist in a postnuclear world; I thrive in a cozy nuclear family living under one roof with a loving wife and two loving daughters. But that does not mean that I want to tell other people how to live their lives. I've lived in a few communes in my time, and confusion over sex was usually the precipitating factor leading to the decay of the community. Free love, at least in theory, makes good sense if someone wants to succeed at a ZEGG-type community. But as a model for the outside world, the ideology has its limitations. Take the issue of children. ZEGG does have some innovative programs for the community's dozen or so kids, but with ten times more adults it still seems overwhelmingly a community of singles.

These are people without much stake in mastering the art of the nuclear family.

Intriguingly, as I get to know the crew better, I will hear many of them declare that they too have tried monogamy, but failed. For them, at the present moment, the ZEGG ideology offers a chance to take part in a grand experiment as well as an exercise in sexual healing. Several crew members openly express a hope that one day they, too, will find true romance in the form of a life partner.

The skipper, for instance, confesses that he does not follow the carrot of free love. Talking with him one day as he mans the helm, I mention that listening to the dolphins mew and whistle and echolocate all day long through the speakers seems to add its own special momentum to the shipboard romances, as if the sounds were underscoring the connection between ZEGG's free love and the free love attributed to dolphins. The captain starts laughing in his good-humored way, and then informs me that a series of future workshops will be devoted to "erotic cruising" and even "the love academy," where "compersion" will be studied in depth.

"Oh, yeah, sure, compersion. I forgot about that," I answer in deadpan.

He stares at me a moment, lowers his glance, and then bursts out laughing again. "It's a made-up English word meaning the opposite of jealousy."

I try to imagine such an erotic cruise, where dolphin sounds end up functioning as a kind of eco-inspirational Muzak to accompany the primary work of the travelers, which is sex. But will it end there, or will the dolphins be promoted to the role of sexual tutors whose species-specific behavior somehow validates ZEGG's experiment in "cultural design"? It's not so far-fetched a thought. I have heard a report of a German woman (unconnected to ZEGG) who is alleged to have mated with a dolphin in the Mediterranean and later described that encounter as the most spiritual experience of her life. You read it here first.

As I question the skipper further, he assures me that my concerns are unfounded. The *Kairos* was built to explore acoustic and perhaps telepathic communication with dolphins. No one wants to turn the *Kairos* into an interspecies loveboat. And no one wants to shut out valid researchers who do not agree with their philosophy of free love. But at the same time, a few of the crew tell me they do not wish to hold workshops or sponsor research that will necessitate a suspension of their sexual experiment.

Fortunately, friendship between me and the crew—men and women alike—develops by bypassing ideology. Aboard the *Kairos,* we all seem to genuinely care for one another. Free love seems to reinforce a spirit of gender democracy. Everyone is equally respected and—even more unusual—equally attractive to everyone else. And despite my own abstinence, these social benefits of the ZEGG sexual experiment fall to me even if I choose not to drink directly from its cup.

Take my relationship with the cook, for example. She is a physically beautiful woman with a huge laugh and an eccentric pair of cowboy boots she wears when going ashore. She's the one who, during our first shipboard meeting, publicly declared her desire to couple with all the new men (and before long had almost achieved that goal). But she has also become like a sister to me. We discuss our mutual admiration for one another one afternoon as I help her prepare a spaghetti dinner for everyone aboard. We seem in agreement. Even as I reap the empathetic afterglow cast by her sexual flame, she expresses an appreciation for me as a man who can be a friend without sex becoming an issue one way or another.

And a climax can take varied forms. Our friendship is consummated one morning when she confides to me a long-held dream to play the bass guitar. Yet, despite being on a boat with several professional musicians, she has not felt comfortable expressing this desire openly. Ironically, she has no problem publicly propositioning men she's hardly met, but feels uncomfortable making music with them. I go find a bass, take out my guitar, show her a simple riff, and turn on the drum machine, and we play "Light My Fire" for the better part of an hour.

On the evening of our fifth day on board, the captain eases his boat into the harbor of the little fishing village of Playa de Santiago, located on the leeward side of Gomera, one of the less populated Canary Islands. All 24 workshop members and crew disembark for an evening on the town. One at a time, we jump from the wooden gunwales onto a quay of huge, freestanding concrete blocks. But our bodies keep on rocking, our leg muscles never stop flexing in rhythm to the now vanished dance partner of the ocean swells.

Even as our pocket utopia grows strong on the boat, so it seems to dissipate a bit whenever we step off the boat. Going ashore and interacting with strangers reminds me of the last scene in *Lord of the Flies*, when adults arrive on the island and, suddenly, the larger-than-life warriors are confronted by the fact that they are actually little children. We, too, feel like graying children. For a brief flickering moment, we live happily (if not ever after)

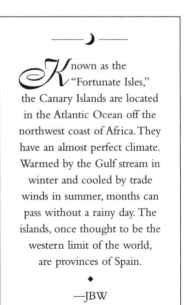

Known as the "Fortunate Isles," the Canary Islands are located in the Atlantic Ocean off the northwest coast of Africa. They have an almost perfect climate. Warmed by the Gulf stream in winter and cooled by trade winds in summer, months can pass without a rainy day. The islands, once thought to be the western limit of the world, are provinces of Spain.

◆

—JBW

within a social bubble of our own creation. It makes me wonder if people join communes—utopian or otherwise—to help each other solve a common problem of keeping the world at bay.

A few members of the group wander through the little Spanish town. Most of us decide on a more plebeian course, journeying no farther than the end of the quay, where we take over a café built inside a cave that fronts the harbor. There, we spend the next few hours sampling the hard local goat cheese, earthenware bowls full of tiny baked potatoes cooked in seawater and lavished with a picante sauce, and bottle after bottle of fruity Spanish red wine. Finally, the paella arrives, a mound of smoky saffron rice topped with seafood.

As always, the conversation starts by going off in any number of directions, but ends up resembling a ball bouncing over the lyrics to the old standard: "I can't give you anything but love, baby." This time, the conversation turns to the dangers of practicing free love. Although ZEGG preaches free sex, group members do not necessarily espouse safe sex—at least as the term is generally understood. Certainly, they do not deny that AIDS exists. But they believe that its infectiousness is overrated. In the words of the man sitting opposite me, "the contagion does not spread where it is not invited." In other words, just as my own vow of monogamy protects me from ever contracting AIDS sexually, so this man and his date both assure me that their own good karma does the same. I catch myself staring at my dinner companion wide-eyed, imagining this happy-go-lucky fellow of 175 pounds reduced to a bag of bones with hollow eyes and sores all over his back.

His companion passes me the goat cheese and asks me about my family. I answer that my wife and I share a belief that our marriage vow is sacred, a lifetime commitment to our children, to our home, and to each other. When she asks if my marriage vow must be difficult to keep in this difficult age—made more problematic by my own occasional immersion in workplaces as unconventional as the *Kairos*—I smile and answer that I don't anticipate breaking my vow.

There's more to this vow than simple attractiveness, dogged willpower, or even the fact that I believe it is my daughters' birthright to be raised by two parents. My wife and I discovered long ago that our fidelity has nurtured a kind of physical magnetism between us that grows more evident and more powerful the longer we cultivate it. It's a force that helps us maintain our emotional grounding and provides an added measure of clarity to all our other relationships. In short, we consider this bond to be a sacred energy.

To cheat on one another would be to trifle with one of the sources of our spiritual existence.

Not everyone, I soon discover, empathizes with my position. One of the women on the boat is a warrior-general in the ZEGG-sexual revolution. She is a strong and creative person with an unerring knack for facilitating our group's daily meetings. Midway through the trip, she stands up during a workshop circle and, in a coy voice, declares to the entire group that she wishes to invite me to her bed. Curiously, another woman lets out a small scream, jumps to her feet, and angrily declares that turning who-sleeps-with-whom into an issue at our daily meetings is a misuse of our meeting time. She, for one, came on board the *Kairos* to meet dolphins.

I turn pensive. I have noticed that none of the ZEGG associates publicly propositions any of the workshop patrons who are coupled up. For that reason, I suspect that this woman's invitation would never have been made if my wife had been on board. In other words, my wife's physical absence renders inconsequential the relationship she and I share. I start to answer by making light of the woman's bold invitation, joking that I'm really a monk, but then veer off that path in mid-sentence to hear myself defending the sanctity of my marriage vow. My tone reveals to this gathering of new friends that I feel that my absent wife is being violated. I stare at my hands a moment and then leave the circle.

It doesn't end there. The next morning is hot and sunny. The captain stops the boat for an hour to permit us to go swimming. The cook puts on a CD and blasts it over the on-deck speakers. It is Seal singing in that rock 'n' roll growl of his: "No, the writers cannot stop us, because the only love they find is paradise." I start to peel off my shorts when suddenly the same woman walks up behind me and pats my bottom. She informs me that the two of us need to swim together. I shake my head and tell her that, actually, I was about to…well…ah…eat lunch. I run downstairs into the kitchen, pulling my shorts up from around my knees, and grab a plate of avocados, orange slices, and dark German pumpernickel.

There's no denying it. I am starting to feel annoyed. Any gesture of friendliness or even nonchalance on my part now runs the risk of getting misinterpreted as a sexual signal. Sex is politics. By not acquiescing, I see myself reflected in her eyes as displaying all the signs of an unliberated male.

That evening after dinner, I sit in the darkness of the aft deck and share a glass of Dalwhinnie single malt and a Kretek with one of the male veterans of the group. This man's sexual behavior sometimes reminds me of a bull elk in rut. Every day I notice him cuddled up with a different woman. Yet he always looks so deeply in love, if not precisely with the lady of the moment or even with love itself. He is instead a mystic lover, enchanted by the spirit of the goddess as she is channeled through every woman. The man seems a veritable superstar in the art of the clean break. That he can change partners so regularly without either his or his squeeze-of-the moment's ever suffering the pangs of separation seems wondrous to me. Of everyone aboard the boat, this man also seems to care the least about communicating with dolphins.

We are sitting quietly, enjoying the stars, when he smiles from ear to ear in that European fullness of expression we so rarely glimpse in the United States. He begins whispering furtively, imploring me to reconsider the woman's public invitation. "You really have no idea what you're missing. Believe me, it is going to be the best experience of your life. You really have to do this."

I don't want to insult the guy. I hardly know him. I turn and stare at him with a droll smirk pasted on my lips, but I am surprised to see that his pleasant smile has vanished. He is wringing his hands. Everything about his demeanor suggests that I am being preached at by a true believer—that the very success of our workshop depends on whether or not I sleep with his "colleague." We continue sipping the whisky in silence when he remarks, "No man could ever resist once he knew what was in store for him."

I'm beginning to understand what it must feel like to be sexually harassed. From this man's perspective, my vow of marriage is a quaint, even dangerous, concept that obstructs the historical imperative of a new social utopia. In other words, my marriage poses a problem not only to my lasting happiness but to his as well. I decide against offering up some retort about harassment masquerading as salvation. Instead, I turn to him and say, "Hey man, I don't want to be in your movie. You go ahead and fuck her for the both of us."

But to linger on this single incident does a disservice to the success of our two-week instant community. I prefer to honor the members of ZEGG for their willingness to experiment with their lives and relationships in hopes of discovering new ways to transform what is too often a demented human sexual environment. That the members of ZEGG sometimes act bewildered by their choices is understandable given the unfamiliar waters they travel.

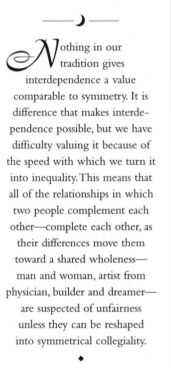

*N*othing in our tradition gives interdependence a value comparable to symmetry. It is difference that makes interdependence possible, but we have difficulty valuing it because of the speed with which we turn it into inequality. This means that all of the relationships in which two people complement each other—complete each other, as their differences move them toward a shared wholeness— man and woman, artist from physician, builder and dreamer— are suspected of unfairness unless they can be reshaped into symmetrical collegiality.

◆

—Mary Catherine Bateson, *Composing a Life*

Living with the members of ZEGG on the *Kairos* made me think long and hard about the "family values" that conservative American

politicians are so fond of promoting as the cure for our social ills.
These societal moralists seem to believe that the secret to family
happiness is a sexless lifestyle right out of *Leave It to Beaver*. What
irony. Living that way only serves to cool down the very passion
that bonds real families together. That is one reason why this rav-
ing monogamist agrees with ZEGG more often than he agrees with
Dan Quayle.

Passion is also the bond that joins the adventurers on the *Kairos*.
But it is not always expressed in sexual terms.

One of the great pleasures on the *Kairos* is listening to the community members sing formally with one another, which they do
at least once a day. Their most breathtaking achievement is a rendition of the Mozart *Requiem* sung in several parts. One afternoon
we are playing reggae when fifteen pilot whales arrive and start
floating just twenty feet off the starboard side of the boat. I put
away my guitar, ring the bell, and gather the members of our little
community into a circle. I take hold of the talking stick and speak
about the pilot whale's inexplicable behavior of stranding on
beaches. "These animals may know how to die consciously. They
seem to have turned it into a community event."

I stare intently at the talking stick and then continue speaking.
"I want to try something. The Mozart you sing so well seems one
of the best human statements ever made about death. I think we
should stand together now and sing for them; sing out our own
species's best death song to these pilot whales who seem to be
connoisseurs of such matters."

We are a relaxed group. Everyone on board is barefoot. One
man is wearing a *Kairos* t-shirt but nothing below it. One woman
is dressed in a sari, but it barely reaches her hips. Three people are
stark naked. We all stand, lean up along the starboard gunwale, and
watch the black pilot whales rolling and spouting in the waves
right there in front of us. A few of the animals must be eighteen
feet long. There are two babies swimming among them. The
whales can be heard mewing and whistling and clicking through
the loudspeakers.

The *Kairos* chorale leader waves her arm once. The still air is suddenly filled to overflowing with fifteen or more voices singing the Mozart in a clear multiparted harmony. It is achingly beautiful—ethereal, as if a shard of sunlight had suddenly shone down on the deck ready to beam the boat, its passengers, and the whales directly up to heaven. On and on the music rises and falls. The whales are barely moving now. Everyone on board feels their presence, feels their cetacean minds and their cetacean bodies listening to us in their own mysterious way even as we sing to them.

The music subsides, and then ends altogether. I am leaning against the gunwale watching the people as they watch the whales depart. No one moves. All eyes are focused intently on the surface of the water. One whale turns a moment and then raises his head as if acknowledging both our gift and our presence. He turns around and slowly swims off with the rest of them. Every human face bears the same sublime expression.

There, on the deck of the *Kairos,* at that moment, we all experience a profound sense of the sacred in nature. It is a humbling sensation. It cuts through ideology, nationality, gender, and species. And it's my strongest memory of life aboard the *Kairos.*

Writer, musician, and monogamist Jim Nollman lives with his family in Friday Harbor, Washington.

✳

It is the genes that "want" men to have sex with as many women as possible. Sex and power are the nuts and bolts of natural selection. We are designed to seek ephemeral pleasures, to believe that just one more million, the next lover, one last drink for the road, will bring everlasting bliss.... And the force which drives us into illicit pleasures and hides behind the guises of temptation is clearly identifiable now as one whose interests are served by practices which may no longer be appropriate for us. It is the devil we know. Our old ally, the selfish gene.

—Lyall Watson, *Dark Nature: A Natural History of Evil*

* * *

Hindustani Personals

*Female American tourist seeks
good-looking Indian man...*

THE MIDDLE-AGED CLERK ADJUSTED HER SARI AND GLARED AT ME over black-framed spectacles. "For your information, Ms. C. C. George," she began, "the American Express Mail Service is just what the name implies—a *mail* service, not a *dating* service."

Giggles in the background brought the speaker's head sharply around. Her two young assistants covered their mouths and regained composure.

Oh, my God. I'd completely forgotten about the ad I'd run in the *Hindustan Times* a month earlier, before my trip to Nepal.

"Not only did you receive far and beyond the normal limit of letters," continued Ms. Bifocals, motioning her assistants toward a back room, "but several men called our office asking for you. One poor fellow came here twice in person. This is completely unacceptable."

The young clerks reappeared, each lugging a rice sack of letters. I humbly apologized to the head clerk, grabbed my mail, and headed back to Sunny Guest House. The odor of tandoori chicken from a street-side cafe followed me as I dragged the sacks up a dark, narrow staircase and into the lobby.

Just as I was about to reach for my room key, up popped the receptionist from behind the counter and snatched it first. Bose must have been napping on the job, until my arrival awakened him. "What have we here?" he demanded. "More souvenirs?"

"No, no, nothing," I answered quickly. "Can I please have my key?"

"Not so fast, sweetheart," said Bose as he scrambled up onto his bar stool for a better look at my goods. Bose considered himself an eastern Don Juan, but to me he more resembled Groucho Marx with his bushy black eyebrows, thick mustache and crown of receding wild curls. "I had hoped to converse," he continued, "about your auspicious sojourn into the land of the Himalayas. So, tell me, how did thee fare?"

"It was…great. Just…great." I hungrily eyed my room key peeking out from Bose's pudgy fist. "Bose, please, I'm really tired. Give me my key," I said, stretching out an open palm.

As if on cue, two blonde women appeared at the top of the stairwell. Distracted by these apparitions of Nordic beauty, Bose dropped my key on the counter as he hit the desk bell. A servant boy appeared and awaited his orders. Meanwhile, my key and I escaped unnoticed.

Safe inside my cubicle, I dumped the letters out on the cot and began counting them. Two hundred thirty-five! Wow! I never expected such a response!

Ever since I'd arrived in India several months earlier, I'd been fascinated by the matrimonials section of the *Hindustan Times*. I'd buy the Sunday paper and open right away to pages and pages of classified ads for potential brides and grooms:

WELL *settled Jat Sikh match for pretty, slim, homely, M.A. English, employed girl, 25/160/2200, family well settled, decent marriage.*

A SUITABLE *Kayasth match for a very highly placed industrialist, having his own factory, 28/182/fair, very good physique, exact time, date and place of birth of bride be quoted in the first instance.*

Having graduated with a degree in sociology, I tried to analyze the ads from a sociological perspective. Typically, they listed qualifications such as education, religion, salary, family status, age, height, weight, and zodiac sign. Often they included skin color, dowry, caste. Connections abroad mattered: English born, American educated, Canadian passport. Men were valued for money; women for good genes.

Finally, after studying the matrimonials for some time, I decided to do some first-hand research, and possibly publish an article on the results. This is the ad I placed:

FEMALE American tourist seeks good-looking Indian man. Caste, colour, creed unimportant. Must laugh easily and enjoy life. Respond w/photo and personal statement. C.C. George, c/o American Express, Connaught Place, New Delhi.

Maybe I abused my privileges as an American Express customer, but what choice did I have? I couldn't have used Sunny Guest House for a return address because Bose would have surely opened my mail "accidentally." I'd been staying there so often that he considered me part of his personal harem, which he jealously guarded from other men.

Just in case, I locked the door, then began ripping open the letters. I couldn't believe the variety: handwritten, typed, photocopied; Hindus, Muslims, Christians, Sikhs, even Jews; a few wrote in Hindi or other Indian scripts. The oldest were my father's age; the youngest still teenagers, a decade younger than me. And the photos were great. So serious—it was hard to tell if they were homely or handsome.

What really puzzled me was that half of them were addressed to *Mr.* C. C. George. Then I remembered reading that Indian marriages are usually arranged by men. They must have thought that C. C. George was my father, uncle, or brother. I began to organize the letters into three stacks. In one pile I placed all the form letters and resumes, anything mimeographed or photo-copied:

Dear Sir -
Reference your <u>72387-CA</u> , I, the boy in question, am pleased to introduce myself as under: —

Age: —39 years. Height: —161 cms, Wheatish complexioned, hand-some, healthy, clean-shaven bachelor. An early, simple, demandless/dowery-less marriage (girl's merits is main concern) is desired.

Next to the form letters, I stacked the ones which responded to only one word in my ad—American:

I am poor, old man. In shabby position, and down trodden. All that I have to offer you is my love. I will follow you to USA and serve you all the days of my life…

Into the third group I placed the ones that were more personal. I read these first:

I am pleased to appraise you of my brief resume for your perusal. More pleased am I to note the coincidence of your jovial nature and inherent wish to enjoy the pursuits of life. I feel that your quest of a good companion may find a venue in me…

I have no liabilities as my 3 brothers all older to me and all were married to Indian girls (poor guys) (I may be lucky). My mother very sobre lady. Although she doesn't know how to read or write, but modern in her thinking.

——) ——

*I*ndia shows what she wants to show, as if her secrets are guarded by a wall of infinite height. You try to climb the wall—you fall; you fetch a ladder—it is too short; but if you are patient a brick will loosen and then another. Once through, India embraces you, but that was something I had yet to learn.

When I arrived in Delhi it was my ladder that was too short. I wanted everything immediately.

Inevitably I consulted a fortune-teller. "You are married, yes," he stated wisely.

"No," I replied.

"But you are having a companion, I think."

"Yes."

"You are most fortunate, sir. Soon you will be having another one. I am seeing many problems. But do not worry, sir," he added brightly. "They will only be getting worse."

◆

—Mark Shand,
Travels on my Elephant

It took several days to read all 235 letters and several more to respond—with the help of a xerox machine. In my group letter I explained the situation and apologized for not writing personally. Then I took the opportunity to philosophize a bit:

Whether I find a man in India or not, I definitely learned a lot about courtship. For many Indians, marriage is a business deal. Even though I stated in the ad that I don't care about color or caste, probably 75% included this information. I still haven't figured out the caste system or what a wheatish complexion is. I never mentioned my color. Americans come in black, brown, white, and all shades in between.

In the U.S., we marry for love, based on personality and compatibility. I'm sorry, but I just couldn't consider a xeroxed form application as a possible mate. I may sound egotistical, but I like to consider myself as more than a ticket to a green card.

I closed the letter by wishing each of them success in finding a wife. To a few of the most promising letters, I added personal notes.

One night I invited Lisa and Nikki, two Canadian girls, into my room and showed them the letters.

Rahim's photo showed him drinking a beer, looking very handsome and friendly. I liked the tone of his letter:

The girl I am looking for need not be beautiful in the conventional sense. Her response and her reaction in a given situation should be appealing enough to my sense of aesthetics. That is my connotation of physical attraction. To be able to relate on all the three levels, emotional, intellectual, aesthetical is so satisfying. The physical seems so dissatisfying without the fusion of the former three!! And it is so exhilarating to achieve it.

He wrote about his college days at Oxford, which explained his natural use of English. With Lisa and Nikki looking on in anticipation, I nervously dialed Rahim's number.

"Yes, this is Rahim."

"Hi, this is Chelsea George. You answered my ad in the *Hindustan Times.*"

"Chelsea! Smashing! I've been expecting your call."

I explained to him about the trip to Nepal and the 235 marriage proposals, "but you're the only one I've called."

"That's brilliant," he said brightly in a clipped British accent. "Listen, Chelsea. A friend of mine is throwing himself a birthday party tonight. Why don't we meet at my place and go together."

I covered the phone with one hand, then whispered to Lisa and Nikki. "He invited me to a party."

"Let's go!" Nikki said, while Lisa clapped her hands in excitement.

Moments later, I found myself on a dark New Delhi street with four others—Nikki had invited two guys from the guest house to join us—waving our arms madly at a passing auto rickshaw. It stopped. The five of us crammed into the back seat and putt-putted away into the night.

Rahim lived in a part of the city I'd never seen before, graced with huge mansions and foreign embassies, surrounded by fortress walls. Arriving at C 471 Lord Byron Circle, we untangled ourselves from the back seat and paid the driver the pittance he requested.

Han, the tall Dutch guy, whistled softly. "Nice place your boyfriend has," he said.

I rang the bell and before long a well-built light-skinned man threw open the wrought iron gates. Even more handsome in person, Rahim at least pretended not to be surprised by our numbers.

"Come on in, mates," he beckoned. "We can go just as soon as my friend Aloke gets here. We'll probably need two vehicles for all of us." A BMW and two Jaguars were parked inside the iron gates, so transportation didn't seem to be a problem.

"The folks are off on holiday to England," Rahim explained, "so I let the servants take the night off. Ordinarily I wouldn't answer the door myself. So which of you three damsels is the Lady Chelsea?"

I raised my hand and he kissed it gallantly, then led me up the long driveway and into his mansion. The others followed, gazing around in obvious admiration. Up until then, I'd only visited village homes, where everything's low to the ground, foot-high tables, floor pillows, wood-framed woven cots called *charpoys*. But now after months in India, Rahim's European-style furniture gave me culture shock. In fact, everything looked imported: gold-gilt chandeliers, framed landscapes with individual gallery lamps, large screen color TV with remote control and VCR, even *Elle* Magazine and Italian *Vogue*.

Rahim looked as un-Indian as his house, with snug-fit designer jeans, cowboy boots, and feathered haircut. The only other Indians I'd seen who shared his height, slightly olive skin, and hazel eyes were film stars and models. I wondered what he thought of me, with my dark brown hair tied back in a ponytail, dressed in an Indian-print, wrap-around skirt and well-worn sandals.

Aloke arrived as Han and our host were comparing notes on pro soccer. Stockier than Rahim, Aloke also appeared to be in his late twenties, and even more self-assured.

"Well, chaps," said Aloke, slapping poor Ian, the Hungarian, on the back. "Ready to hit the road? Last one out's a rotten potato." He invited Lisa and Nikki to ride with him. They looked at each other a bit uncertainly, then Lisa grabbed Han, leaving me with Rahim and Ian. Some chaperone, I thought, as Ian silently climbed into the back seat of the BMW.

The more I read, the more it became clear that the events of 1947 [Partition] were the key to understanding modern Delhi. The reports highlighted the city's central paradox: that Delhi, one of the oldest towns in the world, was inhabited by a population most of whose roots in the ancient city soil stretched back only 40 years. This explained why Delhi, the grandest of grand old aristocratic dowagers, tended to behave today like a nouveau-riche heiress: all show and vulgarity and conspicuous consumption. It was a style most unbecoming for a lady of her age and lineage; moreover it jarred with everything one knew about her sophistication and culture.

◆

—William Dalrymple, *City of Djinns: A Year in Delhi*

Rahim drove at break-neck speed through the dark and deserted streets, trying to keep up with Aloke's silver Mercedes.

The birthday boy's mansion put Rahim's to shame. Huge picture windows and bright chandeliers revealed a wrought iron staircase that spiraled up four floors. Turbaned waiters in black suits carried silver trays and seemed to float through spacious ballrooms filled with *Vogue* and *GQ* lookalikes.

It was easy to spot Nikki and Lisa in their jeans and t-shirts— the only women without spike heels and priceless jewelry. Han, in cut-offs and sandals, towered over the crowd. Even Ian in a button-down sports shirt and khaki slacks was clearly underdressed. Together we looked like poor little First Worlders begging at a feast of aristocratic Third Worlders.

Rahim made the rounds, kissing each of the women and shaking hands with the men, while I lingered in the foyer, wishing I were invisible. After what seemed an eternity, Rahim came back to retrieve me.

"Chelsea, darling. I want you to meet two of my dearest friends." He led me by the arm over to a cluster of prima donnas near the white Steinway.

"These lovely twins are Jennifer and Jessica. They're Yanks like you. Isn't that too cool? Their father works at the U.S. Embassy."

Identically stunning, they looked me up and down as I did the same to them. Their matching white silk dresses clung to their slinky adolescent bodies. Each of them had fluffed up her fine auburn hair and frozen it in place with at least a can of hair spray. We may have been from the same country, but hardly the same planet.

The twins ignored me, but ooohed and aaahed over Rahim, as only teenage international jetsetters can. Not until Aloke dragged Rahim off to another group, did the twins notice me.

"So what part of the states are you from?" Jessica or Jennifer asked me.

"Santa Cruz, California."

"How quaint," she remarked. "We're from McLean, Virginia. You know, where Bobby Kennedy's family lives."

"Tell me," said the other one. "You're from California. Which is more ritzy, Bel Air or Beverly Hills?"

"I wouldn't know," I said dryly. "It's not my neighborhood."

Tired of slumming, the twins presented me to Sita, a classmate of theirs, then glided off in the direction of two young sheiks. British-born of Indian parentage, Sita was planning to study International Politics at Harvard.

"Isn't it a crime," she said in a hushed voice, "to see such wealth while millions go hungry?" Just when I thought I'd met someone I could relate to, Sita squealed, "Oh, look, there's Debu!" and rushed over to a dashing young millionaire.

I spiraled up the stairs and found Ian and Han seated next to a buffet table, each with a heaping plate of Cornish game hens, butternut polenta, and asparagus embedded in a hollandaise sauce.

"Chelsea," said Han. "This is our new friend, Sur… umm…"

"Suresh," said Suresh, putting his arm around Han.

"And Suresh has just invited the five of us to his family's vacation home in Goa. It has twenty-five rooms and a fabulous ocean view. Isn't that smashing?"

"That's great, Han," I said. "Where are Lisa and Nikki?"

"Oh, they're dancing on the rooftop." He turned towards me, cupping his hand over my ear so Suresh wouldn't hear, "Great party. This is the *creme de la creme* of New Delhi."

Fine. Keep the cream. Just give me skim milk and my humble cot back at Sunny Guest House. I grabbed a shish kabob and slipped out to the balcony, bumping into Rahim and Aloke.

"Well, look who we have here. Cinderella herself!" said Aloke with a face-breaking smile. "I guess I'll leave you two lovebirds alone. You know what they say. Two's company, three's a crowd. Hasta la pasta!" Wink, wink.

My little lovebird put his arm around my shoulder and pulled me closer. I peered over the balcony railing in time to see a crowd gathering in the courtyard below.

"So, whaddaya think so far?" he asked.

"Interesting," I said. Downstairs we could hear a toast, followed by a chorus of "Happy Birthday."

"You're missing your party, Rahim."

"No I'm not. *You* are my party."

He turned me towards him and looked deep into my eyes, Hollywood style. "Whaddaya say, Chelsea baby? Let's split this scene and find somewhere more comfortable, just you and me."

"But I can't abandon my friends."

"Come on, now, they're big boys and girls. They can find their own way home." He tried to pull me closer, but I resisted.

He leaned forward, lips puckered. "So…are we gonna do it or not?

"Are you crazy?" I demanded. "I don't even know you."

"You're American. I know what you like."

"No you don't," I insisted, my voice increasing in volume. "You don't know anything about me.

"Okay, okay, take it easy, but it's your loss," he said, glancing down over the railing to be sure I wasn't creating a scandal. "I'll call you a cab—and don't forget to take your leeches with you."

How ironic, I thought to myself. Initially Rahim attracted me because of his light skin and western ways. I thought I'd be more comfortable with someone less foreign. But when he assumed we'd have sex on the first date, that hit too close to home. Too late, I realized that a more traditional Indian suitor probably would have treated me with more respect.

I rounded up the gang to wait out front for the cab. Eventually, a big black curvaceous Ambassador pulled up to the curb, and the driver jumped out to open the doors for us. An antique grandfather's clock struck twelve as we drove off into the night.

Carole Chelsea George will do almost anything to avoid working nine-to-five; professional racquetball, magazine writing and photography, tramping by freight train, remodeling Victorian houses, self-publishing books, teaching Adult Education, owning a juicebar…and traveling around the world for several years with her grandmother. Currently, she lives in Santa Cruz with her daughter Maya Angela and is working on a book entitled Travels with Oma.

✳

For the large majority of Indians, love and passion have never been synonymous with marriage.

In that sense, the "new" Indian arranged marriage is something of a breakthrough after all. The middle class has essentially created an odd hybrid by grafting the Western ideal of romantic love onto the traditions of Hindu society—yet another example, perhaps, of the Indian talent for assimilating the culture of a foreign invader, much as the country absorbed Persian and Moghul art, architecture and language. In the end, the result is something completely and peculiarly Indian, including the notion that it "works." It is of course possible to match up two people of common backgrounds and interests and then watch as they fall in love. What are the American personal ads and dating services, after all?

—Elisabeth Bumiller, *May You Be the Mother of a Hundred Sons: A Journey Among the Women of India*

✦ ✦ ✦

Drawn to Darkness

Choosing a wild man, the
writer finds peace.

WHEN I FIRST CAME HERE AND TEVITA FORBADE ME TO GO TO visit Malé, saying he was a very bad person and wanted me only for my money, I was suspicious, for didn't Tevita and his family also want me for my money? All of their stories about his badness whetted my curiosity. I have always had a fascination with the semioutlaw; and the things Malé had done, mainly getting drunk and fighting when he was staying in Suva, didn't seem that bad. I was also a little seduced by the possibility of helping him to change his ways, which he had told me he wanted to do.

So, much like the moth to the flame, I flew unhesitatingly to the danger. There was not much basis for the relationship except that Malé wanted to marry me, and I was intrigued by him. Malé is young, and although very skilled as a villager, has no comprehension of what I would consider a love affair or marriage. His idea of a wife—the Fijian idea—is basically another sister you can order around, yet one you can sleep with. We could hardly speak together. Yet the silence, too, was refreshing, for if we couldn't much speak, we couldn't much get into trouble with one another. So we collided like two mute planets in the night, in a quiet explosion of dark and light.

I have always been fascinated and attracted by darkness, by the soft dark night, by the shadows, by the depth of dark eyes. Dark skin seems more functional, and more attractive, to me than light skin, for it doesn't burn in the sun and get lumpy and red, but stays clean and beautiful. My early arguments with my mother, which continue to this day, have to do with my attraction to dark men. So here comes this handsome Pacific Islander who is said to want my money. And what does he have to offer? An island, the dream of beauty, and the possibility of love—and how much is that worth in an age when even a cheap car costs five thousand dollars?

Yesterday I received a letter from my mother. She is very upset. She is old, and I am going farther and farther away. She writes, "We can't understand what you are doing out there, why you have left the soft green paradise of Hawaii, your house and horse, and dog and car and boat, and thrown it all away to go live in a village." Well, Mother, I can't exactly understand it either, especially when there is nothing to eat but boiled breadfruit and when sometimes even the act of getting a drink of water is more than I can manage. I'm sure if you saw me here you would understand even less. Then why?

I once met a man—accomplished, educated, affluent—who told me that he had read in a book that if one does not follow one's dreams, one dies. No matter how long the body stays alive and well, the spirit withers, the soul departs, leaving only an empty shell, a husk lacking psychic vitality. I think it is something like that; the dream is the seed, and if you kill it, it will lie inside like a child never born, poisoning the body and the mind, a rotting clot of something that might have been graceful and beautiful. I'm not sure it matters whether the dream can ever be real, yet the way must always be open for it to materialize.

Three days before leaving Hawaii to come to Fiji for the first time, I spent a sleepless night in the anguish of a full moon. Lying alone in the familiar safe comfort of my bunk on the boat, I longed for a warm man at my side. I wanted to sleep in a grass house, to lie next to an islander under the South Pacific stars. That's what I wanted—not a new dress, or car, or a date to dance in a fancy hotel, but a grass house and the soft sound of the sea and the great dark night, and a great dark man.

The morning light filters into the *bure*, a pattern of stars woven into the coconut matting. The black-and-brown-and-white pattern of the *tapa* hanging over our bed stirs into life; the mosquito net flutters in the breeze. I wake and look at Malé sleeping beside me. Stretched out full and comfortably, his face relaxed, his long lashes covering his intense dark eyes, a bright red *sulu* glowing with huge orange hibiscus flowers thrown over his loins, he is the dream incarnate.

The morning birds are stirring, a soft calling of doves and honey-eaters. I lie next to Malé, warm with his warmth, and remember my longing.

Joana McIntyre Varawa was educated at UCLA and Berkeley. She has written three books, including Changes in Latitude, *from which this piece is excerpted. She lives with her husband Malé in Hawaii.*

*

Love thrives especially well in exotic locales. When the senses are heightened because of stress, novelty, or fear, it's much easier to become a mystic or feel ecstasy or fall in love. Danger makes one receptive to romance. Danger is an aphrodisiac. To test this, researchers asked single men to cross a suspension bridge. The bridge was safe, but frightening. Some men met women on the bridge. Other men encountered the same women— but not on the bridge—in a safer setting such as a campus or an office.

The men who met the women on the trembling bridge were much more likely to ask them out on dates.

—Diane Ackerman, *A Natural History of Love*

MALIDOMA PATRICE SOMÉ

* * *

In the Arms of the Green Lady

A West African initiation into
ancestral ways becomes a
doorway to another world.

THE NEXT DAY I WAS ORDERED TO RESUME MY GAZING EXERCISE.
The others were gone, probably getting on with their initiation. I
had not had time to speak to Nyangoli, either after waking up at
daybreak or during the more opportune time of breakfast, but just
being with him had made me feel better. My friend embodied all
that I was trying to become. To be near him was to have a frame
of reference for all my confused feelings, and that somehow com-
forted me.

As I took up my position in front of the tree, I noticed that I
was not as restless as I had been the day before. I was able to get to
work with a relatively quiet mind that took the task at hand seriously. Today I was more eager to explore the new avenue made
available to me by this opportunity. There was, however, a greater
number of curious elders watching me than the day before. Four
of the five elders had gathered to see me gaze at the yila tree, as if
someone had told them there was an unusual event occurring on
the sidelines of the initiation ceremonies. I felt the anxiety of
someone who is being monitored—stupid, as I had at school when
I sinned and was asked to wear the hated goat symbol.

I had to show these old men that I could do something. I concentrated my sight on the tree. *This*, I thought to myself, *is a gaze that has substance and meaning—the look in my eyes embodies challenge.* I was determined to overcome the opacity of the physical by my commitment to see. By now I had figured out that I was expected to see something other than the tree itself-something that still was the tree, but uninvented, unmediated, pure. I stared intensely. I was more confident than I had been yesterday, and my level of distraction was minimal. For the first time I had stopped asking myself questions. There was a goal to reach, and I did not want to continue lagging behind everybody else. So I attacked the tree with the drill of my sight.

The sun rose, and with it came the heat. It penetrated the depths of my body, cooking every cell along the way. As I locked on to the tree, the heat locked on to me. The contest was hard, for I did not want to waste another day fighting against the sun and other distractions. I was determined to do better this time. I began by deciding the sun did not exist. Only me and my tree existed in this whole universe. But my denial of the heat became more and more impossible to sustain as the sun got closer and closer to the zenith. To make things worse, some insects decided to bite me on my bare back. Instinctively, I reached back and hit myself very hard. I heard the elders laugh at me, exchange some words, then laugh again. Meanwhile, a large area on my back was getting swollen. I guessed that I had been stung by a bee.

Presently, the area needed to be scratched but I could not afford to do so for fear of being laughed at again. It was apparent that they were enjoying watching me wrestle with my ordeal. I decided I was not going to think about my back either. In the meantime, the sweat that the heat of the sun had forced out of me was dripping slowly down my body, tickling me in sensitive areas. I thought about designing a strategy to diminish thinking about sweat running down my body, but I couldn't do it. It was beyond me. Trying to ignore the sweat only made me think about it more. It also served to irritate the part of my body that had been stung. As if envious of my wandering attention, the pain rose sharply from the area of the bite and drew my hand to scratch it. The elders noticed

this and, as before, murmured to one another. I saw them shake
their heads in agreement, then look away from me.

I resolved that I would not continue to torture myself for the
sake of a tree. Since I could not openly defy the elders (that would
have meant the end of me), I would trick them. They expected
me to see something, so I would make something up. How would
they know I was lying? The understanding of traditional education
I had gained from my year in the village had taught me that one
was always introduced to the very thing that is part of one's own
world. I had also learned that the world of the self in the universe
of these elders was autonomous. Knowing meant knowing one's
own world as it truly was, not as someone else told you it should be.

Wasn't this gazing assignment just one of the many contests
designed by the elders to allow each of us to come to grips with
that esoteric universe of the self?

I called out to the elders and told them that I was seeing an antelope staring at me. It was gigantic and brownish, with a white
line on its side and another between its eyes. I said that it was looking at me as if it intended to hunt me, and I asked them. "Can a
tree become an antelope and vice versa?" While speaking, I made
sure I never looked their way because I knew they would then
detect that something was wrong. I wanted to convey the impression that I was fascinated with this apparition. In so doing, I hoped
to increase the credibility of my invention.

Their reaction, however, was the opposite of what I had expected. Though I was not looking at them, I could sense the impact of their surprise in the air around me. They all stood up as if
shocked. Then the elder who had been my supervisor the day
before asked me what else the antelope was doing. I said it was sitting on its hind legs. This time they all burst out laughing and kept
laughing for what seemed like a very long time.

"An antelope sitting on its hind legs?" my supervisor said in
between laughs. "Keep looking."

They cackled and gleefully patted one another on the back.
When they finally calmed down, one of them said, "What did I
tell you? This boy is fighting against himself. I can't believe it.

This falsehood is not his own invention. He would never have thought of this kind of thing himself. The white men have initiated him into acting this way. He has lived around them too long, and now he has become a liar too. If his *Vuur* were not stained with white, he would know that this life has no room for lies."

I felt as if I had been stabbed. I was ashamed of myself, so much so that I felt the urge to bury myself, right on the spot, to escape the presence of the elders. How did they know that I had so stupidly lost it? All I could do was to pretend I did not hear them. After they had their fill of laughter, they ignored me. Tears insidiously crawled out of my eyes and ran down my face, mixed with sweat.

I was crying because of my sense of failure. What was wrong with me that I could not do what I was being asked to? Sitting in front of this tree and failing at my first initiation task made my being different from everyone else even more painful and intolerable. For here I was—being laughed at! Here I was—caught in a lie. My feelings were a mixture of everything: aloneness, broken pride, anger, alienation, ostracism, segregation.

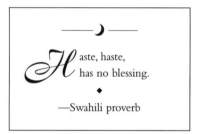

*Haste, haste,
has no blessing.*

—Swahili proverb

Through my tears, I managed to continue keeping an eye on the tree. Then I suddenly began speaking to it, as if I had finally discovered that it had a life of its own. I told it all about my discontent and my sadness and how I felt that it had abandoned me to the shame of lying and of being laughed at. I complained that my failure must have its roots in the fact that the spirit of my grandfather had defaulted from his duties toward me a long time ago. He had brought me here to be humiliated and thrown away like trash. I addressed Grandfather, accusing him of standing between me and this tree and delaying my traditional education. I told him I did not deserve this and begged him to take me away if he could not allow me to have a normal education like everybody else in the camp.

I then spoke to the tree again, not angrily, but respectfully. I told her that, after all, it was not her fault that I could not see, but mine. I simply lacked the ability. What I really needed to do was to come to terms with my own emptiness and lack of sight, because I knew *she* would always be there when I needed to use her to take a close look at my own shortcomings and inadequacies.

My words were sincere: I felt them while I said them. My pain had receded somewhat, and I found I could now focus better on the tree. It was around midafternoon, but I was not really interested in the time. I had something more important to deal with, for suddenly there was a flash in my spirit like mild lightening, and a cool breeze ran down my spine and into the ground where I had been sitting for the past one and a half days. My entire body felt cool. The sun, the forest, and the elders and I understood that I was in another reality, witnessing a miracle. All the trees around my yila were glowing like fires or breathing lights. I felt weightless, as if I were at the center of a universe where everything was looking at me as if I were naked, weak, and innocent. For a moment I experienced a deep fear that I imagined was similar to what one feels when one is told that something must have happened while I was trying to reconcile myself to the shame of being caught in a lie.

To substantiate my impression, I thought about the hardships of the day—the baking heat of the sun and my sweat falling into my eyes and burning them like pepper. I had lost all sense of chronology. I told myself that this is what the world looked like when one had first expired. I felt as if I were being quite reasonable. I could still think and respond to sensations around me, but I was no longer experiencing the biting heat of the sun or my restless mind trying to keep busy or ignoring my assignment. Where I was now was just plain real.

When I looked once more at the yila, I became aware that it was not a tree at all. How had I ever seen it as such? I do not know how this transformation occurred. Things were not happening logically, but as if this were a dream. Out of nowhere, in the place where the tree had stood, appeared a tall woman dressed in black from head to foot. She resembled a nun, although her outfit did not seem religious. Her tunic was silky and black as the night. She wore a veil over her face, but I could tell that behind this veil was an extremely beautiful and powerful entity. I could sense the intensity emanating from her, and that intensity exercised an irresistible magnetic pull. To give in to that pull was like drinking water after a day of wandering in the desert.

My body felt like it was floating, as if I were a small child being lulled by a nurturing presence that was trying to calm me by singing soothing lullabies and rocking me rhythmically. I felt as if I were floating weightless in a small body of water. My eyes locked on to the lady in the veil, and the feeling of being drawn toward her increased. For a moment I was overcome with shyness, uneasiness, and a feeling of inappropriateness, and I had to lower my eyes. When I looked again, she had lifted her veil, revealing an unearthly face. She was green, light green. Even her eyes were green, though very small and luminescent. She was smiling and her teeth were the color of violet and had light emanating from them. The greenness in her had nothing to do with the color of her skin. She was green from the inside out, as if her body were filled with green fluid. I do not know how I knew this, but this green was the expression of immeasurable love.

Never before had I felt so much love. I felt as if I had missed her all my life and was grateful to heaven for having finally released her back to me. We knew each other, but at the time I could not tell why, when, or how. I also could not tell the nature of our love. It was not romantic or filial; it was a love that surpassed any known classifications. Like two loved ones who had been apart for an unduly long period of time, we dashed toward each other and flung ourself into each other's arms.

The sensation of embracing her body blew my body into countless pieces, which became millions of conscious cells, all longing to reunite with the whole that was her. If they could not unite with her, it felt as if they could not live. Each one was adrift and in need of her to anchor itself back in place. There are no words to paint what it felt like to be in the hands of the green lady in the black veil. We exploded into each other in a cosmic contact that sent us floating adrift in the ether in countless intertwined forms. In the course of this baffling experience, I felt as if I were moving backward in time and forward in space.

While she held me in her embrace, the green lady spoke to me for a long time in the softest voice that ever was. She was so much taller than I was I felt like a small boy in her powerful arms. She placed her lips close to my left ear and she spoke so softly and tenderly to me that nothing escaped my attention. I cried abundantly the whole time, not because what she told me was sad, but because every word produced an indescribable sensation of nostalgia and longing in me.

Human beings are often unable to receive because we do not know what to ask for. We are sometimes unable to get what we need because we do not know what we want. If this was happiness that I felt then no human could sustain this amount of well-being for even a day. You would have to be dead or changed into a something capable of handling these unearthly feelings in order to live with them. The part in us that yearns for these kinds of feelings and experiences is not human. It does not know that it lives in a body that can withstand only certain amount of this kind of experience at a time. If humans were to feel this way all the time, they would probably not be able to do anything other than shed tears of happiness for the rest of their lives—which, in that case, would be very short.

Human beings never feel that they would have enough of anything. Oftentimes what we say we want is real in words only. If we ever understood the genuine desires of our hearts at any given moment, we might reconsider the things we waste our energy pining for. If we could always get what we thought we wanted, we would quickly exhaust our weak arsenal of petty desires and discover with shame that all along we had been cheating ourselves.

Love consumes its object voraciously. Consequently, we can only experience its shadows. Happiness does not last forever because we do not have the power to contain it. It has the appetite of a ferocious carnivore that has been starved for a long time—this is how much love and bliss and happiness there is in nature, in the place that was there before we existed in it.

I cannot repeat the speech of the green lady. It lives in me because it enjoys the privilege of secrecy. For me to disclose it would be to dishonor and diminish it. The power of nature exists in its silence. Human words cannot encode meaning because human language has access only to the shadow of meaning. The speech of the green lady was intended to stay alive in silence, so let it be.

I loosened my grip, lifted my wet face up to hers, and read departure in her eyes. I did not know where she was returning to, but wherever it was I did not want her to go without me. My feelings for her were so strong I felt that I would be able to brave anything to stay with her, nor did I think there was any reason we should part after having been separated for so long. Her face, however, said I could not go where she was going and that this was one of those imperatives that one had to respond to without negotiation. Things had to stay as they were. In despair I clung harder to her soft body, unable to do anything else. My eyes closed as my grip tightened, and the soft body under my hands became rough.

When I opened my eyes I realized I was desperately hugging the yila tree. It was the same as it had been before. Meanwhile, the elders had moved closer to me, obviously watching everything I had been doing. I heard one of them say, "They resist and play dumb when there are a lot of things waiting to be done, and then when it happens, they won't let go either. Children are so full of contradictions. The very experience you rejected before with lies, you are now accepting without apology."

This seemed to have been directed at me. I looked up at the elder who spoke. He met my eyes, and I felt no further need to be holding on to the tree.

"Go find something to eat, and make your bed for the night," he said gently.

It was then I noticed that the sun had set. My experience had lasted several hours, but the time had felt so short!

When I arrived back at the camping circle, the students were almost done making up their sleeping places. Nyangoli in his faithfulness was discreetly waiting for me. He looked relieved when

I appeared, so relieved that, for the first time since we had arrived at the camp, he spoke to me first. "You're still alive! *Walai.*"

"Yes—of course," I replied, feeling in the mood to chat. "The day was challenging but not too bad."

"I feel you are gradually becoming a bush person. That will help a lot in the days to come. I don't know how to tell you this, but I've been afraid for you since the first day. Now I do not think I should worry anymore. I can see in your eyes that you are getting over to the other side. You were not there when you arrived."

"What is the other side?" I inquired, feeling that I had learned nothing so far and that this might be my chance to satisfy my curiosity.

"When you arrived here, your Siè was out of you. That is dangerous for what we are doing here. You have to keep your Siè inside to make sure you can be pulled back to this side of reality after you've done your learning. Otherwise your soul will forget that it is connected with your body and abandon you. Somebody must have done something to heal you today."

"You mean a medicine person performed a ceremony to fix me from a distance?" I asked. "But who?"

I knew what it meant when the Siè is out of a person. That person is prone to unnecessary pride and passion, loses his humility, and can't tolerate feeling vulnerable. I knew too that the only way this situation could be rectified was by performing a ceremony with a black chicken. When I returned from the seminary, my father had done this once without explaining to me what he was doing. After the ritual he had told me that a foreknowledge of its function would have voided its effectiveness. I had never heard of this ceremony being done from a distance before, but obviously something in me had been strengthened and helped.

It was getting dark, and my sleeping place had not been replenished. Nyangoli helped me change the leaves, and together we joined the rest of the group for the customary fire ceremony.

Malidoma Patrice Somé was born in Upper Volta (now known as Burkina Faso), West Africa and educated at the Sorbonne and Brandeis University.

He was initiated in the ancestral traditions of his tribe and is a medicine man and diviner in the Dagara culture. He has written several books, including Ritual: Power, Healing and Community *and* Of Water and Spirit: Ritual, Magic and Initiation in the Life of an African Shaman, *from which this story was excerpted. He currently lives with his wife in Oakland, California and conducts intensive workshops around the United States.*

✳

To ritualize life, we need to learn how to invoke the spirits or things spiritual into our ceremonies. This means being able to pray out loud, alone. Invocation suggests that we accept the fact that we ourselves don't know how to make things happen the way they should. And thus we seek strength from the spirits or Spirit by recognizing and embracing our weakness. This way, before getting started with any aspect of our lives—travel, a project, a meeting—we first bring the task at hand to the attention of the gods or God, our allies in the Otherworld.

—Malidoma Patrice Somé, *Ritual: Power,*
Healing and Community

⋆ ⋆ ⋆

Little Mi

In China a bridge between two
cultures is short and steep.

"TEACHER MARK—CAN I TROUBLE YOU?"

"What can I do for you?"

"I have a relative. She is my wife's cousin. She is a doctor visiting from Harbin, attending a conference in Changsha for a few days. She speaks very good English and is very interested in learning more. Could I take her here to practice with you? It would only be once or twice, that would be more than enough."

Because of the overwhelming number of relatives and friends of students, not to mention perfect strangers, who were very interested in learning English, I had to be protective of my time. I explained this to my student and apologized for not being able to help him.

"Oh dear, this is terrible," he said, hanging his head and smiling sheepishly. "Why?" I asked. "Because...I already told her you would." I tried to let my annoyance show, but the harder I frowned, the more broadly he smiled, so at last I agreed to meet with her once. The student, much relieved, said he wanted to tell me a bit about the woman before I met her.

"Her name is Little Mi. She is very smart and strong-willed. She was always the leader of her class and was even the head of the

Communist Youth League in her school. During the Cultural Revolution she volunteered to go to the country-side. There she almost starved to death. At last she had a chance to go to medical school. She was the smartest in her class, and she excelled in English."

Little Mi sounded like a terrific bore; I cleared my throat, hoping that my student would simply arrange a time and let me be, but he continued: "Her specialty was pediatrics. She wanted to work with children. When the time came for job assignments after graduation, though, some people started a rumor that she and some of the other English-speaking students read Western literature in their spare time instead of studying medicine. They were accused of *fang yang pi!* (Imitating Westerners, literally "releasing foreign farts.") So instead of being sent to a good hospital, she was sent to a small family planning clinic outside of the city. There she mostly assists doctors with abortions. That is how she works with children. But saddest of all, she has leukemia. Truly, she had eaten bitter all her life. I know that talking with you will cheer her up; you are really doing a very kind thing. When can I bring her?"

I told him they could come to my office in the Foreign Languages Building that evening for an hour or so. He thanked me extravagantly and withdrew.

At the appointed time someone knocked. I braced myself for an hour of grammar questions and opened the door. There stood Little Mi, who could not have been much older than me, with a purple scarf wrapped around her head like a Russian peasant woman. She was petite, unsmiling and beautiful. She looked at me without blinking.

"Are you Teacher Mark?" she asked in an even, low voice.

"Yes—please come in." She walked in, sat down and said in fluent English, "My cousin's husband apologizes for not being able to come. His advisor called him in for a meeting. Do you mind that I came alone?"

"No—not at all. What can I do for you?"

"Well," she said, looking at the bookshelf next to her, "I love to read, but it is difficult to find good books in English. I wonder if you would be so kind as to lend me a book or two, which I can send back to you from Harbin as soon as I finish them." I told her to pick whatever she liked from my shelf. As she went through the books, she talked about the foreign novels she had enjoyed most; among them were *Of Mice and Men, From Here to Eternity* and *The Gulag Archipelago*. "How did you get *The Gulag Archipelago?*" I asked her. "It wasn't easy," she answered. "I hear that Americans are shocked by what they read in it. Is that true?"

"Yes, I guess so. Weren't you?"

"Not really," she answered quietly.

"You are a pretty tough girl, aren't you?"

She looked up from the magazine she had been leafing through with a surprised expression, then broke into a smile and blushed.

"Do you think I am?"

"You seem that way."

She covered her mouth with her hand and giggled nervously. "How terrible! I'm not like that at all!"

We talked for over an hour, and she picked about five books to take with her. When she got up to leave, I asked her when she would be returning to Harbin. "The day after tomorrow." Against all better judgment I asked her to come visit me again the next evening. She eyed me closely, said "Thank you—I will," then disappeared into the unlit hallway. I listened to her footsteps as she made her way down the stairs and out of the deserted building; then, from the window I watched her shadowy figure cross the athletic field in the moonlight.

She came the next night at exactly the same time. I had brought from the house a few handsome picture books of the United States and a few short story collections I thought she might enjoy. She marveled at the beautiful color photographs in the picture book, especially the ones taken in New England during the fall. "How beautiful," she said over and over. "Just like a dream." I could not openly stare at her, so I contented myself with gazing at her hand as she turned the pages of the book, listening to her voice as she talked, and occasionally glancing at her face when she asked me something.

We talked and talked, then she seemed to remember something and looked at her watch. "Oh my…" she gasped, looking suddenly worried. "What is it?" "Look what time it is!" It was after ten o'clock—nearly two hours had passed. "I've missed the last bus!" She was staying in a hospital on the other side of the river, a forty-five minute bus ride and at least a two-hour walk. It was a bitter cold night; even if she was strong enough to make it by foot, she would get back after midnight and arouse considerable suspicion. The only thing to do was to put her on the back of a bicycle and ride her. That in itself would not attract attention, since that is how most Chinese families travel around town. I had seen families of five on one bicycle many times, and young couples ride that way for want of anything else to do at night. The woman usually rides side-saddle on the rack over the rear wheel, with her arms around the man's waist, leaning her shoulder and face against his back. A Chinese woman riding that way on a bicycle powered by a Caucasian male would definitely attract attention, however. I put on my thick padded Red Army coat,

---

)

When I went for coffee in the morning, I had spotted a small bicycle shop off Jianguomenwai Avenue and people bringing bicycles in for repair and rental. Unable to communicate a single word, I pantomimed again with my hands. I held out money. The man took it and I was off.

First I rode through residential streets to test my skill before entering the throng on Jianguomenwai. Women doing their wash held up babies, who waved at me. Men squatted by the side of the road, smoking, spitting. I rode past people's houses, their gardens, their laundry. People shouted as I went the wrong way down a one-way street. I rode on like a deaf-mute until I crashed into a man with a bike loaded down with live ducks. He cursed me under his breath, the ducks squawking.

◆

—Mary Morris, *Wall to Wall: From Beijing to Berlin by Rail*

tucked my hair under a Mao cap and put on a pair of Chinese sunglasses, the kind that *liumang*, the young punks, wear. To keep my nose out of sight I wore a surgical mask, the way many Chinese do to keep dust out of their lungs. She wrapped her scarf tightly around her head and left the building first. Five minutes later I went out, rode fast through the gate of our college, and saw her walking a few blocks down the street, shrouded in a haze of dust kicked up by a coal truck. I pulled alongside her and she jumped on before I stopped.

The street was crowded, so neither of us said a word. Trucks, buses and jeeps flung themselves madly through the streets, bicycles wove around us, and pedestrians darted in front of us, cursing the "*liumang*" if we brushed too close to them. Finally I turned onto the road that ran along the river, and the crowd thinned out. It was a horrible road, with potholes everywhere that I could not see in time to avoid. She, too shy to put her arms around my waist, had been balancing herself across the rack, but when we hit an especially deep rut, I heard her yelp and felt her grab on to me. Regaining her balance, she began to loosen her grip, but I quickly steered into another pothole and told her to hold on. Very slowly, I felt her leaning her shoulder against my back. When at last her face touched my coat, I could feel her cheek through it as if my back were naked.

We reached the bridge and I started the long climb. About halfway up she told me to stop riding, that we could walk up the bridge to give me a rest. When we got to the top of the bridge, we stopped to lean against the edge and look back at the dim lights of the city. Trucks and jeeps were our only company, so we talked quietly before going on.

"Does this remind you of America?" she asked, gesturing toward the city lights with her chin.

"Yes, a little."

"Do you miss home?"

"Very much. But I'll be home very soon. And when I get home, I will miss Changsha."

"Really? But China is so...no, you tell me: what is China like? I want to hear you tell me what China is like."

"The lights are dimmer here."

"Yes," she said quietly, "and we are boring people, aren't we?" Only her eyes showed above the scarf wrapped around her face, and they stared evenly at me. I asked her if she thought she was boring. She continued to stare at me, then her eyes wrinkled with laughter.

"As a matter of fact, I am not boring. I believe I am a very interesting girl. Do you think so?"

"Yes, I think so." She had pale skin, and I could see her eyelids blush a faint pink.

"When you go back to America, will you live with your parents?"

"No."

"Why not?"

"I'm too old! They wouldn't want me to hang around the house. They would think it was strange if I didn't live on my own."

"How wonderful! I wish my parents felt that way. I will have to live with them forever."

"Forever?"

"Of course! Chinese parents love their children, but they also think that children are like furniture. They own you, and you must make them comfortable until they decide to let you go. I cannot marry, so I will have to take care of them forever. I am almost thirty years old, and I must do whatever they say. So I sit in my room and dream. In my imagination I am free, and I can do wonderful things!"

"Like what?"

She cocked her head to one side and raised one eyebrow. "Do you tell people your dreams?"

"Yes, sometimes."

She laughed and shook her head. "Well, I'm not going to tell you my dreams."

We were silent for a while, then she suddenly asked me if I was a sad man or a happy man.

"That's hard to say—sometimes I'm happy, sometimes I'm sad. Mostly, I just worry."

"Worry? What do you worry about?"

"I don't know—everything, I guess. Mostly I worry about wasting time."

"How strange! My cousin's husband says that you work very hard."

"I like to keep busy. That way I don't have time to worry."

"I can't understand that. You are such a free man—you can travel all over the world as you like, make friends everywhere, and see places that most of us can't even imagine. You are a fool not to be happy, especially when so many people depend on it."

"What do you mean?"

"My relative says that your nickname in the college is *Huoshenxian*—an immortal in human form—because you are so…different. Your lectures make everyone laugh, and you make people feel happy all the time. This is very unusual. You should always be that way; it makes sad people happy. Isn't that important?"

I agreed with her that making other people happy was important, then asked her if she was happy or sad. She raised one eyebrow again, looking not quite at me.

"I don't have as many reasons to be happy as you." She looked at her watch and shook her head. "I must get back—we have to hurry." As I turned toward the bicycle, she leaned very close to me, almost touching her face against mine, looking straight into my eyes, and said, "I have an idea."

I could feel her breath against my throat. I asked her what it was. "Let's coast down the bridge—fast! No brakes!"

I got on the bicycle. "Are you getting on?" I asked her.

"Just a minute. At the bottom I'll get off, so I'll say good-bye now."

"I should at least take you to the gate of the hospital."

"No, that wouldn't be a good idea. Someone might see me and ask who you were. At the bottom of the bridge I'll hop off, and you turn around. I won't see you again, so thank you. It was fun meeting you. You should stop worrying." She jumped on, pressed her face against my back, held me like a vise and said, "Now—go! As fast as you can!"

Mark Salzman is a summa cum laude graduate of Yale with a degree in Chinese Language and Literature. He is the author of four books, including Iron and Silk, *from which this story was excerpted. He lives with his wife and various animals in Los Angeles.*

✳

I can tell sometimes, as I look out over the classroom, that something like love is happening in there. It scares me. My students are convinced I look like a Western movie star. If I wear my shoulder-length hair up in a twist on a hot day, I can predict that at least a dozen of them will have their hair in a twist the next week. If I roll my jacket sleeves, they will roll theirs. My Oral English class has fun imitating my American slang, especially my habits of saying "Oh wow!" They have fun telling me their culture's secrets. They have fun making jokes and laughing and speaking English, hair in a twist, sleeves rolled.

Maybe that's my function. Not very consequential but perhaps necessary. "Visiting Foreign Teacher" is the official title on my visa. The students call me "*sensei*," but I'm not like other *sensei* in the Japanese scheme of things. I am exotic and I am temporary. My embittered colleague might be right. In the sum total of their existence, it doesn't matter greatly that their English has improved. At my most cynical, I think of myself as a diversion, a respite from frenetic Japanese life, the pedagogical equivalent of the *sarariiman's* whiskey.

But I don't think you can be a teacher unless you believe in the possibility of change. When I'm feeling optimistic, I like to think I give my Japanese students the same thing I try to give my American students back home: a space in which to speak and be heard.

—Cathy N. Davidson, *36 Views of Mount Fuji: On Finding Myself in Japan*

PART FOUR

IN THE SHADOWS

** *

Feast of Fatima

*The right thing is the wrong
thing in another culture.*

A LITTLE WARNING TO THE READER: THIS IS A SEA STORY. I WAS
serving on board the light cruiser *USS Oklahoma City* in the early
'70s, known as the "Gray Ghost of the Vietnam Coast." Being sea-
men, and forward deployed, we had little opportunity to meet the
nice kind of ladies you'd like to bring home to Mom. To be blunt,
the only women with whom we could find sure association were
the port women in various waterfront establishments. I'm not
making excuses, nor am I voicing regrets. We had two choices: take
vows and become maritime monks, or consort with whores. The
whores won, by a big margin.

This is a story about a certain Ghost Man and a certain whore.

We sailed to the island of Penang, down near the equator. It be-
longs to Malaysia these days, and it used to be a part of British
Imperial Malaya until about 1950. It sits at the western mouth of the
Straits of Malacca, right where the Pacific and Indian oceans meet.

It was a magical place. An Island of the Gods, where all the
world's great religions and civilizations meet and live in harmony
under the law willed to them by the Empire and the enlightened
rule of the Sultan. About a third of the people are Malays, a third
Chinese, and the remainder Tamils, Sikhs, Thais, and Europeans—

mostly Brits and Aussies. Most of the people lived in the principal community of Georgetown.

We were coming in for R&R, Rest and Rehabilitation; although we called it Rape and Riot. We came into port that day as ready to invade as to visit.

But the instant we rushed ashore, we could sense a difference and we slowed like a sea wave coming up the beach. There were no neon signs. Didn't need them either; the place was colorful enough with all of God's houses. There were none of the usual waterfront people waiting on the docks to sell us worthless junk, do our laundry, or pick our pockets. Life in Penang went on as usual. The air was slow and silky. And there were sounds, like the music of *gamalangs* and the chants of *muezzins*, but there were no harsh sounds, no grating sounds, no clanging-banging sounds. No one seemed to be in a hurry.

> Penang Island, with its urban center of Georgetown, is Malaysia's most popular tourist destination. And for good reason. Unlike most other Asian towns, which have lost their distinctive identities through modernization and urban development, Penang has stayed wonderfully nostalgic by retaining its old architecture, narrow alleyways, extravagant temples, lively street markets, authentic ethnic neighborhoods, and, perhaps most importantly, its gracious sense of disorder.
>
> ◆
>
> —Carl Parkes,
> *Southeast Asia Handbook*

I heard the "ring ring" of three little bicycle bells as pedicabs rolled up. Their drivers had fixed umbrellas over the love seats, for it was hot that day. Two of them smiled; the other was stoic. Six of us got in and had an easy rolling trip into town. My five mates were: burly, Castro-bearded Sam Robinson; curly blond Ricky Young; Al, the preacher's son; Jack "Tarkus" Wells, who was a misfit seaman although his dad was a Navy captain; and Tiny Rowan, the yeoman.

We rolled past money changers and jade dealers sitting cross-legged on the ground, their goods spread out on lengths of cloth. The walls of Indian temples, simple of design, extruded gods in sculpture, and their portals spilled them forth in deluge.

I think the essence of the magic of Penang is in the uniqueness of its air. Like a drug in its ability to dissipate tension, it's thick, it's moist, it's warm: a tactile sensation. It has a viscosity like some unknown element between air and water. You can glide slowly through it like a boat on a still pond.

As we sailed in our little three-wheeled vessels through the viscous and scented air, someone said, not altogether sarcastically, "Well, this is all very nice, but I, for one, have had a long voyage, and I'm thirsty."

"Beer." Sam growled.

"Yeah!" We affirmed. "Beer!"

"Well I, for two, have had a long voyage, and I am hornier than a three-peckered billy goat in the spring!" Ricky yelled.

"Yeah!"

"Naked skin!"

"There is nothing like a dame," we sang.

We wanted to swim through a sea of beer to a soft woman for an island. We yearned to leave behind the haze gray and steel, the bark of commands, the uniforms and guns, the great machines, and the smells of men.

Our three drivers pedaled us to several different places where we were able to sample the drink, to eye, and be eyed by, the women and unwind after a long and stormy crossing. The drivers always knew of yet another establishment where the beer was colder and the women were prettier. At one point we paid them extra to race. And they raced us to the Chung King Hotel & Bar at 398-A Chulia Street. A short hallway led into a parlor with rattan and stuffed furniture. On the right was a counter, behind which a middle-aged-looking Malay, lean and wrinkled but not gray, and kind of dour, bent over a ledger. At the far side, a door led out to an atrium or courtyard, and some narrow stairs went up to the rooms on the next floor. About a half-dozen girls looked up eagerly as we came in. A well-fed but otherwise nondescript Chinese man introduced himself as Tang, and said he was the owner. The Malay at the ledger was his "clerk," Ohsman.

Tang must have encouraged a competitive environment, because the girls rushed us. One was a Tamil in a sari, the darkest person I'd ever seen. Two were Chinese, one tall and thin, one short and not so thin.

There was one who didn't get up and rush us with the others. She was sitting on a couch wearing a long red velvet dress. She wore no makeup; it would have been superfluous, as her lips were full and well-shaped and her brows were naturally dark and framed her large eyes that seemed to reach out and touch me. She held a book on her lap. She was Malay, very dark. And red was the perfect color for her to wear.

As the other men were appreciating the ladies, laying their claims and ordering beer, I walked over to the quiet one. She watched as I approached. When I stood over her, and she was looking up at me, I thought I would say something, but all I did was look at her, hard.

"Hello," she said. And she smiled. A real smile. Not a whore smile; not a stewardess smile or a beauty queen smile, but a real smile with lots of very white teeth.

"What's your name?" I asked.

"Fatima."

She pronounced it FAHtima, not FaTIma.

"What's your full name?"

"Fatima Binti Abdulla."

"That's beautiful. My name's Richard. Sometimes my buddies call me Dick."

"Do you want to sit with me for a little?"

"Yeah, yeah, that would be nice," and I sat down with about a foot of space between us and put my arm on the back of the couch. Her hair smelled of coconut oil, and her skin gave off the faintest suggestion of burnt clove.

"What are you reading?" I asked her.

"Oh, just a book," she said, closing it and smiling self-consciously. Book didn't rhyme with "look," it rhymed with "duke." And the word started at the back of her throat and traveled the length of her tongue to arrive at her parting lips. "Just a book," she repeated, stroking its worn cover.

"Do you like reading books?" she asked, her R trilling.

"Yes, yes I do. I read novels. And poetry too. I like Kipling, maybe you've heard of him. And I read *Playboy* and all those other magazines with naked women," I grinned.

She blushed. It surprised me to see a hooker blush, but she did, her cheeks turning from mahogany to rosewood. She brought her book up to her face, just beneath the eye, like a fan, and smiled and blushed at me over its pages. A real smile! Again. The smile melted, the blush cooled, and her large eyes danced as they took me in. The book came down slowly.

"You are in the American ship?" she asked.

"Yes." The boisterous voices of the other men and women had grown infinitely smaller. A thread had spun between her and me. A thin, tenuous thread, tied one end to her and one end to me, taut. It vibrated, ever so slightly. I believe it was red, like her dress. I could have touched it, but I'm sure it would have broken if I had because it was so delicate, like spider's silk.

"We just got into port this morning," I told her. "We're only staying a few days this time, but we'll be coming back."

We talked a little about nothing and something. She asked me about my voyages and travels and if I were a war hero or something.

"We're all heroes. Just ask us," I joked. I was watching her lips purse as they formed words like book that rhymed with duke. She hadn't fondled me or anything, and yet she had touched me.

"Well, are ya? I heard someone say from the distant periphery. I looked up to see Ricky Young standing over us, repeating his question. "You gonna stay here all day making goo-goo eyes or come with us?"

"You're leaving?"

"We been here a fuckin' hour, man. Where you been?" He took Fatima's hand and shook it saying, "By the way, my name's

Ricky B. Young and people call me the Youngster. Maybe you and me will do some business later on, but right now I've got to take Dickie away."

I had to go. You don't separate from your mates when you're on the beach together. Not till the end of the day. It's the buddy system; you take care of your buddies, they take care of you. Nobody comes between you.

I didn't want Ricky or anyone else getting his hands on Fatima. So I paid for her, giving the money to Ohsman, and made arrangements to stay in her room on the upper floor that night. I paid a little extra, too, to keep her from having to work while I was gone. "I'll come back later tonight," I told her. "In the meantime, you've got the day off." She smiled that real smile, with lots of teeth and crinkles at the eyes. I left her with the scent of coconut and clove lingering in my senses.

At 11 o'clock the temperature was still near eighty degrees, and I wore a fine, light sweat as I walked the narrow street that led back to Fatima's place. The palm trees lining the street hung their fronds limply in the moist, windless air.

When I reached the Chung King, it had the only light on Chulia Street still burning. Fatima was sitting on the couch again, the only person in the room. She had changed into a white cotton sarong and was still reading *The Drifters,* slowly, using her dictionary. When she saw me, she marked her place with a ribbon, got up, and smiled. She smiled just as real as before, but this time it was a little smile. Not the broad smile of meeting, but the little kind that says, "I know you." In her flat sandals, Fatima reached my collarbone. She had a rich black profusion of hair that hung down her back and over her shoulders. Her most remarkable feature was her skin. It was dark, warm and lustrous, as though she had been burnished or rubbed with oil.

"Ohsman said you're not going to come but I told to him no. I said he's going to come. Richard will come, I'm sure. Or do you like to be Dick?"

I told her, "For you, I'm Richard," because of her luscious trill of the R.

"Got any more beer here?" I was thirsty after the hot walk. She got a bottle of Anchor out of the cooler, from the bottom, nice and cold. When she turned away to get it, I noticed that her sarong was backless, exposing a vast amount of that beautiful shining skin, the muscles and spine working beneath it.

"I'm putting it on your bill," she said as she wrote it down in the ledger on Ohsman's countertop.

"I have something else for you," she told me. "Maybe you were too busy to take your dinner tonight, so I brought you these." From a paper bag, she took out four little pleasantly brown half-moon pastries, each a little larger than an egg. "Curry puffs," she said. "Very popular in my country."

So I sat on the couch where we first met, and I took the little meal that Fatima had saved for me. For such a simple dish, the curry puffs were a remarkably sophisticated marriage of textures, flavors, and aromas: a chewy crunchy pastry smelling of good oil; shrimp, bean sprouts and chives bringing together the sea, the shore, and the earth; all knit together in an Indian spice bouquet.

"I didn't know Malayans were fond of curry," I said. "I thought it was an Indian dish."

"My country is many places."

She brought me another beer, a large one. Marking it on the ledger, she asked, "Are you ready to go?"

Her room was neat and spare. A plain wooden floor, two wooden chairs, a wood table, a dresser, and two double beds that sagged a little. The sheets were clean but had been through many launderings and were wood-ash gray. The whitewashed walls were bare except for a small hanging of some local design. The room itself was large and airy. Double windows opened out onto the courtyard, and I could smell the pungent, musky-sweet flowers outside. As I pulled up a chair, Fatima handed me a bottle opener and a single glass.

"None for you?" I asked.

"No, thank you. Do you want to relax a little?"

"Yeah, yeah, I will," and I took off my shoes and put my feet on the bed. As she took off her earrings and sandals I asked, "Where did you learn English?"

"Convent school. At home, in Malacca."

"You're Catholic?"

"No, Moslem. Mother sent me anyway."

"How long?"

"Three years. I'm going to close the light now?"

"Sure." And when she had and it was dark, very dark in that room, I could see the white sarong come off and lie across the other chair as though under its own will. Her dark shape then moved toward the bed and got in, pulling the sheet up to her waist. She was a silhouette, reclining on large pillows and outlined with perfect clarity against the wall. In the darkness of the room, I couldn't tell where her skin and hair met, but her outline looked drawn with ink and a fine pen. Her breasts pointed upward. Her belly rose and fell with her breathing. Her lips moved. I listened. No sound. Yet I could see them move.

I sipped the beer for a few moments as she lay still. Then, looking up from my glass, I saw that she was facing me, her head propped up on one hand.

"Tell me about your family, Fatima," I asked.

Fatima was tracing circles on the mattress with her palm. "I have my mother, in Malacca. Sometimes I visit her, or send her some money."

"What about the others?"

"No others. Will you come to bed to me now?" she asked as I poured. I hesitated. I was suddenly afraid. I didn't know of what. Of Fatima? How could that be? I had paid the fare, she was mine, I could do what I liked. What's to be nervous about? It was that smile that said, "I know you." I heard it in her voice. It was black in that room, but she could see me. I felt a little like I wanted to hide.

At length I brought my hand up to her face. With it, I began to trace the line of her jaw, just with my fingertips. With the back of my index finger, I felt her lips. They were full and bow-shaped. I crooked my finger. The knuckle pressed against her lips, and they parted. My curved finger slid into her mouth, her teeth scraping against it, and she bit down, almost hard. The pressure shot through my whole body. Finger and groin throbbed. Gut shivered.

I uncrooked the finger, and she let it go, sliding out wet. I crooked my middle finger and returned, into her mouth. She bit. Harder. Hard enough that I pulled, and she didn't release. I pulled harder, and her head came off the pillow, my body came off the sheet, and I pulled myself atop her as her legs parted. Her body took mine, I uncrooked my finger, and she released it. And I was one with her.

Her hands were on my shoulders, and I could feel her long nails against my skin. Her knees were bent, the soles of her feet against my legs, my face in her billow of coconut-scented hair. Then, before I began to move, the muscles of her vagina twitched, then flexed and gripped. It felt like five warm fingers, each gripping after the other. And that was a way of speaking. She didn't need to make that effort. She might have lain there, quite still, her mind in some cool, other place. It was her prerogative. But she didn't.

Again her body spoke, and almost imperceptibly her hips began to rock. It spoke again. She was saying, "Enjoy. You paid."

About the axis of our bodies, the universe slowly rolled and brought the pillow softly to my head. Fatima's body released mine and gave it back to me. My breath, for a while, came in deep, even draughts. Her fingers twined and untwined through my hair, and they said, "There. There, mariner. There. And now sleep, for that too comes with the price. It's all in our bargain. And there's a bargain for you." Though I had no sea to rock me, I didn't wake till morning.

Before leaving Fatima for the ship I gave her the price of her time for the coming day and night. "Here," I said. "Check yourself out and pay Ohsman when he comes in. I'll be back as soon as I can."

Things were slow on board, and I finished by ten o'clock. I had worn civvies the day before, but I thought that Fatima might like to see me in uniform. She had asked about my military career. So I put on my best dress whites with new ribbons. The suit itself was custom-tailored in Hong Kong and I had one of those belt buckles with the ship's logo on it.

She did like it. She grinned hugely when she saw me come into the Chung King. She took my arm and turned me around for a good look-see. She was in black jeans and the usual sandals. She wore a magenta blouse made from wrinkly cotton from India.

The day before, I had had a tour of all the bars on the island. This day she was going to show me its less-sordid side. We saw a pedicab whose driver, an old, short, wiry Malay, was lounging outside the house. Fatima negotiated the fare, in Malay, telling where she wanted him to take us. We got in, and the wizened little man began laboring down the road.

We went to a curio stall where I was looking at some odds and ends when I noticed her buying something. She took out her wallet and found two old, nicked and dull coins, one copper, one aluminum I think, and paid the seller for two iron-on patches in the shape of a Levi's hip pocket. They each bore the logo of Camel cigarettes. She was vastly pleased with them and insisted on paying for them herself; I tried to buy them for her, but she said no, thank you.

Back in her room that evening, I sat in the same chair sipping beer while Fatima was in the shower. I could hear the muffled voices of the people downstairs as they partied. She came into the room wrapped in a thin cotton towel that clung moistly to her body. At the top, her nipples protruded against it, and at the bottom it conformed closely to her mons. I could see the impression of the thin, dark hairs there. Her glossy skin shone with moisture. She hadn't wet the hair of her head, but it was disheveled and so thick, so long and wild that it looked like a lion's mane. She was so beautiful it made me ache. I knew that if I spoke just then that my voice would crack. I felt seasick, but without the nausea.

As she knelt to put away her shower kit in a lower drawer, she noticed my attention on her. She stopped what she was doing and exchanged gazes with me. Then she came over to me and stood next to the chair. With the long nail of her forefinger, she began to comb through one of my ear-length sideburns. She moved to the hair on my arm, and stroked it, tugged lightly on it, combed her nails through it.

At that moment I felt honored by Fatima, the port girl. I swear I couldn't move for fear I would disintegrate. That's when she kissed me. She put her arms around my shoulders and pressed her face against the side of mine, then kissed and inhaled through her nose sharply to take in my scent. I had read about that way of kissing in Malaya, but I had never see it. She did it again. And again.

Prostitutes don't kiss their clientele. It's just not done. It's an unwritten code of conduct. They may perform any act, natural or unnatural, but they don't kiss. One reason is that many of the clients don't want a whore to kiss them. But even more than that, kissing is reserved for affection. It's the one thing she doesn't sell. She has to have something to give, after all. Everybody has to have something to give. What good are you without it?

But maybe Fatima didn't see it that way. Her eyes were dancing at me just like that first time we met such a long day and night ago. She sat on the bed as she retucked her towel, keeping her modesty. She laid her hands on my outstretched legs, unthinkingly gripping and ungripping them. She kneaded them, all the while her eyes dancing at me, dancing. The muscles in her jaw clenched and relaxed, clenched and relaxed. Her liquid eyes came to a tense stop, locking on mine, and her hands held tightly. She was a wound-up spring. Then her face began to soften and her grip to weaken. Suddenly she exhaled a smile and let go of me. She laughed. I smiled. And we embraced. And I kissed her.

The world was exceedingly, quietly alive when I awoke. Outside the first raven squawked. A pedicab driver chimed his little bell and another answered him from farther off. A pushcart clattered its way to the open market. And Fatima, her face hidden beneath her hair, was just beginning to draw deeper, waking breaths.

As I was dressing she sat up, covering herself only partially now, and looked at me through sleep-narrowed eyes above a subtle, satisfied smile. A cat with a mouthful of canaries. I smiled. My shoes had gotten kicked under the bed, so I sat on the floor next to it to reach them and put them on. Fatima suddenly loomed over me on hands and knees and barked a sharp, triumphant animal sound. A beast of prey saying "gotcha!" She grinned, exposing all of her white canines.

It was the first time I had seen her naked in the light. Her lion's mane fell around her face and neck and shoulders and down her back. Her limbs were spread out, her hind section cocked slightly back, ready to spring. "Yes, you are a lion," I thought. "A bronze lion. Not a lioness but a lion woman. You're a griffin, you're a sphinx. You're a mythical creature."

Getting to my feet, I suddenly realized that in forty-eight hours I would be leaving. I began to miss her already. "Fatima, listen," I said, rubbing my ear as she got out of bed and wrapped the sheet around herself, togalike. "How would you like it if we go somewhere else tonight, to stay? Someplace nice, someplace very nice."

"To stay for all night? In a very good room?" She trilled.

"The best!"

"With air conditioner?"

"Yes! The best place in all Penang. What is it?"

"No, that's E & O." That was only for fine folks.

"Then it's E & O." She looked a little pensive, and I figured it was concern that she'd be seen and thrown out or otherwise embarrassed. "Don't worry," I said. "Here's what we'll do. I'll go get the room and pretend that I'm alone. I'll come tell you what number it is, and you come later, on the sly."

I pulled out my wallet and started counting out the cost of Fatima's time for the rest of my stay.

"Here, take it," and I held it out. She reached out and lightly tapped the back of my hand and withdrew. It was the old Malayan way of polite refusal.

"You go to the hotel," she spoke in a low voice. "Get the room and you can wait me. Ask to somebody to tell me its number. When the house is closed I'm going to come to you."

I looked stupidly at her and at the money, thinking only in practical terms. "But you'll have to work."

"I'm going to tell to Ohsman that I have a woman sickness."

"Ah. Yeah, sure. I should have thought of it myself," I said with a wink, dropping the money into her purse. She reached in and gave it back to me. She wrapped my hand around it, held that in her two hands and said, "I'm going to come to you."

I had a lot of things to do on board that day, so I wasn't able to get away till the afternoon. As soon as possible, Ricky Young and I went to the E & O and I got a room fronting the beach. It ran about $100 Malaysian (roughly $20 U.S. at that time). Ricky agreed to tell Fatima which one.

After dinner at the E & O, I walked along the beach to my room. The moon was rising and glittering over the sea to the west. The ocean seemed to sigh contentedly. The moist, warm equatorial breeze ran ahead of me as if to lead the way.

In temperate zones the wind always seems cold and violent. It's something that strikes you, stings your ears and fingers, and makes your nose red and runny. It's out to blow away your newspaper, deposit leaves on your lawn or dust in your eyes.

But in the tropics, the wind is a woman. A sensuous, lascivious woman who titillates your nerve endings and whispers in your ear. It is Aphrodite.

I entered my room and called room service for coffee. After it was served, I sat down to sip and to wait. Just as she said she would, a little after midnight, Fatima tapped on the sliding glass door that opened onto the beach. I slipped the door open and the breeze billowed in, carrying her coconut and clove scent. Wisps of her black hair reached up and touched my face. She looked up at me and smiled a little nervously. I kissed her lightly on the lips, and she pressed her face against my neck and smell-kissed me, in the Malayan way.

"Did anyone see you come?" I asked as she entered the room.

"No. I came around the back."

She wore a red batik sarong *kebaya*.

"You have been swimming?" she asked, pointing to the swimsuit I had changed into.

"No, but I thought you and I might go. It's such a warm night."

"But I have nothing to wear."

Raising my brows and smiling, I asked, "Have you ever heard of skinny-dipping?"

"Skin dipping?"

"No. Skinny-dipping."

"Mmmmm, no," she said cautiously. "This is something from America?"

"It's going swimming with nothing on," I grinned conspiratorially.

"Oh. Well, anyway, I don't swim."

"Well, you don't have to swim. You can just play in the water. That's why we don't call it skinny-swimming."

"You do this?" she asked, looking at me askance.

"Of course. Everybody does," I said, turning out the light.

"Women too?"

I climbed out of my suit and picked up a towel.

She looked out to the beach to see if anyone was there, then quietly slipped out of her sarong. I looked up and down the beach. Satisfied that we were still alone, I took her hand, and we walked past the palms, where the breeze whispered in the fronds, toward the gentle Indian Ocean surf. In the light of the full moon, her darkness stood out against the white, sandy beach. The luster of her skin caught the moonlight and reflected it so that she looked like a luminous shadow. We stood there for a while and felt the sensuous breeze caress our bare bodies with its humid fingers.

We waded into the dark, silky sea and played and splashed and spoke in laughing whispers. The water glistened as it ran down her face and hair in rivulets. It made a sheen on her breasts, and I tasted the salt on her nipples. The moon was so bright I could see into her eyes, and I looked into them, holding her shoulders, for a long moment. She gave a little laugh, and the breeze echoed it high up in the palms. We walked arm in arm to a place under a palm and lay down. I nuzzled my head against hers and smelled the sea in her wet hair, long, thick and black, clinging in arabesques to her brown face and shoulders. She bit my arm gently. The sand gave way like pillows beneath our bodies. Warm flesh melded. The moon peered mischievously through the palm fronds and the breeze, Aphrodite, flowed warmly over us.

When it was very late, we went back to the room to sleep a little.

The sun was up, and Fatima woke with a start. Her motion woke me and I heard her give a little cry. I opened my eyes to see her dressing hurriedly.

"What's the matter?"

"I have to go," she said tersely. Then under her breath, "Already I will get five slaps."

"Huh? What?"

"Nothing."

"No, wait a minute. You said five slaps. What do you mean five slaps?"

"Five slaps of the face," she said, looking in the mirror.

"Why are you going to get 'five slaps of the face'? And who the hell is going to give them to you?"

"Ohsman, of course," she replied, quickly brushing her hair.

"Ohsman? Tang's errand boy?"

"Ohsman is Mr. Tang's manager of the house." She seemed surprised at me.

"So why is Ohsman going to slap you?" I demanded as I got out of bed.

"Because I left the house without permission."

I stood staring at her, not wanting to comprehend.

"We're not supposed to leave without getting permission," she explained. "Especially for visiting a man. I have to go now."

She turned to the door but I caught her by the arm, pulled her back to me, and said, "Now wait a minute! Just wait a minute. You mean to tell me that he's just going to go ahead and hit you, slap you, five times?"

Seeing that I was getting upset, she tried to calm me. "Oh, don't worry. He's not going to hit me hard. If he does, then I will be ugly, and nobody will want me. He's only going to do it for the noise."

"I don't believe I'm hearing this! Listen, I don't care what that bastard's intentions are. I'm going there with you, and if he feels like slapping somebody, he can try it on me. Then we'll see what he gets for his trouble!"

"No! If you go to see Ohsman it's only going to be worse for me. Please…no…you stay here, Richard. It's our rule. I broke the rule. It's all right. I wanted to see you for a while, so I came here. I know the rule. So, all right, please, stay here."

"No! I won't. A guy that slaps women around needs to get some of it himself. Listen now, don't you worry. He's not going to touch you as long as I'm there."

"But you're not going to be there always! You're going to leave with your ship. And you don't have to worry. And maybe you don't come back." Her eyes were misty and she said, "And maybe you come back and you want another girl. Then I'm alone with Ohsman. And he tells Mr. Tang, and he will make me leave the house. Then they're going to tell everybody that I make trouble, and I won't get another job, so stay here. You have to stay!"

She picked up her bag and went out into the hot morning, down the beach, without turning back, her five-foot, red-clad frame moving slowly home to Ohsman. I stood there, naked, looking after her.

Slowly, realization sank in. "Oh my God. Oh no, no. Fatima, I'm sorry. I didn't realize. I didn't think."

At four in the afternoon, I opened the Chung King's door loudly. Ohsman was at his counter. Fatima was standing near the other girls. They all looked my way as I came in. I looked aside at Ohsman, and he glowered at me, his sour mouth puckered up like a prune. Yeah, he was pissed; we had cheated him out of a few bucks. I locked eyes with Fatima and slowly walked toward her. She stood rock still. She was wearing her white sarong, the backless one, and was ready for work. I could feel Ohsman's eyes on me as I passed him. I refused to acknowledge him, but his glare was boring a hole in my head anyway. Nearing Fatima, I looked for signs of violence against her and so far saw none. "He couldn't have hit her. He wouldn't. No way." Then it occurred to me that he could have hit her on the back of the head, or somewhere on her body.

In her left eye, the little weblike blood vessels were broken. The eye was blood-shot. I looked closely for marks on her face and there were none, but the texture of the skin on her left cheek was different. It had no luster. It was dull, about a hand's width, and it wasn't smooth. She saw that I had seen and looked at the floor.

He had hit her. The son of a bitch had hit her. My mind cried out. Anger pumped up my chest. My hands made fists without my bidding them to. Arm muscles throbbed, bicep, tricep, and forearm. Power trembled in them. I would break something in him. "I'll break his face! I'll hit him in the gut, and I'll open up his face. And if I can't do it alone, I'll get some guys, and we'll all stomp the shit out of him."

I jerked my head his way. He looked at me, his gaze unwavering. The wrinkles of his mouth shifted over to one side, and it curled itself into a tiny, scornful smile. My chest heaving, I realized that if I made a move on Ohsman, he'd just call the cops. He'd probably dealt with guys like me before. Maybe he even had a weapon. And even if I did slug him and get away with it, he would simply take it out on Fatima.

I turned back to Fatima, realizing that I was causing a scene and embarrassing her. But I was still angry, and yet unable to take action on it because it would just come back on her. I thought, "I'll give her some money," but I couldn't do that either. That pig Ohsman would just take it away from her, saying she owed it to him. "Damn!" My ears started to ring. "I'll have Sam bring her the money in an envelope," I thought. "With a note, a letter."

What the hell else could I do? Take her on board as a stowaway? Send her a monthly allowance for life? Float her a big loan or send her home to my mother? I couldn't help her. I couldn't do one stinking, infinitesimal fucking thing! It was her life, and she was stuck in it.

There was a groan or a cry in me wanting to get out, when Fatima reached out toward me and said shyly, "I want to see you again." Her long-nailed fingers reached my abdomen and traced five lines down my shirt. My insides screamed at her touch, "What the hell's the matter with you?" I thought. "Don't you have any buddy system? Don't you have any rights? Don't you have anything?"

Tears were rising up from the bottom. They would soon be at my eyes. I couldn't let that happen in front of Ohsman. Or in front of Fatima, for they were coming to her also.

I took a step back and croaked, "Well, we're leaving in the morning, you know."

"Wait," she said, and grabbed her purse and dug through it. It didn't take long, there wasn't much in it. She drew out those two Camel patches that she had fancied so much. "Here." She handed them to me, sniffling and trying to smile. "For a little remembrance," she said, rolling the R.

I swallowed and took them, forcing my hand not to shake. I took another step backward. Holding the patches in one hand, I waved a few fingers at her with the other, then turned, kind of half-saluted, and left while I had time. On the way out, I heard human sounds through the buzzing in my ears, but I don't know what they were.

I walked out onto the street. The sun was dropping, and I walked toward it. The esplanade lay in that direction; there was privacy in a large space. All the colors of Penang swirled around me: people in their batiks, gaudy pedicabs, pushcarts, dogs, ravens, jade dealers, money changers, all coming, going, doing, being—a maelstrom of people, colors, sounds, and smells. I was nearing the esplanade, and the tears were making a movie on my remembering eyes. In it was Fatima, dressed in her white sarong, the backless one, ready for work, and the next man; a bruised eye; and Ohsman.

Richard Sterling is a writer, editor, and lifelong gourmet. He is the editor of the award-winning Travelers' Tales Food: A Taste of the Road *and author of* The Fearless Diner *and* Dining with Headhunters: Jungle Feasts and Other Culinary Adventures. *He lives in Berkeley, California.*

⋆

It's for real, but not for long.

—The Shepherd of Richfield

BARBARA BAER

⋆ ⋆ ⋆

The Veil of
Kanchenjunga

Encountering the real India
brings passion and pain.

THE LITTLE TRAIN WITH WOODEN CARS AND BLUE ENGINES ON
both ends steamed up the last steep switchback, gave a final puff of
triumph and stopped. I stepped onto the platform in Darjeeling,
jewel of Himalayan hill stations. Spires above me pierced a rolling
mist. I breathed air that felt blessedly cool after the scorching
Indian plains.

I saw him before he saw me, slender, in black, as good-looking
as Indian film stars, but finer-featured, Tyrone Power or Alain
Delon, ideally dark and handsome.

I flicked the black *pullau* scarf over the shoulders of my green
Punjabi tunic. He was greeting an older Sikh gentleman stepping
off the train when he saw me. The rickshaw boy repeated, "Mrs.
Winchell's Guest House, *Memsahib*?" I nodded, looking back, finding the stranger's eyes.

The *Sahib* and *Memsahib* crowd, as well as genteel Anglo-Indian
couples in the parlor of Mrs. Winchell's Guesthouse, fell silent
when I walked in. My friend Mohan in New Delhi warned me
that Darjeeling was a getaway for the ex-Colonial British, the ones
who had stayed on. Henrietta Winchell was British Empire herself,
short, stout, fluttery as she showed me a gone-mad-in-floral room

on the second floor. Serious now, hands on her ample hips, she stated the rules, which were many, including management of various keys, towels, hours for meal times, and curfews. When she'd bustled out, I asked myself, why had I come here? Because Mohan, my scruffy, angry, hard-bitten political journalist friend, feared I wouldn't find a room. We were Press Club buddies, we drank cold beer together, talked Sixties talk. I was barely twenty-four and having the adventure of my life.

At the lunch table, the ladies wore floral frocks and had tight heads of curls. My Indian dress must have been a "gone native" alert. They pursed their lips, tucked their napkins into their belts, said Grace, and slurped up their mulligatawny soup.

Mrs. Winchell's soup and boiled meat only sharpened my appetite for kabob sizzling on spits in the lower market town. So I wandered to where cobbled lanes turned muddy, flies buzzed, animal and human smells were strong—this was my India. I would ask for my week's deposit back and find my own room. I looked up to the fairy tale spires.

"The Windemere Hotel," I heard a voice behind me. The extraordinarily handsome man from the station was only a few feet away. "The Prince of Sikkim wooed his American wife there," he said.

His eyelashes were so long, he was so good-looking. I trembled. I don't know how I remembered Queen Hope of Sikkim.

"Darjeeling's a romantic place," I said.

"Romantic? Darjeeling is a crossroads and a no-man's land. Traders and bandits come from Bhutan, Tibet, even China with their goods."

"You live here?"

"I came recently from Bombay. Previously London. I was born in a part of India that is now called Pakistan. My home is gone. I have no home."

Looking into his eyes I was hearing his heart; we were in a capsule of timelessness on a moving earth.

"I am Vikram Singh." He folded his hands together and I did the same.

"You look very well in the *shalwar-kameez*. Most western women will not wear it so naturally."

I told him about Mrs. Winchell's, the guests' disapproval.

"You must see Darjeeling with one who approves. I would be honored."

Vikram expertly guided me through the traffic of rickshaws, bicycles, animals. Darjeeling seemed to divide itself into an upper and lower town—British homes, the great hotels above, the polyglot bazaar, and small houses tumbled below as if a glacier had dropped them there. Over us all loomed Kanchenjunga, Goddess of the Snows, shrouded in clouds.

Beneath a two-story building in need of paint, a sign, Snowview Hotel, swung on a single hook.

———⟩———

*T*he *salwar kameez* is worn primarily in the northwest states of India, including the Punjab and Kashmir. The dignified ensemble is made up of long trousers, the *salwar*, and a tunic, the *kameez*. The outfit is graced by a complimentary long flowing scarf, or *dupatta*, that is draped with all the mystery and élan a woman can muster.

◆

—JBW

"I have recently taken charge here as payment of a debt," Vikram told me. "Please excuse its condition." The Sikh I'd seen at the station opened the door for us. The foyer was dark and the walls smelled of curry. Vikram spoke Hindi to several bearded men, Sikhs by their wrist bangles and turbans, who sat around a dimly lit lobby in longjohns.

"We Sikhs are economical," Vikrim said as we climbed a dark flight of stairs. "I allow cooking in their rooms. This is my room where I live."

High windows made it less dingy than the downstairs. Books on the shelves and writing materials on a desk. I knew Vikram lived for more than business. The bed was neatly made with a lace cover and white curtains at the windows swayed in and out with the breeze.

As I looked out the window, a pair of rangy Pathan horsemen passed on the street below, the tops of their stiff white turbans bobbing with their ponies' trot. I was in Darjeeling, talking to the most devastatingly attractive man who was pouring me cups of sweet milky tea and telling me his tragic life story.

Dinner time at Mrs. Winchell's came and went. Lights went on all around us, thousands of candles. For an instant the clouds parted and I saw Kanchenjunga with moonlight swirling on its peak like a veil.

I didn't realize I was cold until he said, "Let me fetch you a wrap."

The shawl he placed on my shoulders was the softest white Kashmiri wool embroidered with blue flowers. "No one else has worn it. It was given by my father to my mother many years ago, in happier times." He sighed. My heart fell miles. I knew what was happening and I didn't know what would happen. This closeness was as real as breathing, as surreal as the immensity of the white mountain outside in the night.

"I have the solution to your problem," he said, and proceeded to invite me to live in his room. "I am travelling outside more than I am here. Many goods pass through here without a government stamp."

"Do you mean you smuggle?"

He looked like a tragic fallen prince. "We lost everything in Partition. My father, my brothers, all the males murdered. I saw this before Mother dragged me to safety. I've done what I could to forget. I would like to have been a writer, a teacher…"

I told him I didn't care. A smuggler seemed glamorous to me. I repeated what Mohan said. In India, the politicians were the criminals.

I didn't return to Mrs. Winchell's that night. Vikram tucked me into his bed with a chaste kiss that made me all the more passionate for him. Some hours later, still in darkness, he woke me with a cup of tea. He had borrowed a jeep to take me to see Kanchenjunga from Tiger Hill. That dawn, she came forth like a bride from her veils, inspiring the sun to rise, a mountain like a solid white heaven above earth. We walked to the far side of Tiger Hill where a Tibetan Buddhist monastery stood with prayer flags flying and Darjeeling lay bathed in mist below. On lower slopes, waves of green interlaced with wheat terraces, postcard villages. Kanchenjunga hung like a giant negative, almost transparent, overlaying the sky. We kissed. The earth moved.

In bed, he was modest, unaware of his beauty. He preferred darkness, darkness for our bodies that were too hungry our first love-making to really do it right.

Vikram never left my side and I never wanted him to. We explored back alleys, Chinese restaurants, Tibetan beer shops where young monks drank the sour white liquor they brewed from barley. We had high tea at the Windemere, whose very name evoked Deborah Kerr and a dark hero. Vikram didn't like waiters' eyes lingering and accused a busboy of staring. I heard his remarks but they didn't warn me the way his stories of his childhood caring for his widowed mother, straight out of Kipling or Dickens, moved me to tears.

India at that time was in a state of high alert against China— there had already been a border war. The hill stations like Darjeeling were sensitive military areas. Foreigners needed permits. When my first week's permit expired, I extended it for two without questions, but the police told me I'd have to give reasons to stay longer.

Vikram assured me there would be no problem. He read me love poems in Hindi. He fussed with my short hair as if he could make it grow longer overnight. A tailor made me tunics with long sleeves and more bloomery trousers. There were daily gifts in Kashmiri boxes.

The true Sikh never cut a hair on his body, but Vikram had been clean-shaven for years. Still, he was a Sikh at heart, he said. Sikhs were a warrior caste, the fiercest men in India, and the most ardent lovers. I could attest to that. I hadn't known such a ravenous desire, almost too much attention to pleasure and to me, in my life. We were always getting into bed. My contraceptive cream was fast running out, as were the days on my extended permit.

When we published the *banns* for our engagement, he said, I could stay indefinitely.

"The *banns*?" I asked.

"We will marry, won't we?"

How could I refuse? We'd made love every day and spent the rest of the time talking about the future. We would have engagement pictures and publish our *banns*.

When the photographs arrived from the studio, I saw myself for the first time in my prospective situation. The photographic artist had even given me thicker brows and made my hair appear as if it were long and up. Standing protectively behind me, Vikram was the picture-pretty movie star I'd seen the first day, but my husband?

The day my permit expired, Kanchenjunga hid behind clouds and Vikram brought me a square blue India air letter from New Delhi on my breakfast tray.

"Who is this Mohan Ram?"

I reached eagerly for the letter. "Mohan is my friend in New Delhi."

"Any fool can see that by looking. What kind of a friend is he?"

"Good friend. May I have my letter?"

"I must know what kind of friend."

"Mohan is a journalist. We understand each other's work."

"Such an understanding should have ended." He

I'd been in Darjeeling three days and still hadn't seen Kanchenjunga, the dominating presence that I knew lay out there just beyond the clouds. Each morning I'd rise at dawn and peer out the window to a heavy fog, until one day something felt different in the air. I sat up and actually gasped. There, sprawling across the horizon, seeming to take up every inch of space, was a mountain of such power that I could scarcely breathe. Dusted pink by the rising sun, it pulled me in completely. I'd never seen anything so magnificent.

◆

—Larry Habegger,
"Searching for Sikkim"

pinched the letter between his index finger thumb, squeezing as if it were an ear. "You will not keep a second man."

"Second man?" I felt at a disadvantage being in bed. "The letter came to me."

Vikram paced to the window. "How does he know this address?" He pulled down the window sash. "You have written him, Barbara."

"I sent a card with a picture of the mountain when I was alone here…"

"You have been to bed with this Delhi pig?"

"With Mohan!" A wicked laugh came from my throat. "No I did not go to bed with Mohan. He is clever and bright but I never found him attractive."

"If you found him as you say attractive, you would have been in his bed as quickly as you were in mine, almost any stranger's bed. I have been a fool." He rolled his great dark eyes. "Mother forgive me."

I felt a wave of shame, then relief, hot shame followed by cold reality. We would reconsider the engagement, go more slowly, admit to different standards.

Vikrim ripped the air letter, scanned a line or two, then steely cool, said, "This is no friendship. He speaks of your breasts!"

Since Mohan had done a story on Allen Ginsberg along the Ganges, he'd fancied himself a beatnik poet. "He's talking about any woman's breasts," I said. "When we said good-by at the station it was so hot I wasn't wearing a bra and…"

Before I could finish my words, Vikram hit me so hard my ears roared. I backed to the farthest corner of the bed.

"You shame the memory of my mother."

"I never asked to take her place."

"How can you even think it, whore!"

He seemed about to hit me again, then walked to the window where the curtains fluttered. I was scared to move.

"I'm sorry. Please forgive me." He knelt at the bedside. "I believe you are innocent. I beg you to forgive me."

Yes, I am innocent, I thought. This time I am, but another time

I won't be. I saw the swelling on my cheek, dressed with my back to him, and pulled out my suitcase.

"Please, my darling. Pressure has been great. I was not able to leave Darjeeling and money is short."

"I'm going away for a while, Vikram. I have to think. I have work to do."

"Tell me what I must do to prove my love. I will take a room down the hall."

"My permit expires today. You said it didn't matter. I think it does."

"I wanted no trouble with the police." He pushed his hands through his beautiful dark hair. "Then I'll come to New Delhi and we'll marry there. Yes, I'll get money, lots of money. It was too great a shock to realize you knew other men but now it's clear. You are an independent woman. Indian women never learn independence."

I started for the door with my suitcase. He called the boy to take it.

"I will accompany you. It will look badly but I must not care."

"I'll go alone. I'm sorry, Vikram. It's my fault. I wasn't honest…"

His face started to flush, then he said, "No, darling, I'm to blame. You are perfect and you'll love me again. You will write to me here? You'll write soon?"

I looked up at the SNOWVIEW HOTEL sign still hanging askew.

"Yes," I said. "I will write." I did not turn back to see if he watched.

The little blue train with one engine pushing and one pulling was making its slow climb around the switchback turns when I arrived. I wished it would hurry. People crowded the platform, familiar faces among them, possibly from Mrs. Winchell's table, or others who had seen me so obviously flaunting their ways. Darjeeling was a village. In India, women who thought they could bend rules, supposed they could ignore differences, ended up with a black eye.

As the train pulled in, I looked up and saw Kanchenjunga. She watched and found me lacking. Once I'd asked Mohan about love.

Ironic and cynical about all else, he said that Indian men were the last great romantics. I vowed Vikram would be my only romance with an Indian.

The engine that had been the caboose began to pull the little blue train in the other direction, down the mountain, back towards the plains.

In the mid-1960's, Barbara Baer, fresh with an M.A. in English from Stanford, taught literature to young ladies in south India, wrote articles, studied classical dance, traveled and got in the way of adventures, romances, and scrapes. Her writing has appeared in anthologies and periodicals, and last year she began Floreant Press, whose first book, Cartwheels on the Faultline, *is in its third printing, and whose second collection,* Saltwater, Sweetwater, *has recently been released.*

*

How could one not love India? And, loving India, how could one not love? The real reason women fall in love abroad is not that they are free of domestic inhibitions but that they translate their love of stone and place into love of flesh.... Is this true?

— Barbara Grizzuti Harrison, *An Accidental Autobiography*

MICHAEL LANE

✦ ✦ ✦

The Firing Squad

*Two travelers find that love
and terror coincide.*

THIRTEEN TRUCKS STOOD SIDE BY SIDE. THE BORDER WAS JUST A
strip of sand away. Almost as many trucks were on the other side,
all with their tails facing us. There was no fence, no flag, no wall.
Just a shantytown full of leathered faces peering out of cardboard
boxes and wooden crates.

So this was the end of the road, Contraband City, where the real
deals were made. A dozen men were waving their arms in the air.
It wasn't exactly a homecoming committee, just a tribe of Berbers
getting a rise out of seeing *girls*.

The Berbers were a shade more civil than our Moroccan drivers. A tall, elegant man wearing trousers and a turban was direct-
ing our truck in. When we finally came to a metal-crunching stop,
we all jumped down so fast we left tread marks on the rails.

We unloaded our bags and kissed that stinking truck goodbye
forever, without even a nod of thanks to our drivers, who were
laughing like fools and spreading the news about the pack of idiots
they'd found to pay them money for such a ride.

We walked toward the guard station and stood in a line. It did
seem a bit absurd. There was no one in the station. And nothing
but a small gate crossing to distinguish the border.

The Moroccans were freely walking back and forth, shifting cargo from truck to truck. Finally Joseph went to ask about the border.

The border only opened once a week, and tomorrow was the big day. That's why the smugglers were all there—to exchange contraband before the officials showed up. We were told that a military bus from El Aaiún brought a captain up for the weekly opening. Once he stamped our passports, we could catch a ride on the bus.

So we dug in for the evening right there on the sand. We watched them tear off the tarps and that wretched smell of rotting goats overtook the camp like a plague. The Berbers were all gagging, pulling scarves over their faces. Our Moroccan drivers were puking on the tires. All seven of us just stood there with our hands on our hips, nodding our heads saying one big, "Uh huh."

It was sweet revenge.

By evening all the trucks had exchanged cargoes and the Moroccans were back on their way. The Turk yelled, "See you in hell," and he had a point. If there was a hell they'd be there.

That night we partied. We were stone-happy drunk to be off that miserable rotten truck. The Germans dug out a bottle of wine, the Berbers brought over their hash and the Swedes pulled out tin cans of sardines while the Turk and I did a little soft-shoe on the desert floor. We had ourselves a virtual feast at the invisible border of Spanish Sahara.

The rest of us just fell asleep like exhausted soldiers after a forced march.

Bright and early in the morning we heard the roar of a bus barreling across the sand. Joseph was the first to jump up and see a cloud of dust as high as the sun. It was the military bus from El Aaiún.

We were all scrambling for our passports. None of us wanted to be left behind in this charming little place.

The bus came to a stop and half a dozen sloppy-looking soldiers climbed out. The captain stepped out toward the small shack of a guardhouse. He looked tough as nails. They opened the door, set up a table, and the square-faced captain seated himself in front of his papers, clicking his heels.

The border was officially opened.

As the others lined up I trotted out to a field for my morning squat. The captain made a note of this.

Slowly each of us waddled through the guardhouse, rubbing sleep from our eyes, and waited for the stamp of approval before boarding the bus. Joseph went through and that only left Peter and me.

Peter stepped into the guardhouse. The captain wanted to see his passport and money.

He'd been asking this of everyone in line. If you didn't have a hundred dollars cash in your pocket, he wouldn't let you through. Neither Peter nor I had paid attention to this. When they asked Peter to show his money, he drew a blank. Joseph was carrying Peter's wallet in his pack.

The captain scowled when Peter yelled at Joseph to give him his wallet. He was a ruthless, play-by-the-book old fart. He refused to let Joseph give Peter his wallet. The guards stepped up and blocked Joseph. Peter argued until he was pink in the face trying to convince the captain to let Joseph give him the wallet.

But the captain didn't care. He said it was a trick and that if Peter didn't have the money on him then it wasn't his. The guards shoved Peter back and motioned me forward.

Now, I definitely did not have money—at best, ten dollars left to my name. I was trying to come up with something good to say on the money front. But the captain wasn't concerned about my money. He wanted to know why I was out there taking a long shit in the field. Then he asked to see proof of my cholera shots.

What the hell was it with cholera shots? For the second time I was refused entry across a border for lack of a shot.

The captain slammed his books shut and motioned to the guards to push us back to Morocco. Before we knew it, the bus had started.

We were left standing in Morocco with Joseph, Sylvia, the Germans and the Turk all looking on in horror. They screamed as the bus took off. It left us behind in a swirl of dust, but not before Joseph tossed Peter's wallet out the window. Joseph yelled from the bus that he'd wait for us in El Aaiún.

As the dust settled I turned to Peter and gestured to ask him what we ought to do. I felt like the fool because, come to think of it, Peter and I had never spoken a word to each other.

We turned in a big circle looking at where we were. No TVs. No radios. No cars. No crooked hawkers trying to steal our last coin. It *was* the end of the road.

But we were not alone. It just felt that way.

About thirty yards away a hairless old man with a set of wooden teeth peered out from his curtained door. Two wooden crates turned on their side were his home. Actually, they were his store.

He brought us over to his little hut, no bigger than a bread truck, and let us peer inside. He had all sorts of stuff in there, from AA batteries to canned pears. The shelves were jammed with over-flow contraband from the trucks. He made it known that every-thing was for sale.

This was reassuring in an odd sort of way.

We walked outside and let out the biggest sigh. It looked like we had no choice—we were going to have to wait a week. There was no way in hell either of us was going to take another truck back through Morocco after what we'd undergone.

We took a cue and made ourselves a home out of an evacuated box. It was a nice box, made out of cardboard and high enough to squat in. There were two small broken toaster ovens inside to weigh it down from the wind. At four by eight feet, it had enough room for two men to sleep in.

That night Peter and I just quietly fell asleep in separate cor-ners of the box. We didn't have anything to say because we couldn't talk.

I lay there for the longest time, staring at the roof of the box, listening to Peter sigh. He still looked ever so much like a god, only a depressed one. Then this god started to snore. Not just a sweet-little-baby snore but a dirty-old-hairy-man snore with phlegm in every ground-rattling breath.

I didn't get a wink of sleep.

The following morning my eyes were glued closed with a ton of grit, and I stretched my legs outside of our cardboard box. I stood up and crossed the desert floor like I was walking on a crunchy pie. The wind off the dunes blew sand up into the air, in my hair, up my nose and into my lungs. I sort of enjoyed breathing sand. It was better than stinking exhaust or rotting goats.

I went foraging for scrub brush to build a fire for tea. Then I saw Peter pop out of the box and run after me. He had a smile on his face and sailed in the wind with his turban fluttering behind. His golden skin and blue eyes mirrored the hills and sky before us. His mood had changed.

He yelped. I laughed. And off we sped in a chase up the dunes, over the crest toward the rising sun. We laughed—parched, guttural laughs that crackled through the earth. Peter was fast. He caught the corner of my robe, pulled me down, and met me eye to eye.

What a tease he could be.

Up he went again, running along the top of a mountain-sized dune. The sun kissed our faces as we raced along.

When we came to one crest, we stopped.

Across the valley we saw a band of men far away on a neighboring dune. At first we were startled.

The more we studied their silhouettes, the more we could see they were a military patrol. They rode two abreast on camels, their rifles hoisted in the air. They cast long shadows across the valley. We began waving. And then we ran. Ran like speeding bullets, ran with the wind, not away from but toward them.

Most people might have seen a band of gun-toting camel riders and hid behind a hill. But most people hadn't watched *Lawrence of Arabia* a million times.

We were electrified to see such a scene. Men in robes, turbans and gun belts, all riding behind a fluttering flag. Off we sped like two desert foxes into a snare.

By the time we hit the bottom of the dune, they had seen us. Suddenly, in full fury, they charged. Two shots rang past our ears as soon as our feet touched the valley floor. The riders thrust their heels into the camels' flanks, scattering dust and spit. We were alarmed. Those bullets seemed a little too real.

Within minutes we were encircled, rifles aimed at our heads. Very confused, I stood there grinning a stupid-looking grin.

Peter was the first to go down; a man took a swing with his boot and kicked him to the ground. Then I was hit on the back of the legs and fell too. They were yelling in Spanish in loud, angry voices. A soldier got down from his camel and pulled us up by the scruff of our necks.

They then tied our wrists behind our backs. Four men dismounted, jammed rifles into our ribs and shoved us forward.

Terrified, we didn't know what to do. They were asking for our passports, which we'd left back in our cardboard box. We were in a sorry state.

For the next two hours we marched ten kilometers through the valley of dunes. We didn't have a clue where we were going or why these guns were pointed at our heads. My legs were bruised from the rifle butt that struck me. A trickle of blood ran from Peter's neck. I was ready for a commercial break and a glass of cold milk. But this wasn't TV.

When we finally arrived at a small outpost, we learned what we had done. We'd crossed into Spanish Sahara without knowing. This was the border patrol. It was serious. At the headquarters, a small clay hut in the desert, sat an official.

He was a mess of a man. If our fate lay with him, I was seriously worried. Even though he wore the uniform of an officer, with his ruthless laugh he had the attitude of an illiterate peasant. His cap

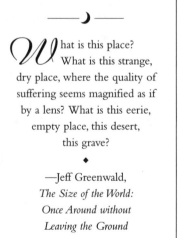

What is this place? What is this strange, dry place, where the quality of suffering seems magnified as if by a lens? What is this eerie, empty place, this desert, this grave?

♦

—Jeff Greenwald,
*The Size of the World:
Once Around without
Leaving the Ground*

and jacket were worn through with holes. His teeth were rotten and black. He smoked a chillum and drank sweet mint tea.

They kept us outside, with a guard looking over us. Peter looked scared.

Only half an hour had gone by when a woman appeared at the door. She was a small, pretty woman in jeans and a sweater. She had curly brown hair and wore lipstick the color of the sunrise. She eyed us sadly and asked if we spoke Spanish. I asked if she spoke English. Peter asked if she spoke Swedish. But there were no common languages until Peter struggled to ask if she spoke French, which she did. Neither of us could speak it, but we could understand a word or two.

She told us that she was the official's wife. Then came the bad news. She told us we had been arrested as spies. Our robes and turbans, she said, made them think we were impersonating Arabs. And with downcast eyes she said that they were going to shoot us.

"Shoot us?"

Both Peter and I jumped at this thought.

"You mean, with bullets?" I said.

Only a few hours ago we had been dancing like fools on the dunes. And now this?

Then we learned of the tensions at the border between Morocco and Spain. There were armies and there was war. Our little morning walk had been a big mistake.

She began to cry. Things did not look good.

We stood there, shaking. *Shot for spying? No court, no judges, no jury?* If this was true, then we would be buried in the desert sands in our Moroccan garb. And no one would ever know.

We just sat down on the ground, swollen with pain, and feeling the seconds of our lives tick away.

The heat was now upon us and my lips were cracked from the dry air. My legs ached from the march. Peter was shaking, but the blood from his wound had dried on his neck. We looked at each other with question marks in our eyes.

At any moment we expected someone to set us free. But such was not the case. We could hear the brutal talk from inside, the voices desperate. The captain spoke in strong, forceful tones. The official was slow to anger, but it seemed as though a quarrel was taking place. Our pretty friend asked where we were born and if we were Christian.

She ran back to the men, perhaps to speak in our favor. We hung on every word, every nuance in her voice, straining to hear the response. But it didn't sound good.

Finally the captain came storming out of the hut with several men at his side. He was yelling orders.

Time began moving quickly, too quickly to protest or think of other options.

Soldiers raised us up. One wielded a knife, quickly slicing our ropes and freeing our hands. But this was not freedom. They shoved rifles in our backs and forced our hands to our heads.

The official came out of the building. He rocked on his heels and spat on the dirt with his hands on his hips. His wife began pleading, holding his arm, tears on her face. She yelled at the captain as he mounted his camel.

Peter was crying. I was, too.

They pushed and shoved us out toward a flat stretch of ground. More soldiers mounted their camels. We were forced to face the sun, side by side. The captain fired a shot in the air, sending terror through us.

We both now felt death coming. Our hands dropped to our sides, and the woman was screaming hysterically. The captain ordered everyone to mount his camel. Every remaining man swung up on his saddle and they all cocked their rifles in the air. The captain barked more orders and the men formed their camels into a semicircle, facing us. The camels were champing their bits restlessly.

I remember looking up the barrels of the guns as they were lowered at us.

Peter moved even closer to me. Our bodies pressed hard together, shoulder to shoulder, arm to arm, our fingers touching. We looked straight ahead while the captain ordered the guns readied.

I remember birds in the sky circling around and a cloud floating across the horizon. I noticed ants in the sand and an abandoned shoe on the dirt. An old cane leaned against the hut and a cross hung over the door.

I could smell Peter in my soul, his fear mixed with mine. Moments turned into long rivers of time, and fleeting thoughts took on lives of their own.

I looked at the men and could see them clearly. I could see their whiskers, one by one, the roots of their hair and the moles on their cheeks. I could smell the breath of the camels, hear their gurgling stomachs and shifting limbs.

I looked at the men again and could hear their thoughts.

And I could hear Peter thinking of me.

It was as if we could finally speak. I felt myself asking him if he loved me. I felt us talking in our heads. The guns were cocked and the sights steadied on our hearts. The barrels wavered in the air before taking accurate aim. The captain's voice barked a command. Our feet touched the desert and I could feel a drop of Peter's sweat on my arm. Even in Spanish, we knew what he was shouting.

"Ready!"

And the breathing was in sync between Peter and me. The last breath was drawn before the impact of lead.

"Aim!"

I felt Peter inside me, screaming my name. I could feel the desert consuming our bones and the birds singing our death song.

"Fire!"

A volley of bullets exploded all around, deafening us. Bullets whizzed through the air slightly above our heads and off toward the dune.

They had missed! And we were still standing!

Peter and I looked at each other, expecting another round.

With a loud whoop the captain shot his gun in the air, and they all began shooting off bullets. They circled around, spitting in our faces. They circled once more. And then they raced away into the desert, laughing like dogs.

They left us alive. And free.

The woman came running up once they were gone. She cursed

the captain and begged us to run back to our camp before he changed his mind.

She was shaking with relief and swore the captain was insane.

We agreed.

Peter and I sprinted across the desert. We ran faster than the wind. Finally we saw the encampment of cardboard boxes, a welcome refuge. We ran and ran until we were back in our box, safe from the border patrol.

Michael Lane grew up in trailer parks throughout the South, landed in the Haight-Ashbury scene at seventeen, and for the last several decades has chased life relentlessly. Co-creator of Monk *magazine, which* Newsweek *described as "Charles Kuralt meets Jack Kerouac with Laurel and Hardy thrown in," he is co-author of* Mad Monks on the Road, *and author of* Pink Highways: Tales of Queer Madness on the Open Road, *from which this story was excerpted.*

＊

Love is one of the answers humankind invented to stare death in the face: time ceases to be a measure, and we can briefly know paradise.

—Octavio Paz, *The Double Flame*

✳ ✳ ✳

Bo'sun Seduction

"Very sexy 'ooman" cannot compete
with a sailor's greatest love.

THE SMALL, WHITE FREIGHTER GLIDED THOUGH A WARM NIGHT LIT by constellations of the Southern Hemisphere, stars that I had dreamed of seeing all my life. Papeete lay behind us, Pago-Pago straight ahead. After hours of gazing at the sky and phosphorescent swells, I had come inside reluctantly, knowing that the cook would be whistling me out of bed before dawn.

I was starting to slip off my sundress when a soft knock brought me to the door. Against a background of slowly moving stars loomed a blond giant, cinematically handsome, wearing cutoffs and a turquoise net singlet the exact color of his eyes. This vision cradled two liquor bottles, a triangle of brie laid precariously across their caps. His strong fingers scissored the stems of two brandy snifters, and his bulging bicep pinned a Tahitian baguette. His massive free hand grasped a tape deck and a nylon cassette bag.

"Can I come in?" he murmured.

Stifling my first response ("Trick question, right?"), I considered the situation in the light of recent history.

A month earlier, I had been thrilled when the Scandinavian shipping agent called, only a week after our interview, to offer a job on a Norwegian freighter. So many of my queries about working on a freighter had been met only with derisive laughter. American flagships never hired women, and foreign flagships never hired Americans. How had I ever conceived such an idea in the first place? And I had already quit my San Francisco office job? What a romantic fool!

When I finally reached the shipping agent at his unlisted phone number, he tried to get rid of me by promising to mail an application. But insisting on an interview, I trotted down to the Customs district wearing a becoming red suit, high heels, and the glow of youthful innocence and enthusiasm. The agent seemed impressed by my willingness to serve meals and wash dishes, my strong sense of responsibility, and my friendly personality.

The *Thor I's* seedy air and its leisurely, unplanned route seemed the essence of adventure. We would be traveling for two to three months, perhaps as far as New Guinea. There were only thirteen passengers to worry about, and plenty of free time between meals. Having laid in a supply of Maugham and Conrad, I prepared to wallow in the atmosphere.

But the sailors had their own ideas. Every time I paused, someone—more often two or three someones—would be right there. Noticing that the other crew women, two Norwegians and a pair of Tongan sisters, had chosen sweethearts, I began to suspect that everyone was waiting for me to make a choice, or even better, sleep around. Had I been hired for my entertainment value?

The only one who remained aloof was the Bo'sun, by far the handsomest man on board. He had a name, but no one used it, giving him a mysterious air. Imagine a

A bo'sun (the shorter version of boatswain) is a petty officer on a merchant marine ship who is in charge of rigging, cables, anchors, sails, the ship's hull, and related equipment. He supervises a crew which welds, paints, and maintains the structure of the ship.

♦

—JBW

Nordic god striding about the ship, deeply tanned body displayed in brief cutoffs, sunstreaked hair flying in the constant breeze, a frequent sneer revealing startlingly white teeth. In fact he was a little picturesque for my taste. I was more attracted to the First Engineer, a bear of a man with dark, sleepy eyes. However, Bjorn was married (a problem for me, not for him), while someone had said the Bo'sun had no wife, not even in Norway where most wives were stashed. It was flattering to be noticed by such a gorgeous creature. On the other hand, as the one and only available female on this ship, just how flattered could I feel?

I awoke from this debate to find the Bo'sun already inside the cabin. Glancing up and down the corridor, I shut the door behind us.

Bare feet planted in a take-charge stance before the dressing table mirror, my guest appeared to be surveying the cabin in this backward way. Fortunately I had gone to some trouble with the decor. With the aid of manicure scissors and travel sewing kit, I had made curtains and pillows covers of polished cotton, deep blue with tropical scenes outlined in gilt. In Tahiti I had found coconut-leaf fans and cowrie necklaces for the walls. My Tongan roommate had abandoned me for the First Mate, and her bunk beneath the port hole made a fine spot for entertaining.

The Bo'sun nodded his approval. Setting his offerings on the dressing table, he lit the utility candles kept ready for the frequent power failures. Then he switched on the tape player, igniting the bewitching rhythm of Tahitian drums.

Meanwhile I inspected the refreshments. The baguette was fresh, still fragrant, unlike the previously frozen things we had been breaking our teeth on during the two weeks between Los Angeles and Papeete. The brie was ripe and soft around the edges, with a tantalizing pungency. I would have preferred French wine, but these dusty bottles looked interesting. As for seduction, apparently also on the menu, surely I could make my mind up later about dessert?

Taking silence as consent, the Bo'sun began to mix drinks.

"What is this?" I asked, taking a well-filled snifter.

"Carry-Me-Home," he said with a glance at my bare legs. "Brandy and Benedictine." I gazed at the dark concoction, gauging its aphrodisiac effect. Considerable, if I didn't pass out first.

I began to think, "Why not?" The night was young and so was I. The Chief Steward could hardly expect me to do breakfast duty in a waking state every single morning, for the pittance he was paying (not to mention pocketing my tips). And Tahitian music has a beat that goes straight to the…well, let's just say it puts a person in the mood.

Tearing off a piece of bread and slathering it with brie, a precaution against passing out, I curled up in one corner of the couch. With a parting scrutiny of his mirrored self, the Bo'sun lowered himself beside me a bit stiffly, like a heroic statue not intended to sit down. He leaned toward me, face eloquent of the desire to bridge the gap between one soul and another. But he couldn't seem to find the words.

At last the chiseled lips parted. "How's your sexability?"

"Beg your pardon?"

He frowned. "This is English word, ja?"

"Not really. Well, I think I know what you mean, but we don't usually ask people things like that. At least, not right away."

He settled back, chagrined, and combed his hair. Then he brightened. "You know, I will never look in ooman's purse."

I couldn't think of anything to say but, "Oh?"

"Never," he affirmed with pride. "One time I'm drinking with ooman in a bar in San Francisco. She gets drunk, she passes out. I want to get her car keys, drive her home, but I will never look in ooman's purse. So I have to call another ooman—hey, come over here and get her keys."

As I smiled and nodded, damned if the Bo'sun didn't launch into another example of how he never looked in ooman's purse. I didn't have a clue why this was so important to him. Purse as metaphor? An obscure form of political correctness? Beginning to fear that this was his idea of conversation, I gulped another inch of Carry-Me-Home to encourage my sexability.

The Bo'sun slid a little closer. "Sven says you are very sexy ooman."

"Sven? AKA the Visigoth? How would he know?" I asked indignantly.

"Sven said you are very very hot. Terrific lay."

"He said what? That jerk!" I sat bolt upright, Carry-Me-Home waves sloshing up the sides of my snifter. "What really happened was, he tried to rape me!"

It had been a terrifying experience. Before he metamorphosed into the Visigoth, Sven had been one of my best friends on board—friendly, understanding, even affectionate in a brotherly way—and I accepted his invitation to tour Papeete by night without a qualm. After margaritas at the notorious Quinn's (wickedest bar in the South Pacific), where we met the entire crew getting plastered while trying to sort the exquisite women from the exquisite transvestites, he said that he was driving me back to the ship. Instead he drove to a deserted spot and switched off the headlights. Darkness fell: absolute and almost palpable, like a blanket thrown over my head. Then he attacked. I fought to the point of exhaustion before resorting to hysterics—which, miraculously, discouraged him. Then he had the nerve to say I hadn't fought all that hard; other girls had fought harder!

This sordid episode had evidently been embroidered.

"Listen, Sven is a big, fat liar." Fury and frustration brought tears to my eyes. "No lay, terrific or otherwise. Understand?"

"Sure, sure, I understand," the Bo'sun said, his deep voice a touch too soothing. "Hey, want to dance? Tahitian dancing, very sexy."

I stared at him unhappily, trying to recapture my former mood. Nothing had changed, really. The warm air was still billowing the curtains of Hawaiian cotton. Nothing had happened to the candlelight, the music, or the soothing motion of the sea. The man was still gorgeous beyond belief. All the ingredients for romance were here, and I was ripe and ready, damn it.

"Right." I set the snifter on the floor. "Let's dance."

The Bo'sun was right: Tahitian dancing is very, very sexy. It all happens in the hips, and ours seemed glued together, causing me to notice that the Bo'sun's sexability was on the rise, so to speak.

He began to kiss my lips and eyes and neck, without interrupting the flow of our dancing. The insistent beat vibrated through our bodies, hijacking my mind. The Carry-Me-Home purred along my bloodstream. As he slid my dress up and down to the rhythm of the music, his big, warm hands began to move beneath the fabric. I was leaning back against his locked arms, savoring the many pleasurable sensations, when I felt one massive arm give way.

I opened my eyes. The Bo'sun was combing his hair again, studying his reflected face and body with transparent satisfaction. And I sobered with the realization

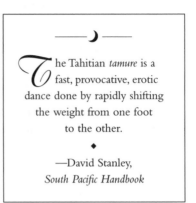

The Tahitian *tamure* is a fast, provocative, erotic dance done by rapidly shifting the weight from one foot to the other.

◆

—David Stanley,
South Pacific Handbook

that this man's real romantic interest was over there, in the mirror.

The atmospheric backdrop fell away. Subtract the Norwegian freighter, the South Pacific, and the Tahitian music, and what was left? Your garden variety one-night stand, complete with candles and "liquor is quicker" recipe for seduction. Take away his gorgeous surface, and the Bo'sun was a man I wouldn't want to spend a minute with. And what was so romantic about drifting year after year, unattached to anyone or any place? It seemed to be a life of considerable pain, judging by the amount of time the crew spent seeking oblivion in one form or another.

The Bo'sun didn't have the faintest idea why I was pushing him out the door, but he didn't lose face by protesting. Loading up his bottles, his baguette, and his brie, he balanced the tape deck on his head and danced out to the music: a terrific exit.

Maybe he was just as happy to go back to his cabin and make love to himself. Or maybe his main interest was in recounting his exploits to his shipboard buddies, in which case it really didn't matter what we did tonight. What really mattered, to him and to his envious listeners, was the fantasy.

And fundamentally, weren't the two of us in the same boat?

Meredith Moraine's other adventures include hopping freight trains in British Columbia, herding cows in the Swiss Alps, and back-packing extensively in Asia. A sojourn in Bali produced a murder mystery, The Kris of Death, *co-authored with Jerrold Steward.*

★

The conception which unites the whole varied work of [Robert Louis] Stevenson was that romance, or the vision of the possibilities of things, was far more important than mere occurrences: that one was the soul of our life, the other the body, and that the soul was the precious thing. The germ of all his stories lies in the idea that every landscape or scrap of scenery has a soul: and that soul is a story. Stevenson stands for the conception that ideas are the real incidents: that our fancies are our adventures.

—G. K. Chesterton

MICHAEL WAYNE HUNTER

* * *

Mother Teresa on
Death Row

*A special traveler visits the mind
and heart of a condemned man.*

IN THE SUMMER OF 1987, I HAD JUST FINISHED MY THIRD YEAR ON
San Quentin's death row. Warehoused on the old death row, or
"the shelf" as we call it. (The state of California had never antici-
pated the current [400-plus] population on death row, so another
part of the prison holds the overflow.)

On this particular day, I came onto the tier at 8:30 a.m. on my
way to work out with my friend Bobby Harris. After lifting
weights for a while, I was off to my cell to change into gym shorts
to play basketball.

As I sat on the tier, double-tying my shoes, the guard on the gun
rail came down and asked what I was doing.

"What does it look like?" I asked him. "I'm getting ready to go
rock up on the roof (where the shelf's exercise yard is
located…right next to the gas chamber exhaust stack—nothing
like a daily reality check, you know.) "That's what I do every day
after I lift weights," I added.

"You're going to miss Mother Teresa," the guard said. "She's
coming today to see you guys."

I looked at him with a cynical smile. "You cops will do anything
to keep from running us to the yard, won't you?" I said. "I'm not

missing my sunshine. If she shows, tell her to lace up some high tops and meet me on the roof. I can post her up to the hoop, probably, and shoot over the top of her."

"Okay," the guard said. "But don't say I didn't warn you." Then he turned and walked away.

Whereupon a couple of alarm bells went off in my head. The guard, I told myself, had given up too easily. Maybe Mother Teresa was coming. Then I thought, "Get real, Hunter." And I finished getting ready to rock, heading up to the roof with everyone else.

But afterwards, walking down the stairs back inside, I heard the guard on the gun rail call: "Don't go into your cells and lock up. Mother Teresa stayed to see you guys, too."

So I jogged up to the front in gym shorts and a tattered basketball shirt with the arms ripped out, and on the other side of the security screen was this tiny woman who looked 100 years old. Yes, it was Mother Teresa.

You have to understand that, basically, I'm a dead man. I don't have to observe any sort of social convention; and as a result, I can break all the rules, say what I want.

But one look at this Nobel Prize winner, this woman so many people view as a living saint, and I was speechless.

Incredible vitality and warmth came from her wizened, piercing eyes. She smiled at me, blessed a religious medal, and handed it to me. I wouldn't have walked voluntarily to the front of the tier to see the Warden, the Governor, the President, the Pope. I could not care less about them. But standing before this woman, all I could say was, "Thank you, Mother Teresa."

Then I stepped back to let another dead man come forward to receive his medal.

As I stood there looking at the medal, I knew my wife was going to treasure it. After all, in her youth, she seriously considered becoming a nun. It occurred to me that her sister was going to be absolutely jealous. Perhaps, I thought, I should try to get a second medal.

Taking a chance, I walked the few steps back and asked Mother Teresa for a medal for my sister-in-law. She smiled, blessed one, and handed it to me. Once again, the warmth of her presence surrounded me, then Mother Teresa turned and pointed her hand at the sergeant on the shelf. "What you do to these men," she told him, "you do to God." The sergeant almost faded away in surprise and wonder.

That night, as I wrote my wife and sister-in-law and sent their medals, I told them I couldn't help reflecting on how this woman had chosen to live her life and what she had accomplished, and how I in contrast had just thrown my life away. It was a humbling experience.

So Mother Teresa came and went. The sergeant was affected by her words for a whole day and a half.

My wife, who is also named Teresa (though I call her Terri) started wearing the medal on a chain around her neck. It became one of her prized possessions.

As time went by, however, I began to forget how powerful I had found Mother Teresa's presence. Usually, in talking about her visit, I would just joke that she kept the sarge at bay for 36 hours.

Then, in 1989, my fifth year on death row, my wife told me that she couldn't remain married any longer. It was one of the toughest experiences of my life, right up there with when my mother died. Terri told me that she still loved me, but being married to a dead man was just too difficult. We divorced shortly after my death-penalty appeal was rejected by the California Supreme Court. I was at my lowest ebb emotionally. This is when I began to recall the strength and warmth I had felt in Mother Teresa's presence.

I wrote to Terri and asked if I could borrow the religious medal that Mother Teresa had blessed for me.

The medal would be hers, of course. I just wanted to borrow it to recapture some strength from that remarkable woman. I would return the medal when I left death row, probably upon my execution.

Terri sent it to me with a chain, telling me she did not wear it anymore. Since our divorce, Terri had started wearing my wedding band (the one I had worn during our marriage and returned to

Terri) on a chain around her neck instead. It made her feel closer to me, Terri said. But she did not miss San Quentin or walking past the gas chamber to see me each week. We began to correspond regularly again, and Terri, through her letters, has become very much a part of my life once more.

Now I wear Mother Teresa's medal every day. I feel linked by it to both the woman who blessed it and the woman who wore it during marriage. It continues to lend me strength in my darkest moments.

Michael Hunter is a condemned prisoner at San Quentin.

★

There is a terrible hunger for love. We all experience that in our lives—the pain, the loneliness. We must have the courage to recognize it. The poor you may have right in your own family. Find them. Love them. Put your love for them in living action. For in loving them, you are loving God Himself.

It is not how much we do, but how much love we put in the doing. It is not how much we give, but how much love we put in the giving.

To God there is nothing small. The moment we have given it to God, it becomes infinite.

You have to be holy in your position as you are, and I have to be holy in the position that God has put me. So it is nothing extraordinary to be holy. Holiness is not the luxury of the few. Holiness is a simple duty for you and for me. We have been created for that.

—Mother Teresa

PART FIVE

THE LAST WORD

✦ ✦ ✦

Remember Africa?

A life of travel bestows a final gift.

"WHO ARE YOU?" FRANK DEMANDED WHEN RUTH WALKED INTO the room. She sighed and eased gently down on the bed next to him, folding his age-shrunken hand in hers. He recoiled from her uncertainly, fear widening his eyes.

"I'm Ruth, your wife," she said, forcing a polite smile and patting his hand.

His eyebrows shot upward as he bolted upright in bed. "Wife?"

"We've been married forty years, Frank."

"No." Frank shook his head vigorously. "No. I don't remember you."

Ruth nodded and closed her eyes. It was a conversation they had had nearly every day during the past few months. The illness had not much weakened Frank's body, but his mind faded, day to day, like color from an oft-washed cloth.

"That's okay, dear," Ruth answered. "I love you whether you know me or not." She adjusted the pillow between his back and the wooden headboard, then straightened the covers around his waist. "Oh Frank, we've had so many wonderful years. We've sure had a good life together."

He smiled back at her tentatively, eyes still clouded in confusion.

"Was I a good husband?"

She chuckled. "You devil," she said, pinching his cheek softly. "The best. You were always kind and gentle and lots of fun. Even now, you try, don't you?"

He nodded. Her words seemed to reassure him. He looked around the room, as if desperately searching for clues. "Our family…?"

Ruth hesitated. "We never had children, Frank. We tried, but we couldn't. But we have so many friends and loved ones. You've lived eighty-two good, long years now. People have always loved you, Frank. And you've touched so many lives."

"Hmmm."

He nodded, but his eyes kept that faraway gaze, unable to connect with any familiar faces. "Well, what did we do?"

"Well, mister, we worked. We worked hard and we built up your family business and we went to church and we enjoyed ourselves just fine. And we traveled all over the world."

"Oh?" His eyes danced, just a flicker of light. "Where?"

"Everywhere, Frank. We went to so many beautiful places. Do you remember Edinburgh, Frank? The castles and the countryside of Scotland? You loved how green it was, even when we were freezing. And you wore this silly plaid cap that made me laugh." She searched his eyes, but the light had passed.

Frank slipped back down on the pillow and stared at the ceiling. His profile was nearly the same as her first sight of him 40 years earlier, as he stood in her doorway, coming to pick her up for a ride to church camp. When she opened that door, his eyes had grown wide with interest, and he gave her that devilish grin she'd come to love so much. Now his mouth was drawn tight, grim with irritation.

"And Japan. Remember Tokyo, Frank? Remember the lights and those crowded streets, and the temples? How you bought all those tiny mechanical toys, and the radio as small as your fingernail?"

She held up his hand to show him, but his eyes were squeezed tight, his mind fruitlessly searching for his memories. He shook his head, a frown deepening on his face.

A moment passed. He blinked and stared at her again, at the face he had awakened to every morning for 40 years.

His eyes narrowed. "Who are you?" he asked, his voice edged with fear.

She drew a long, steady breath, looking into his bewildered eyes. "Africa, Frank," she said slowly. She took his hand back, gripping it tightly. "Do you remember our travels through Africa?"

"Africa…" he repeated quietly.

"We saw animals…" she ventured softly.

"Lions…" he answered. She sat silently, waiting.

"We saw lions," he said, pulling himself up slowly beside her. "We sat in the Land Rover and the lions were surrounding us, coming right up to us. And there were elephants, and a huge one with the huge tusk that came crashing out of the bush right at us…"

Ruth nodded, smiling back at him.

"You were there with me. You were sitting next to me." His eyes were clearing, shining; she could feel the tears begin to well in her own.

"And the flamingoes," he said, his voice rising. "We stood at the edge of the lake and watched them fly. There were so many of them, it was just like a pink cloud rising up from the water."

His words slowed, and his eyes closed.

"Frank…" she said, and he sat still, not moving, not answering.

"Frank, remember the night in Uganda, when the children sang to us? We were in that little village near the river…"

"The children! Yes," he said, opening his eyes again. "They were so young, so sweet…"

"And their round little faces all lit up…"

"…they were all holding candles! And afterward, we ate in that man's home, with the dirt floor. We sat in the candle light, and they brought us the food in those huge black bowls…"

"Remember how strange that food looked?"

Frank laughed, then groaned. "We didn't know if it was raw, or worms, or what. And, and…were we with missionaries?"

She nodded. "Yes, we were visiting missionaries who had a church in the village."

"Yes, yes," he said. "I can see them now. And the missionary told us how he prayed before he ate. He prayed, 'Lord, I'll put it down if you keep it down!'"

As they laughed, she took in every detail—the blueness of his eyes, the curve of his cheekbones, the wrinkles surrounding his smile.

Then Frank looked toward the window, where sunlight streamed in through a crack in the curtains. "Ruth," he asked worriedly. "Why am I in bed so late this morning?"

"You're not well today, Frank."

"I am feeling tired," he said, yawning. He slid back down onto his pillow, smiling dreamily up at her. "Ruth, what were those waterfalls?"

"Victoria Falls?"

"Yes, Victoria Falls. Ruth, I remember standing there, feeling the spray from the falls, and you were scared and holding onto my arm so tight. And you said it was the most beautiful sight you had ever seen. And I told you no, you were still more beautiful to me."

He curled up and kissed her softly on the cheek. She was shaking, holding as tight to his arm as she had at the edge of the falls.

"And you still are beautiful."

"You are something else, mister," she laughed.

"I love you, Ruth."

"And I love you, Frank."

His eyes were blinking, fading.

"Why don't you dream about those waterfalls?" Ruth said. "I'll be right here."

With that, he gave a sigh and relaxed, his sparse gray hair flattening against the pillow.

Ruth pulled the covers up around his chest and kissed him, listening to his breath rise and fall. His mind was drifting back in the fog, away from her and the world they had shared. When he woke, he would again recoil from her. And she knew the sight of his face and the warmth of his skin were a gift, a brief glimpse too soon lost to memory. Someday, even the vast continent would not have the power to bring him back to her.

Jo Beth McDaniel is a journalist and author living in Long Beach, California. Ruth and Frank are her great aunt and uncle. This essay is based on talks McDaniel had with her aunt Ruth. She says their story introduced her to the importance and mystery of travel.

*

Recommended Reading

We hope *Travelers' Tales: Love & Romance* has inspired you to read on. A good place to start is the books from which we've made selections, and these are listed below along with other books that we have found to be valuable. Some of these may be out of print but are well worth hunting down.

Ackerman, Diane. *A Natural History of Love.* New York: Random House, Inc., 1994.

Armington, Stan. *Trekking in the Nepal Himalaya.* Hawthorn, Victoria, Australia: Lonely Planet, 1994.

Auden, W. H. *The Dyer's Hand and Other Essays.* New York: Random House, Inc., 1962.

Bateson, Mary Catherine. *Composing a Life.* New York: Plume, a division of Penquin Books USA, Inc., 1989.

Bumiller, Elisabeth. *May You Be the Mother of a Hundred Sons: A Journey Among the Women of India.* New York: Random House, Inc., 1990.

Chamberlain, Basil Hall. *Japanese Things: Being Notes on Various Subjects Connected with Japan.* New York: Charles E. Tuttle Company, 1971.

Chatwin, Bruce and Paul Theroux. *Patagonia Revisited.* New York: Houghton Mifflin, 1986.

Dalrymple, William. *City of Djinns: A Year in Delhi.* London: HarperCollins Publishers (UK) Ltd, 1993.

Davidson, Cathy N. *36 Views of Mount Fuji: On Finding Myself in Japan.* New York: Plume, a Division of Penquin Books USA, Inc., 1993.

de Botton, Alain. *How Proust Can Change Your Life: Not a Novel.* New York: Random House, Inc., 1997.

Derman, Bruce Ph.D. with Michael Hauge. *We'd Have a Great Relationship If It Weren't For You.* Deerfield Beach, Florida: Health Communcations, Inc., 1994.

Ehrlich, Gretel. *Islands, The Universe, Home.* New York: Penguin Books USA, Inc., 1991.

Freuchen, Peter. *Peter Freuchen's Book of the Eskimos.* Cleveland, Ohio: World Publishing Company, 1961.

Greenwald, Jeff. *The Size of the World: Once Around without Leaving the Ground.* New York: Ballantine Books, a division of Random House, Inc., 1997.

Gutkind, Lee. *The People of Penn's Wood West.* Pittsburgh, Pennsylvania: University of Pittsburgh Press, 1984.

Harrison, Barbara Grizzuti. *An Accidental Autobiography.* New York: Houghton Mifflin, 1996.

Hesse, Hermann. *Wandering: Notes and Sketches.* Translated by James Wright. New York: Farrar, Straus & Giroux, 1972.

Iyer, Pico. *The Lady and The Monk.* New York: Vintage Departures, a division of Random House, Inc., 1991.

Lane, Michael. *Pink Highways: Tales of Queer Madness on the Open Road.* New York: Birch Lane Press, 1995.

Lowe, John. *Into Japan.* Salem, New Hampshire: Salem House, 1985.

Maran, Meredith. *What It's Like to Live Now.* New York: Bantam, 1996.

McCormick, John and Mario Sevilla Mascareñas. *The Complete Aficionado: A Comprehensive Survey of the Art and Technique of Modern Toreo.* Cleveland, Ohio: World Publishing Company, 1967.

McDaniel, Judith. *Sanctuary: A Journey.* Ithaca, New York: Firebrand Books, 1987.

McQueen, Ian L. *Japan - a travel survival kit* (3rd edition). Hawthorn, Victoria, Australia: Lonely Planet Publications, 1989.

Millman, Lawrence. *Last Places: A Journey in the North.* New York: Vintage Departures, a division of Random House, Inc., 1992.

Morris, Doug. *Italy Guide.* New York: Open Road Publishing, 1996.

Morris, Mary. *Wall to Wall: From Beijing to Berlin by Rail.* New York: Penguin Books USA, Inc., 1991.

Parkes, Carl. *Southeast Asia Handbook.* Chico, California: Moon Publications, Inc., 1994.

Paz, Octavio. *The Double Flame.* Orlando, Florida: Harcourt Brace Company, 1995.

Salzman, Mark. *Iron and Silk.* New York: Vintage Departures, a division of Random House, Inc., 1986.

Shand, Mark. *Travels on my Elephant.* London: Jonathan Cape, Ltd.; Woodstock, New York: The Overlook Press, 1991.

Somé, Malidoma Patrice. *Of Water and the Spirit: Ritual, Magic, and Initiation in the Life on an African Shaman.* New York: Jeremy P. Tarcher, 1994.

Somé, Malidoma Patrice. *Ritual: Power, Healing and Community.* Portland, Oregon: Swan/Raven & Company, 1993.

Stanley, David. *South Pacific Handbook* (4th Edition). Chico, California: Moon Publications, Inc., 1989.

Sterling, Richard. *Dining with Headhunters: Jungle Feasts and Other Culinary Adventures.* Freedom, California: The Crossing Press, 1995.

Taylor, Chris, Robert Strauss, and Tony Wheeler. *Japan - a travel survival kit* (5th Edition). Hawthorn, Victoria, Australia: Lonely Planet Publications, Inc., 1994.

Varawa, Joana McIntyre. *Changes in Latitude: An Uncommon Anthropology.* Covelo, California: Yolla Bolly Press, 1989; New York: Atlantic Monthly Press, 1989.

Ward, Tim. *Arousing the Goddess.* Toronto: Somerville House Publishing, 1996.

Watson, Lyall. *Dark Nature: A Natural History of Evil.* New York: HarperCollins Publishers, 1995.

Index of Contributors

Acknowledgements

It would be difficult to read through hundreds of essays on romance, as was necessary to find the gems in this book, if one didn't have a romantic to call one's own, and I have that in my remarkable husband, Frank Wylie, a writer, editor, clear thinker, and friend. I thank him for his understanding, his optimism, and his willingness to break out a bottle of wine when things got tough. He's an inspired traveling companion, on the road as in life.

Just when it struck me how much work this book was going to be, Susan Brady, Production Coordinator for Travelers' Tales, sprang to the rescue, speaking in a calm voice, answering frantic questions with good cheer, and otherwise showing a formidable competence combined with a wicked wit. I agree with another Travelers' Tales editor, Christine Hunsicker, who said she was against cloning unless it was for Susan Brady. The world could use at least of a dozen of you, Susan.

One of the best things about joining the Travelers' Tales family as an editor is getting to know and work with series editors Larry Habegger and James O'Reilly, who have a grand vision of what the series should be; Tim O'Reilly, publisher of O'Reilly and Associates; at-large editor Sean O'Reilly; and other warm and wonderful people who care about travel as a way to grow. Jennifer Leo, Leili Eghbal, and editor Richard Sterling have also been wonderfully supportive and encouraging.

I'd like to thank James's wife Wenda for weeping over her toast at breakfast one morning while reading "Remember Africa," which tipped me off that other people could be as touched by it and other stories in this collection as I had been.

Throughout this process, Larry Habegger, a fine editor and writer and always a reasonable and thoughtful sounding board, has been my guide, earning my special respect and thanks.

Thanks also to Helene Brown, who trudged to the library and used book stores in the earlier months of this project, helping me to find wonderful writers I had not met. I am fortunate to live in a town with a terrific library and staff, the Santa Cruz, California City-County Public

Library. The depth of their collections is remarkable, and staff members were unfailingly helpful.

And to other writers, editors and friends who listened, gave insight or helped give the book a wider audience, many thanks, including Eileen Brown, Debra Birnbaum, Joan Scobey, Carolyn Koenig, Judy Wade, Harvey and Jo Ann Stedman, Nancy Howe, Marcia Lipsenthal, Madeline Kaufman, Jean Taylor Lescoe, Kelley Lavin, and Bee Cook. Special thanks to my sister Marcia Boynton for her careful reading. During the process of working on this book we lost my mother, Louise Boynton, who never failed to be excited and pleased by the work I chose to do. She was looking forward to its publication, and I dedicate this effort to her.

"Leaving Los Pájaros" by Iris Litt published with permission from the author. Copyright © 1998 by Iris Litt.

"The Working Class" by Judy Wade published with permission from the author. Copyright © 1998 by Judy Wade.

"The Bridge at Mostar" by Frank Hahn published with permission from the author. Copyright © 1998 by Frank Hahn.

"Sachiko-san" by Pico Iyer excerpted from *The Lady and The Monk* by Pico Iyer. Copyright © 1991 by Pico Iyer. Reprinted by permission of Vintage Departures, a division of Random House, Inc.

"Day in Capri" by Beth Ann Fennelly published with permission from the author. Copyright © 1998 by Beth Ann Fennelly.

"The Lucky Thing" by Cat Gonzalez published with permission from the author. Copyright © 1998 by Cat Gonzalez.

"Sweet Mystery of Life" by Lee Gutkind excerpted from "Scotty and Mama" from *The People of Penn's Woods West*, by Lee Gutkind, copyright © 1984. Reprinted by permission of the University of Pittsburgh Press.

"Animal Crackers" by Susan Feinberg published with permission from the author. Copyright © 1998 by Susan Feinberg.

"Lila's Ballet Shoes" by Gordon Langdon Magill published with permission from the author. Copyright © 1998 by Gordon Langdon Magill.

"Twenty-Four Hours" by Cheryl Herring published with permission from the author. Copyright © 1998 by Cheryl Herring.

"Equal Pressure" by Frank X. Case published with permission from the author. Copyright © 1998 by Frank X. Case.

"Hotel Paradis-o" by Robert Strauss reprinted from the August 31, 1997 issue of the *Chicago Tribune*. Reprinted by permission of the author. Copyright © 1996 by Robert Strauss.

"Black Hair and a Bull's Ear" by Mary Ellen Schultz published with permission from the author. Copyright © 1998 by Mary Ellen Schultz.

"Wind in the West" by Claire Tristram published with permission from the author. Copyright © 1998 by Claire Tristram.

"Feast of Fatima" by Richard Sterling published with permission from the author. Copyright © 1998 by Richard Sterling. A version of this story appeared in *Dining with Headhunters: Jungles Feasts and Other Culinary Adventures* by Richard Sterling.

"The Veil of Kanchenjunga" by Barbara Baer published with permission from the author. Copyright © 1998 by Barbara Baer.

"The Firing Squad" by Michael Lane excerpted from *Pink Highways: Tales of Queer Madness on the Open Road* by Michael Lane. Reprinted with permission from Carol Publishing Group. Copyright © 1995 by Michael Lane.

"Bo'sun Seduction" by Meredith Moraine published with permission from the author. Copyright © 1998 by Meredith Moraine.

"Mother Teresa on Death Row" by Michael Wayne Hunter reprinted by permission of the author. Copyright © Michael Wayne Hunter. This story originally appeared in *Catholic Digest.*

"Remember Africa?" by Jo Beth McDaniel published with permission from the author. Copyright © 1998 by Jo Beth McDaniel.

Additional Credits (arranged alphabetically by title)

Selection from *36 Views of Mount Fuji: On Finding Myself in Japan* by Cathy N. Davidson. Copyright © 1993 by Cathy N. Davidson. Used by permission of Dutton Signet, a division of Penguin Books USA Inc.

Selection from *An Accidental Autobiography* by Barbara Grizzuti Harrison. Copyright © 1996 by Barbara Grizzuti Harrison. Reprinted by permission of Houghton Mifflin Company. All rights reserved.

Selection from "Advice to the Lovelorn" by Rajendra S. Khadka published with permission from the author. Copyright © 1998 by Rajendra S. Khadka.

Selection from "Afternoon in Tokyo" by Jina Bacarr published with permission from the author. Copyright © 1998 by Jina Bacarr.

Quote by Buckminster Fuller reprinted by permission from *The Christian Science Monitor.* Copyright © 1974 The Christian Science Publishing Society. All rights reserved.

Selection from "Chinese Like Me" by Jennifer Leo published with permission from the author. Copyright © 1998 by Jennifer Leo.

Selection from *City of Djinns: A Year in Delhi* by William Dalrymple. Copyright © William Dalrymple 1993. Used with permission of HarperCollins Publishers (UK) Ltd.

Selection from *The Complete Aficionado: A Comprehensive Survey of the Art and Technique of Modern Toreo* by John McCormick and Mario Sevilla Mascareñas. Published by The World Publishing Company. Copyright © 1967 by John McCormick and Mario Sevilla Mascareñas.

Selection from *Composing a Life* by Mary Catherine Bateson. Copyright © 1989 by Mary Catherine Bateson. Used by permission of Grove/Atlantic, Inc.

Selection from "Conversations" by Lynn Magruder published with permission from the author. Copyright © 1998 by Lynn Magruder.

Selection from "No Travelin' Man" by M. Eileen Brown published with permission from the author. Copyright © 1998 by M. Eileen Brown.

Selection from *Patagonia Revisited* by Bruce Chatwin and Paul Theroux reprinted by permission of Aitken & Stone. Copyright © 1986 by Bruce Chatwin and Cape Cod Scriveners Company.

Selection from *Peter Freuchen's Book of the Eskimos* by Peter Freuchen. Copyright © 1961 by Peter Freuchen Estate. Published by The World Publishing Company.

Selection from "Pilgrimage to Muktinath" by Larry Habegger published with permission from the author. Copyright © 1998 by Larry Habegger.

Selection from "The Politically Incorrect Orgasm" by Sara Davidson reprinted from the July 1996 issue of *Mirabella*. Reprinted by permission of the author. Copyright © 1996 by Sara Davidson.

Selection from *Ritual: Power, Healing and Community* by Malidoma Patrice Somé published by Swan/Raven & Company. Copyright © 1993 by Swan/Raven & Company.

Selections from *The Romance of Isabel Lady Burton: The Story of Her Life* by W. H. Wilkins. Copyright © 1897.

Selection from *Sanctuary: A Journey* by Judith McDaniel. Reprinted by permission of Firebrand Books, Ithaca, New York. Copyright © 1987 by Judith McDaniel.

Selection from "Searching for Sikkim" by Larry Habegger published with permission from the author. Copyright © 1998 by Larry Habegger.

Selection from *The Size of the World: Once Around Without Leaving the Ground* by Jeff Greenwald preprinted by permission of the author. Copyright © 1996 by Jeff Greenwald.

Selections from *South Pacific Handbook* (4th Edition) by David Stanley reprinted by permission of Moon Publications, Inc. Copyright 1989 by Moon Publications, Inc. and David Stanley.

Selection from *Southeast Asia Handbook* by Carol Parkes reprinted by permission of Moon Publications, Inc. Copyright © 1994 by Carl Parkes.

Selection from "Tahiti Casts a Romantic Spell on Visitor" by Ron Butler published with permission from the author. Copyright © 1998 by Ron Butler.

Selection from "The Virgin Bride" by Jill Eisenstadt reprinted from the June 16, 1996 issue of *The New York Times Magazine*. Copyright © 1996 by The New York Times Company. Reprinted by permission.

Selection from *Thunder on the Left* by Christopher Morley. Copyright © 1925 by Christopher Morley.

Selection from *Travels on my Elephant* by Mark Shand. Copyright © 1991 by Mark Shand. Reprinted by permission of Jonathan Cape Ltd. and The Overlook Press, 2568 Rte. 212, Woodstock, NY, 12498.

Selection from *Trekking in the Nepal Himalaya* by Stan Armington reprinted by permission of Lonely Planet Publications. Copyright © 1994 by Stan Armington.

Selection from *Wall to Wall: From Beijing to Berlin by Rail* by Mary Morris. Copyright © 1991 by Mary Morris. Used by permission of Bantam Doubleday Dell Publishing.

About the Editor

Judith Babcock Wylie has longed to travel ever since she rode a big yellow school bus to school through the farmlands of Ohio and wished every day that the bus would veer off on a great adventure. After graduate school, followed by many years of administrative work in universities, she took the leap into full-time travel writing fifteen years ago, and has not looked back.

Since then she has eaten bird's nest soup in Hong Kong, sailed to Bali, rounded up cattle with a ranch family in California, trekked to see parrots in Jamaica's cockpit country, gawked at the temples in Mandalay, and swum with penguins in the Galapagos. She is an editor with *Romantic Traveling,* which can also be seen on the web site "Thrive," a joint effort of America Online and Time, Inc.; writes a weekly column, "Travel Help: On Line and In Print," for the Paddock Publications newspaper group in Illinois, and writes travel features which have appeared in many publications, including *Travel & Leisure, New Woman, TWA Ambassador, Modern Maturity, Honeymoons and Romantic Destinations,* and newspapers such as the *Miami Herald,* the *Plain Dealer* in Cleveland, and the *Atlanta Constitution.*

She has contributed essays for a number of Travelers' Tales volumes: *Hong Kong, Gutsy Women, A Dog's World,* and *Fodor's Los Angeles Guidebook;* and is co-author of *The Spa Book* and *The Romance Emporium.*

She regularly teaches travel writing workshops at New York University, the University of California at Berkeley, and the University of California, Santa Cruz. She loves Hawaii and has won a Big Island of Hawaii Journalism Award.

Judy and her husband Frank live on an organic farm in Santa

Cruz, California, with their dog Moxie, cat Fearless, assorted deer, bobcat, and coyote, and 300 apple and pear trees. She writes in a cabin office at the edge of an orchard overlooking the Pacific Ocean.

TRAVELERS' TALES GUIDES

LOOK FOR THESE TITLES IN THE SERIES

Women's Travel

A MOTHER'S WORLD
JOURNEYS OF THE HEART

Edited by Marybeth Bond and Pamela Michael
ISBN 1-885211-26-0, 234 pages, $14.95

"Heartwarming and heartbreaking, these stories remind us that
motherhood is one of the great unifying forces in the world."
—John Flinn, Travel Editor, *San Francisco Examiner*

A WOMAN'S WORLD

Edited by Marybeth Bond
ISBN 1-885211-06-6, 475 pages, $17.95

***Winner of the Lowell Thomas Award for Best Travel Book —
Society of American Travel Writers***

"I loved this book! From the very first story, I had the
feeling that I'd been waiting to read these women's tales
for years. I also had the sense that I'd met these women
before. I hadn't, of course, but as a woman and a traveler
I felt an instant connection with them. What a rare pleasure."
—Kimberly Brown, *Travel & Leisure*

GUTSY WOMEN
TRAVEL TIPS AND WISDOM FOR THE ROAD

By Marybeth Bond
ISBN 1-885211-15-5, 124 pages, $7.95

Packed with instructive and inspiring travel vignettes,
Gutsy Women: Travel Tips and Wisdom for the Road is a
must-have for novice as well as experienced travelers.

GUTSY MAMAS
TRAVEL TIPS AND WISDOM FOR MOTHERS ON THE ROAD

By Marybeth Bond
ISBN 1-885211-20-1, 150 pages, $7.95

A book of tips and wisdom for mothers traveling with their
children. This book is for any mother, grandmother, son,
or daughter who travels or would like to.

Special Interest

THE GIFT OF TRAVEL
THE BEST OF TRAVELERS' TALES
Edited by Larry Habegger,
James O'Reilly & Sean O'Reilly
ISBN 1-885211-25-2, 234 pages, $14.95

"The Travelers' Tales series is altogether remarkable."
—Jan Morris

We've selected some favorite stories from the books in our award-winning series, stories about simple but profound gifts travelers have received from people, places, and experiences around the world — from an unforgettable language teacher in Bangkok to the tambourine men of Recife, from a tomato festival in Spain to a mutton feast in Tibet, from a Barcelona train station to a Baja desert. *The Gift of Travel* will light a match in the firebox of your wanderlust. Join us on the quest.

LOVE & ROMANCE
TRUE STORIES OF PASSION ON THE ROAD
Edited by Judith Babcock Wylie
ISBN 1-885211-18-X, 294 pages, $17.95

"...a passion-filled tribute to the undeniable, inescapable romance of the road."

—Debra Birnbaum, Feature Editor, *New Woman*

A DOG'S WORLD
TRUE STORIES OF MAN'S BEST FRIEND ON THE ROAD
Edited by Christine Hunsicker
ISBN 1-885211-23-6, 232 pages, $12.95

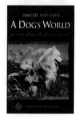

"The stories are extraordinary, original, often surprising and sometimes haunting. A very good book."
—Elizabeth Marshall Thomas,
author of *The Hidden Life of Dogs*

Check with your local bookstore for these titles
or call O'Reilly to order:
800-998-9938 (credit cards only-Weekdays 6 AM –5 PM PST)
707-829-0515, or email: order@oreilly.com

Body & Soul

THE ROAD WITHIN
TRUE STORIES OF TRANSFORMATION
Edited by Sean O'Reilly,
James O'Reilly & Tim O'Reilly
ISBN 1-885211-19-8, 443 pages, $17.95

"Travel is a siren song we are helpless to resist. Heedless of outcomes, we are hooked on the glories of movement, passion and inner growth, souvenirs in abundant supply in *The Road Within*."
—Jeff Salz, *Escape Magazine*

FOOD
A TASTE OF THE ROAD
Edited by Richard Sterling
ISBN 1-885211-09-0, 444 pages, $17.95

"Sterling's themes are nothing less than human universality, passion and necessity, all told in stories straight from the gut."
—Maxine Hong Kingston, author of
The Woman Warrior and *China Men*

THE FEARLESS DINER
TRAVEL TIPS AND WISDOM FOR EATING AROUND THE WORLD
By Richard Sterling
ISBN 1-885211-22-8, 139 pages, $7.95

A pocket companion for those who like to see the world through food. Bold epicures will find all the tips and wisdom needed to feast with savages, break bread with kings, and get invited home to dinner.

Country Guides

BRAZIL
Edited by Annette Haddad & Scott Doggett
ISBN 1-885211-11-2, 433 pages, $17.95
"Only the lowest wattage dimbulb would visit Brazil without reading this book."
—Tim Cahill, author of *Jaguars Ripped My Flesh* and
Pecked to Death by Ducks

NEPAL
Edited by Rajendra S. Khadka
ISBN 1-885211-14-7, 423 pages, $17.95

"Always refreshingly honest, here is a collection that explains why Western travelers fall in love with Nepal and return again and again."
—Barbara Crossette, *New York Times* correspondent and author of
So Close to Heaven: The Vanishing Buddhist Kingdoms of the Himalayas

Country Guides

SPAIN

Edited by Lucy McCauley
ISBN 1-885211-07-4, 452 pages, $17.95

"A superb, eclectic collection that reeks wonderfully of gazpacho and paella, and resonates with sounds of heel-clicking and flamenco singing—and makes you feel that you are actually in that amazing state of mind called Iberia."
—Barnaby Conrad, author of *Matador* and *Name Dropping*

FRANCE

Edited by James O'Reilly,
Larry Habegger & Sean O'Reilly
ISBN 1-885211-02-3, 432 pages, $17.95

"All you always wanted to know about the French but were afraid to ask! Explore the country and its people in a unique and personal way even before getting there. Travelers' Tales: your best passport to France and the French!"
—Anne Sengés, *Journal Français d'Amérique*

INDIA

Edited by James O'Reilly & Larry Habegger
ISBN 1-885211-01-5, 477 pages, $17.95

"The essays are lyrical, magical and evocative: some of the images make you want to rinse your mouth out to clear the dust."
—Karen Troianello, *Yakima Herald-Republic*

THAILAND

Edited by James O'Reilly & Larry Habegger
ISBN 1-885211-05-8, 483 pages, $17.95

"This is the best background reading I've ever seen on Thailand!"
—Carl Parkes, author of *Thailand Handbook,* *Southeast Asia Handbook* by Moon Publications

WINNER
BEST
TRAVEL
BOOK
LOWELL THOMAS AWARD

MEXICO

Edited by James O'Reilly & Larry Habegger
ISBN 1-885211-00-7, 426 pages, $17.95

Opens a window on the beauties and mysteries of Mexico and the Mexicans. It's entertaining, intriguing, baffling, instructive, insightful, inspiring and hilarious—just like Mexico."
—Tom Brosnahan, coauthor of Lonely Planet's *Mexico – a travel survival kit*

City Guides

HONG KONG

Edited by James O'Reilly,
Larry Habegger & Sean O'Reilly
ISBN 1-885211-03-1, 438 pages, $17.95

"*Travelers' Tales Hong Kong* will order and delight the senses, and heighten the sensibilities, whether you are an armchair traveler or an old China hand."
—Gladys Montgomery Jones
Profiles Magazine, Continental Airlines

PARIS

Edited by James O'Reilly,
Larry Habegger, & Sean O'Reilly
ISBN 1-885211-10-4, 424 pages, $17.95

"If Paris is the main dish, here is a rich and fascinating assortment of hors d'oeuvres. *Bon appetit et bon voyage!*"
—Peter Mayle

SAN FRANCISCO

Edited by James O'Reilly,
Larry Habegger & Sean O'Reilly
ISBN 1-885211-08-2, 432 pages, $17.95

"As glimpsed here through the eyes of beatniks, hippies, surfers, 'lavender cowboys' and talented writers from all walks, San Francisco comes to vivid, complex life."
—*Publishers Weekly*

SUBMIT YOUR OWN TRAVEL TALE

Do you have a tale of your own that you would like to submit to Travelers' Tales? We highly recommend that you first read one or more of our books to get a feel for the kind of story we're looking for. For submission guidelines and a list of titles in the works, send a SASE to:

Travelers' Tales Submission Guidelines
P.O. Box 610160, Redwood City, CA 94061

or send email to *ttguidelines@online.oreilly.com*
or visit our web site at **www.oreilly.com/ttales**

You can send your story to the address above or via email to *ttsubmit@oreilly.com*. On the outside of the envelope, *please indicate what country/topic your story is about*. If your story is selected for one of our titles, we will contact you about rights and payment.

We hope to hear from you. In the meantime, enjoy the stories!